Social Work Practice and Social Justice

Social Work Practice and Social Justice

From Local to Global Perspectives

KAREN M. SOWERS
College of Social Work
The University of Tennessee

WILLIAM S. ROWE
School of Social Work
The University of South Florida

THOMSON
━━━✦━━━ ™
BROOKS/COLE

Australia • Brazil • Canada • Mexico • Singapore • Spain
United Kingdom • United States

THOMSON

BROOKS/COLE

Social Work Practice and Social Justice: From Local to Global Perspectives
Karen M. Sowers and William S. Rowe

Senior Acquisitions Editor: Marquita Flemming
Assistant Editor: Alma Dea Michelena
Editorial Assistant: Sheila Walsh
Technology Project Manager: Inna Fedoseyeva
Executive Marketing Manager: Caroline Concilla
Marketing Assistant: Rebecca Weisman
Senior Marketing Communications Manager: Tami Strang
Project Manager, Editorial Production: Christine Sosa
Creative Director: Rob Hugel
Art Director: Vernon Boes
Print Buyer: Linda Hsu

Permissions Editor: Kiely Sisk
Production Service: Abigail Greshik, Pre-Press Company, Inc.
Copy Editor: Mark Mayell, Pre-Press Company, Inc.
Cover Designer: Larry Didona
Cover Images (clockwise from top): © Chad Baker/Ryan McVay/
Getty Images, © Adrian Arbib/CORBIS, © Ron Giling/Peter
Arnold, Inc., © Chris Hondros/Getty Images, © Abbas/Magnum
Photos, © Ian Berry/Magnum Photos
Cover Printer: Webcom
Compositor: Pre-Press Company, Inc.
Printer: Webcom

Library of Congress Control Number: 2005938579
ISBN 0-534-59214-7
Thomson Higher Education
10 Davis Drive
Belmont, CA 94002-3098
USA

For more information about our products, contact us at:
Thomson Learning Academic Resource Center
1-800-423-0563
For permission to use material from this text or product,
submit a request online at
http://www.thomsonrights.com.
Any additional questions about permissions can be
submitted by e-mail to
thomsonrights@thomson.com.

We dedicate this book to Karla Edwards, principal secretary at the College of Social Work, University of Tennessee, and to Trevor Dooley, graduate assistant at the School of Social Work, University of South Florida. Their support, contributions, and advice on this manuscript were invaluable. We also dedicate this book to all those who view diversity as a strength; to those who see community as the vehicle for local and global change; and to those who can see the world through the lens of others while recognizing that we have more to learn than we have to teach.

Contents

CHAPTER 3   Global Standards for Social Work Practice: Implications for Generalist Practice   28

Preface

SOCIAL WORK PRACTICE IN A CHANGING WORLD

Social work practice was developed by and largely in response to local needs—most often to serve the powerless and disadvantaged. The profession also developed expertise in helping victims of tragedy or catastrophic illness, and managing the developmental challenges of everyday living. As populations expanded and immigration and migration grew, it became clear that the challenges facing people in achieving their individual and collective goals were in many ways more similar than they were different.

The effects of globalization have made this all the more apparent in the past few decades. As a result there has been steady pressure to assume that social work practices in developed countries, supported by their advanced training and relatively high levels of funding, were the most desirable and effective and needed only simple cultural adjustments to be applied to human and social problems everywhere.

In reality, no single location or country has the preferred methods for all, although various countries may have exemplar programs or best practices that can be instructive to others. When a tsunami struck Indonesia in December 2004 the world rushed to provide aid. In addition to the 200,000 lives immediately lost, the tragedy had created a situation in which more than 35,000 children were orphaned in the city of Bande Ache alone. Countries all over the world rushed to offer their services, including offers to provide homes for these children through adoption. For many in Indonesia, this was not seen as a solution—the country had already seen its youth scattered throughout the world through both legal and illegal means of human trafficking, often to provide general labor or specific services to wealthy families. What was needed, rather, was an Indonesian solution that allowed the country to get the support that it needs, while at the same time continuing to embrace its children, the country's future.

In December 1991, after the fall of the Soviet empire, Ukraine declared its independence Government services of all kinds simply closed and were not replaced. One of these was the child welfare system. With no history of foster care or volunteerism, children in need of foster support were put by the tens of thousands into total care institutions. Modern social work practice is fully aware of the disastrous results of warehousing children with no connection to a family experience. What is needed by the citizens is an opportunity to develop a foster care system that is based on the strengths and traditions of the Ukrainian people.

Still other countries built poorly planned housing projects when faced with the need to redevelop slum areas, much like the failed initiatives in the United States in the 1940s and 1950s. Neighborhoods are destroyed and traditional support systems are broken up, with the inevitable result of community fragmentation and its attendant crime, disillusionment, addictions, and family violence.

In the same way that we find one country's form of social work to have disastrous results, we also recognize that there are some extraordinary successes when practices are applied in another country. Exemplars, when understood in context, can have amazing positive results. A key purpose of this book is to highlight the main concerns that require social work intervention, identify the key elements of those areas, and describe how they can best be responded to regardless of location. In this book students and practitioners will easily recognize programs and solutions that are peculiar to the United States, but they may be surprised at how the same issues are handled differently and, in some cases, much more effectively in other countries and other cultures. It is not the purpose of this book to create a hierarchy of preferred social work practice. Rather it is to widen the lens for all social workers to take advantage of what can be the positive aspects of globalization—global citizenship, extra-statism, and embracing diversity as strength.

GOALS OF THIS PRACTICE TEXT

We chose the title *Social Work Practice and Social Justice: From Local to Global Perspectives* deliberately. We are referring to social justice not in the sense of the large-scale political meaning but rather in the context of practitioners' contribution to social justice in the practice arena. Through high-quality, value-based, and evidence-supported social work practice, social workers set the stage to move towards social justice worldwide. It is the authors' hope that this book will raise the consciousness of many social work educators, students, and practitioners regarding the dynamics of economic and social globalization and its impact on the poor, oppressed, and vulnerable of the world. We hope to underscore the critical role of international social work in combating global impoverishment. A view of the world as an ecological social system underscores the increasing interconnectedness of nations and states. Vulnerability on one part affects the world configuration. Dysfunctions in any parts of the global fabric result in self-reinforcing vicious cycles, and a transformation of planetary magnitude. The critical state of hunger, oppression, and poverty in the world today creates an impelling need for social workers who are prepared to enter the arena of global social work practice. Social work educators around the world need to equip their students with the knowledge, tools, and change strategies to empower people, communities, and organizations to reclaim and uphold human rights for all.

STRUCTURE AND PEDAGOGY

This book addresses social work practice in the global arena and provides an understanding of the interconnectedness of social work and social development endeavors across the globe. The book is divided into five major sections addressing global social work practice. Part One places social work practice in the global context and moves the reader from national or local practice perspectives to one that is holistic and global. Part Two focuses on the human perspective of global practice and highlights specific populations vulnerable and at risk throughout the world. Part Three addresses global social challenges and highlights practice exemplars from around the world to address specific social problems. Part Four delineates macro practice perspectives and effective community development initiatives as well as describes future organizational trends for global social work practice. Part Five of the book provides a synopsis and conclusion that frames the critical importance of global practice cast in a culturally relevant and respectful paradigm for effective, empirically based practice. Each chapter of the book provides chapter ending summaries, discussion questions, and specific practice exemplars from around the world. The Book Companion Website at http://www.thomsonedu.com/author/sowers contains carefully selected InfoTrac® College Edition articles that provide students with additional readings on specific topics. Please note that access to InfoTrac College Edition is given for free with purchase of new copies of the text but is an optional resource that will need to be ordered with the text.

Social Work Practice and Social Justice

Global Social Work

PART 1

An Emerging Perspective

Social workers around the world come from diverse professional, disciplinary, cultural, social, and geographic contexts. As our diversity adds to our richness so do we find similarities and common ground. Part One of this book provides a background to understand the evolution and history of global social work. It discusses the leading international social work organizations and describes how they are shaping the profession's ethical and practice-related principles. These organizations' commitment and expertise, combined with the developing knowledge and experience of a new generation of social work professionals, promises to promote a greater international social well-being.

This we know, the earth does not belong to man, man belongs to the earth. This we know, all things are connected, like the blood which unites one family. All things are connected. Whatever befalls the earth, befalls the sons of the earth. Man did not weave the web of life. He is merely a strand in it. Whatever he does to the web, he does to himself.

Chief Seattle

1 CHAPTER | # The Evolution of Social Work Around the World

The promotion of social change, empowerment, and problem solving in human relationships are the hallmarks of the social work profession. Social work seeks to liberate people and enhance their well-being. Social work views the person within the context of his or her environment and intervenes at the point where people intersect with their environments. Drawing upon many interdisciplinary theoretical perspectives, including theories of human behavior and social systems, social work intervenes with individuals, families, groups, communities, and organizations. Applying principles of human rights and social justice, the profession utilizes methodology based on knowledge derived from evidence-based research and practice evaluation. The inclusion of knowledge specific to local and indigenous peoples, cultures, and contexts guides the profession in its pursuit of culturally sensitive, relevant, and competent social work practice. Social work recognizes that the interactions between people and their environments are complex and that people have the capacity to be affected by and to influence their environments. To help analyze complex situations involving individuals, organizations, societies, and cultural change, the social work profession draws on theories and interventive methodologies that are grounded in empirical support, such as theories of human development and behavior and social systems (International Association of Schools of Social Work, n.d.).

Social work training first emerged in advanced industrialized countries such as the United States and the United Kingdom and was subsequently transferred to other societies. As Midgley (1981) contends, a form of professional imperialism ensued, anchored to the premise that social work had an international identity and a universally relevant methodology. The initial approach to developing a worldwide perspective on social work was termed *international social work* and was concerned with comparing social work as it exists in different cultures and countries. Increasingly, as social work has grown and matured worldwide, an effort has been made to address social work from a *global perspective*—as one profession practicing in many different countries (Morales & Sheafor, 2001). Beginning in the 1970s, the multicultural and multiracial nature of practice started to receive attention.

The 1980s and 1990s focused on the problems of adapting social work to communities in developing countries (Al-Drenawi & Graham, 2001). Some studies have elaborated difficulties encountered by students and practitioners attempting to adapt Western principles of intervention to the problems of non-Western societies (Roan, 1980; Kulkarni, 1993). A second set of research studies focused on how practitioners have applied the profession differentially from one country to the next (Campfens, 1997; Hokenstad, Khinduka, & Midgley, 1992). A third focus on global social work practice advocated the indigenization of social work knowledge and skills (Drucker, 1993; Ewalt & Mokuau, 1995; Nagpaul, 1993). The indigenization approach allows for the articulation of minority voices and the promotion of a knowledge base in which local metaphors replace those that are considered universal (Leonard, 1997; Martinez-Brawley, 1999). The current literature on global social work continues to reflect these three conceptual strategies.

Global interdependence has grown enormously over the past several decades. Since the nineteenth century social work has attained a significant degree of professionalization. But only recently has the profession of social work begun to recognize and accept the extent to which its practice and professional environment are shaped and influenced by global interdependence. Globalization is viewed by some as a phenomenon responsible for increasing disparities and inequities between rich and poor countries, between the northern and southern hemispheres, between European Americans and societies of color, and between the East and the West (Van Soest, 1997). Global social forces and events, including the movement of populations, have changed the face of social work practice in many countries. However, all too often social work is defined as a locality-specific discipline. No longer can social workers simply rely on a few knowledgeable specialists to work with migrant or refugee groups. And, regardless of one's social work specialization, poverty, inequality, and human distress are issues to which social workers respond everywhere around the globe (Caragata & Sanchez, 2002). As such, global social work practice must go beyond the national level and students should be prepared to work in a world that increasingly demands labor mobility among the professional classes. Capable social work practice in most countries now requires new knowledge and competencies to cope with the social problems and conditions emerging from interdependence (Healy, 2001). The actions of one country socially, politically, and economically affect other countries' social health. All social work is enmeshed in the global processes of change (Lorenz, 1997), and developing countries are expanding their social welfare structures (Popple & Leighninger, 2002).

International social work activities are conducted by myriad organizations. Some of these organizations are specialized, dealing only with global issues related to social work. Some are domestic organizations with international linkages and international organizations in other specialties, such as economic development and health (Healy, 1995). Major groups of organizations in global social work include the intergovernmental agencies within the United Nations (UN); U.S. government agencies; and private, nongovernmental organizations (NGOs). The major international organizations and organizations with international linkages that impact global social work practice will be addressed throughout the book.

Social work in different countries shares many of the same distinctions. Direct practice is the most widely used professional method. Most social workers are employed by the state but may also work in voluntary agencies. Except in the United States, few are employed in the private commercial sector or engage in private practice (Midgley, 1995). Despite the profession's many common characteristics, it faces diverse challenges in different countries. Social work in the industrial countries has been challenged by the rise of radical right-wing ideology, and in some cases has been the object of ideological attack (Jones, 1992). In the Third World, social work is faced with identifying practice methods that contribute positively to economic and social development (Bose, 1992; Khinduka, 1971; Midgley, 1981), and in countries such as Chile and South Africa, the profession has been challenged to cope with political adversity and oppression (Jimenez & Aylwin, 1992; Mazibuka, McKendrick, & Patel, 1992). In Eastern Europe, social work is seeking to adapt to new economic and political realities (Talyigas & Hegyesi, 1992).

Social workers throughout the world are becoming increasingly sensitive to issues of gender and cultural diversity and there has been an increased questioning of Western social work theories and approaches. Social workers have become more aware of the need for a greater sensitivity to cultural differences in an increasingly multicultural world (Davis & Proctor, 1989; Devore & Schlesinger, 1981), and of the need to generate theories and practice methods that are appropriate to their own social and cultural situations (Midgley, 1989). In the midst of significant ethnic conflict around the world, one of the most pressing global issues is facilitating and mediating cross-cultural social welfare issues (Hokenstad, Khinduka, & Midgley, 1992).

FROM SOCIAL WORK TO SOCIAL DEVELOPMENT: MOVING FROM NATIONAL TO GLOBAL PERSPECTIVES

Initially, international social work was concerned with comparing social work as it exists in different cultures and countries. The definition of social work differs greatly across cultural contexts (Payne, 1998). The professionalized conception of the social worker—especially the social worker who provides individual clinical services—originated in Western industrialized countries but most societies have always had a role for individuals who worked to improve conditions for their fellow community members. Although clinical practice may be more characteristic of industrialized countries, community organizers in Western countries have learned many of their strategies and skills from their peers in developing countries (Rowe, Moreno, & Mould, 2000).

Increasingly, as social work has grown and matured worldwide, an effort has been made to address social work from a global perspective—as one profession practicing in many different countries (Popple & Leighninger, 2002). Whereas *social work* is the term commonly used in the United States, other developed nations often use the terms *social development* or *developmental social welfare*. As a global perspective developed, international professional organizations began to form and develop a mutually agreed upon single concept of the profession.

Two international organizations provide the basic leadership for the globalization of social work. One, the International Federation of Social Workers (IFSW), is structured to work through various national professional membership organizations and the professional trade unions of social workers that exist in some countries. The second leading international social work organization, the International Association of Schools of Social Work (IASSW), includes more than 400 member social work education associations and individual schools from 72 countries.

In 1996, the IFSW established a task force to develop a global definition of social work. In 1997, the task force reached agreement that, rather than being a collection of social professions at different stages of development, sufficient commonality existed to attempt to define social work as one profession (Morales & Sheafor, 2001). In June 2001 in Copenhagen, the IFSW (n.d.) and IASSW (n.d.) jointly agreed upon an international definition of social work:

> The social work profession promotes social change, problem solving in human relationships and the empowerment and liberation of people to enhance well-being. Utilizing theories of human behavior and social systems, social work intervenes at the points where people interact with their environments. Principles of human rights and social justice are fundamental to social work.

Both IASSW and IFSW note that social work in the twenty-first century is dynamic and evolving, and caution that no definition should be regarded as exhaustive.

GLOBAL QUALIFYING STANDARDS FOR SOCIAL WORK PRACTICE

The Global Minimum Qualifying Standards Committee was set up as a joint initiative of IASSW and IFSW at the IASSW/IFSW Conference in Montreal in July 2000. That committee developed a standards setting document that elucidates what social work represents on a global level and identifies certain universals to be used as guidelines to develop national standards with regard to social work education and training. Given the enormous diversities across nations and regions, the standard setting document was developed to be sufficiently flexible to apply to any context, specifically taking into account each country's or region's sociopolitical, cultural, economic, and historical contexts while adhering to global norms and standards. According to the Committee (International Association of Schools of Social Work, 2002), the purposes of developing a standard setting document were to:

- protect the "consumers" or "clients" of social work services;
- take account of the impact of globalization on social work curricula and social work practice;
- facilitate articulation across universities on a global level;
- facilitate the movement of social workers from one country to another;
- draw a distinction between social workers and non-social workers;
- benchmark national standards against international standards;
- facilitate partnerships and international student and staff exchange programs;
- enable IASSW and IFSW, in developing such standards, to play a facilitative role in helping those faculties, centers, departments or schools of social work that lack resources to meet such standards; and
- give practical expression to the aim of IASSW, as some saw the formulation of global qualifying standards to be the core business of IASSW.

DEVELOPING AND PROMOTING EXCELLENCE IN SOCIAL WORK PRACTICE GLOBALLY

By developing global qualifying standards, IASSW and IFSW intended not to set minimum standards for practice but rather to promote standards that schools of social work should aspire to on a consistent basis. Across the world, social work training and education differ tremendously. In developing the global standards, IFSW and IASSW note that although global standards may be used to benchmark national norms and standards, national and regional experiences and practices must be incorporated into the formulation of global standards. Where national or regional standards do not exist, IASSW and IFSW will collaborate to facilitate the development of standards. Their role, however, is consultive and facilitative and the two groups do not play a role in ensuring compliance with global social work standards.

Promoting excellence in international social work requires that the profession reframe its educational and practice arenas to embrace global interdependence. Healy (2001, pp. 2–3) notes that global interdependence has created significant areas of international responsibility as well as new opportunities for social work impact by reshaping the social work environment in four important ways:

1. International social forces and events, most dramatically the movement of populations, have changed the makeup of social agency caseloads and affected domestic practice in many countries, including the United States. Competent social work practice in most countries now demands new knowledge and skills to cope with the social problems and conditions emerging from interdependence.

2. Social problems are now shared by both more and less economically developed countries far more often than in previous decades, making mutual work and exchange more desirable. Increasingly, it is as likely that practice innovation and potential problem solutions will be generated in places previously labeled less developed, as in the industrialized nations. This aspect of interdependence has led to a growing shared agenda for social work action. Most nations are currently struggling with homelessness and street children, growing numbers of aged, changes in family patterns leading to less available family care, unemployment and underemployment, and many other social problems.

3. The actions of one country—politically, economically, and socially—now directly and indirectly affect other countries' social and economic well-being and the overall social health of the planet. Nations increasingly share social problems, and the actions that any nation takes can directly affect the well-being of the population of other nations.

4. Enhanced opportunities for international sharing and exchanging are made possible by rapidly advancing technological developments in areas such as communication.

These trends must guide the social work profession in reshaping its practice and educational preparation. It will be critical that social workers be prepared to address internationally related case and community problems that arise in their domestic practice, contribute to mutual problem solving on global social programs, and monitor the impact of their own nation's policies on other countries' and peoples' well-being (Healy, 2001, p. 3).

To move the profession forward there is a compelling need to critically analyze existing social policies and practices for both domestic and global practice. Social programs need to be culturally relevant and responsive to indigenous peoples. No simple and universal rules can be applied to all of the world's native groups. Every region and group is unique, with its own set of problems and inherent resources (Durst, 1992). Overall, the social work profession has engaged in little research or even support for indigenous programs (Timpson, 1990). Indigenous groups in most of the world hold self-determination as a primary value. They are intent on controlling their destiny and preserving their culture (Coates & Powell, 1989; Collman, 1988; Rasnake, 1988; Timpson, 1990). Indigenous peoples from the Aborigines of Australia, the Yanomami of Brazil, and the Inuit of the Arctic Archipelago have voiced their concern over societal threats to their right to self-determination and control over their own destiny (Durst, 1992). In promoting excellence in social work practice in general and global social work specifically, the profession must take a greater role in promoting indigenous control over social welfare issues.

SUMMARY

No longer can social work afford to ignore the influence of global interdependence. Recent world events have impacted individuals, communities, economies, and environments. As a result, social workers across the globe are coalescing to promote peace, greater understanding, and the exchange of information to address global and local problems. The greatest challenge to the profession is the education and training of globally competent social work practitioners with knowledge and skills in multicultural and intercultural practice.

Thinking About Practice: From Local to Global Perspectives

1. Select a major theory (for example human development, behavioral theory, feminist theory, systems theory) pertinent to social work practice. Analyze this theory with respect to its utility to global social work practice. How is it useful (or not useful) in understanding different cultures and the impact of world events on individuals, communities, and societies?

2. Review the National Association of Social Worker's "Code of Ethics" (at http://www.social workers.org/pubs/code/code.asp), with particular attention to the right of self-determination. Select one national policy and analyze the policy. Does it protect individual rights to self-determination? How might this policy be improved to promote self-determination?

3. Is self-determination always an individual concern or may it at times be a group concern?

Social Work Practice and Social Justice Website

Please go to the Book Companion Website at http://www.thomsonedu.com/author/sowers to find a rich collection of related articles selected by the authors from Info Trac College Edition.

References

Al-Drenawi, A., & Graham, J. R. (2001). The cultural mediator: Bridging the gap between a non-western community and professional social work practice. *British Journal of Social Work, 31,* 665–685.

Bose, A. B. (1992). Social work in India: Development roles for a helping profession. In M. C. Hokenstad, S. K. Khinduka, & J. Midgley (Eds.), *Profiles in international social work* (pp. 71–84). Washington, DC: NASW Press.

Campfens, H. (1997). Introduction to international study. In H. Campfens (Ed.), *Community development around the world.* Toronto: University of Toronto Press.

Caragata, L., & Sanchez, M. (2002). Globalization and global need: New imperatives for expanding international social work education in North America. *International Social Work, 45*(2), 217–238.

Coates, K., & Powell, J. (1989). *The modern North, people, politics and the rejection of colonialism.* Toronto: James Lorimer.

Collman, J. (1988). *Fringe-dwellers and welfare: The Aboriginal response to bureaucracy.* St. Lucia, Queensland, Australia: University of Queensland Press.

Davis, L. E., & Proctor, E. K. (1989). *Race, gender, and class: Guidelines for practice with individuals, families, and groups.* Englewood Cliffs, NJ: Prentice Hall.

Devore, W., & Schlesinger, E. E. (1981). *Ethnic sensitive social work practice.* St. Louis, MO: C. V. Mosby.

Drucker, D. (1993). *Interpretative interactionism.* Newbury Park, CA: Sage.

Durst, D. (1992). The road to poverty is paved with good intentions: Social interventions and indigenous peoples. *International Social Work, 35*(2), 191–202.

Ewalt, P. L., & Mokuau, N. (1995). Self-determination from a Pacific perspective. *Social Work, 40*(2), 168–175.

Healy, L. M. (1995). International social welfare: Organizations and activities. In R. Edwards & J. G. Hopps (Eds.), *Encyclopedia of social work* (19th ed.). Washington, DC: NASW Press.

Healy, L. M. (2001). *International social work: Professional action in an interdependent world.* New York: Oxford University Press.

Hokenstad, M. C., Khinduka, S. K., & Midgley, J. (1992). Social work today and tomorrow: An international perspective. In M. C. Hokenstad, S. K. Khinduka, & J. Midgley (Eds.), *Profiles in international social work.* Washington, DC: NASW Press.

International Association of Schools of Social Work. (n.d.). *An international community of schools and educators in social work: An international definition of social work.* Retrieved March 10, 2004, from http://www.iassw.soton.ac.uk/ Generic/DefinitionOfSocialWork.asp

International Association of Schools of Social Work. (2002). *Discussion document on global qualifying standards for social work education and training.* Retrieved March 10, 2004, from http://www .iassw.soton.ac.uk

International Federation of Social Workers. (n.d.). *International Federation of Social Workers definition of social work.* Retrieved March 3, 2004, from http://www.ifsw.org/Publications /4.6e.pub.html

Jimenez, M., & Aylwin, N. (1992). Social work in Chile: Support for the struggle for social justice in Latin America. In M. C. Hokenstad, S. K. Khinduka, & J. Midgley (Eds.), *Profiles in international social work* (pp. 29–42). Washington, DC: NASW Press.

Jones, C. (1992). Social work in Great Britain: Surviving the challenge of conservative ideology. In M. C. Hokenstad, S. K. Khinduka, & J. Midgley (Eds.), *Profiles in international social work* (pp. 43–58). Washington, DC: NASW Press.

Khinduka, S. K. (1971). Social work in the Third World. *Social Service Review, 45,* 62–73.

Kulkarni, P. D. (1993). The indigenous base of the social work profession in India. *Indian Journal of Social Work, 54,* 555–565.

Leonard, P. (1997). *Postmodern social welfare: Reconstructing an emancipatory project.* London: Sage.

Lorenz, W. (1997, August 24). *Social work in a changing Europe.* Paper presented to the Joint European Regional Seminar of IFSW and IASSW on Culture and Identity, Dublin, Ireland.

Martinez-Brawley, E. (1999). Social work, postmodernism and higher education. *International Social Work, 42*(3), 333–346.

Mazibuka, F., McKendrick, B., & Patel, L. (1992). Social work in South Africa: Coping with apartheid and change. In M. C. Hokenstad, S. K. Khinduka, & J. Midgley (Eds.), *Profiles in international social work* (pp. 115–128). Washington, DC: NASW Press.

Midgley, J. (1981). *Professional imperialism: Social work in the Third World.* London: Heinemann.

Midgley, J. (1989). Social work in the Third World: Crisis and response. In P. Carter, T. Jeffs, & M. Smith (Eds.), *Social work and social welfare yearbook* (pp. 33–45). Milton Keynes, England: Open University Press.

Midgley, J. (1995). International and comparative social welfare. In R. Edwards & J. G. Hopps (Eds.), *Encyclopedia of social work* (19th ed.). Washington, DC: NASW Press.

Morales, A. T., & Sheafor, B. W. (2001). *Social work—A profession of many faces.* Needham Heights, MA: Allyn & Bacon.

Nagpaul, H. (1993). Analysis of social work teaching materials in India: The need for indigenous foundations. *Indian Journal of Social Work, 36,* 207–220.

Payne, M. (1998). Why social work? Comparative perspectives on social issue and response formation. *International Social Work, 41*(4), 443–453.

Popple, P. R., & Leighninger, L. (2002). *Social work, social welfare, and American society* (5th ed.). Boston: Allyn & Bacon.

Rasnake, R. N. (1988). *Domination and cultural resistance, authority and power among Andean people.* Durham, NC: Duke University Press.

Roan, S. (1980). Utilizing traditional elements in the society in casework practice. *International Social Work, 23,* 26–35.

Rowe, W., Hanley, J., Moreno, E. R., & Mould, J. (2000). Voices of social work practice: International reflections on the effects of globalization. *Canadian Social Work, 2*(1), 65–86.

Talyigas, K., & Hegyesi, G. (1992). Social work in Hungary: New opportunities in a changing society. In M. C. Hokenstad, S. K. Khinduka, & J. Midgley (Eds.), *Profiles in international social work* (pp. 59–70). Washington, DC: NASW Press.

Timpson, J. B. (1990). Indian and native special status in Ontario's child welfare legislation. *Canadian Social Work Review, 7*(1), 49–68.

Van Soest, D. (1997). The global crisis of violence: Common problems, universal causes, shared solutions. Washington, DC: NASW Press.

Weep not that the world changes—did it keep a stable, changeless state, it were cause indeed to weep.

William Cullen Bryant

Social Work Throughout the World

THE GLOBAL DEMAND FOR SOCIAL WORK

Morales and Sheafor (2001) argue that the Industrial Revolution created the need for the professional approach to helping represented by social work. They suggest that as countries have become increasingly industrialized, traditional ways of meeting human needs have been supplemented by special programs and personnel. If the Industrial Revolution created a national demand for social work, then surely it is the Technological Revolution that is moving social work today from a profession oriented to practice in a single country to one with an increasingly global orientation. As technology advances, the world shrinks. The presence of a worldwide economy makes countries increasingly interdependent. The ability of the media to immediately transmit information around the world creates an unprecedented awareness of events as they occur in even remote areas of the globe. And the availability of the World Wide Web allows human services agencies and providers to exchange information through an almost instantaneous process. As boundaries between countries blur, social work is beginning to think of itself as a global profession.

Today poverty, inequality, and human distress are issues to which social workers respond everywhere in the world (Caragata & Sanchez, 2002). Certain social issues transcend nation-states, including environmental changes such as destruction of the ozone layer, global warming, and deforestation; world hunger, population growth, and food production; and national and global policy issues such as external debt, inflation, trade practices, and employment (Stein, 1990).

WORLD POPULATION CHANGES: CREATING A GLOBAL DEMAND FOR SOCIAL WORK

According to the United Nations, the total population of the world grew from 5.7 billion in 1995 to 6.3 billion in 2003, and it is expected to become 7.2 billion by 2015 (United Nations, 2003). Almost all of the increase occurred in developing countries, which is where most of the projected increases are expected to occur. While the annual rate of population growth has declined and is expected to decline further in the next decade in all major regions of the world, the increment to the world population is expected to remain at over 70 million persons per year over the next two decades, due to the large current populations and the youthfulness of populations in developing and least-developed countries (United Nations Population Fund, 2004). Demographic trends indicate that the level of fertility is declining, as is the rate of infant mortality. The contraceptive prevalence rate is increasing, and the level of life expectancy at birth is increasing in all regions. Many developing countries are also experiencing unprecedented increases in the number of elderly persons as well as the number of young people. Many countries are also facing the complex issues of internal and international migration, internally displaced persons, global trafficking in women and children, and influxes of refugees.

Additionally, many countries continue to experience high levels of maternal mortality, and some are experiencing increases in adult mortality due to AIDS. A growing demographic diversity reflects national differences in social, gender, and health situations as well as the divergent paces at which countries experienced their demographic transitions (United Nations Population Fund, 2004).

Technological Change

The extraordinary scale and rapidity of technological change in the twentieth century has had a major impact. From nuclear technology to the Internet to video access to the technological development of arms, technology will continue to influence and impact the globe. In 1986 the disaster at the Chernobyl nuclear power plant shook the world with a devastating impact (Chazin, & Hanson, 2000). The accelerated technological development of arms has turned the civil population of the world into the main victims of conflicts (International Federation of Social Workers, 2002). The products of our technological advances have produced factors that have been associated with the development of mental and behavioral disorders. Evidence suggests that media portrayals exert an influence on levels of violence, sexual behavior, and interest in pornography, and that exposure to video game violence increases aggressive behavior and other aggressive tendencies (Dill & Dill, 1998). Advertising spending worldwide is now outpacing the growth of the world's economy by one-third. Aggressive marketing is playing a substantial role in the globalization of alcohol and tobacco use among young people, thus increasing the risk of disorders related to substance abuse and associated physical conditions (Klein, 1999).

Population Ageing

The number and proportion of older persons is increasing at a faster rate than any other age group in the global population. One out of every ten persons in the world is aged 60 or over. By 2020, the figure will be about one out of every eight (Leete, 2002). Population ageing is an inevitable consequence of the demographic transition—the shift from high to low birth and death rates. It is taking place at a much faster pace in developing countries than was the case with developed countries, simply because of the faster pace of fertility decline in developing countries (International Federation on Ageing, n.d.; United Nations, n.d.). This in turn is closely linked to the past success of reproductive health programs and family planning. Today, women in the developing world are choosing to have half as many children as they did 50 years ago. Worldwide, people are living longer. Today two-thirds of persons aged 60 years and over, approximately 374 million people, live in developing countries, compared with around 231 million in more developed countries. By 2020, the number of older persons in developing countries is projected to nearly double to 706 million and rise to 317 million in the wealthy, industrial countries (Obaid, 2002). It is estimated that the number of persons over 60 throughout the world will increase from about 600 million in 2000 to almost 2 billion in 2050, and the proportion of persons defined as older is projected to increase globally from 10 percent in 1998 to 15 percent in 2025 (International Federation on Ageing, n.d.).

Over the last half of the twentieth century, 20 years were added to the average lifespan, bringing global life expectancy to its current level of 66 years.

URBANIZATION AND MIGRATION

The urban share of the world's population has grown from 30 percent in 1950 to an estimated 47 percent in 2000. By 2015 the urban proportion is projected to rise to 53 percent of total population. Large movements of people from rural to urban areas continue in most developing countries. Rapid urbanization has led to a growing number of megacities that have in many cases overwhelmed the environmental resources and spawned huge urban slums. Urban authorities are challenged to provide adequate infrastructure and basic social services to cope with the development and environmental implications of growing numbers of people. Urbanization has been associated with the development of mental and behavioral disorders. Between 1950 and 2000, the proportion of the total urban population in Asia, Africa, and Central and South America increased from 16 percent to 50 percent (Harpham & Blue, 1995). In 1950, the populations of Mexico City and Sao Paulo, Brazil, were 3.1 million and 2.8 million, respectively, but by 2000 the estimated population of each was 10 million.

Modern urbanization may have severe negative consequences for mental health through the influence of increased stressors and adverse life events, such as overcrowded and polluted environments, poverty, high levels of violence, and reduced social support (Desjarlais et al., 1995). Approximately half of the urban populations in low and middle income countries live in poverty, and tens of millions of adults and children are homeless. In some areas, economic development is forcing increasing numbers of indigenous peoples to migrate to urban areas in search of a viable livelihood. Usually, migration results in high rates of unemployment and substandard living conditions. There is an increased risk of mental disorders among migrants because of the absence of supportive social networks (World Health Report, 2001).

The displacement or forced migration of people within their own countries is today a common global phenomenon. Such migration may be caused by internal armed conflicts, situations of general violence, ethnic fights, mass violations of human rights or international humanitarian law, or natural disasters. According to the United Nations Centre on Human Rights (1994), violent conflicts and human rights violations in more than 50 countries and in practically every world region—Africa, South and North America, Asia, Europe, and Middle East—have resulted in more than 25 million people being considered displaced. Displaced people are highly vulnerable to discrimination, deprivation, and impoverishment (International Federation of Social Workers, 2002). Marginalized within their own society and facing the emotional trauma of their uprooting experience, displaced people suffer loss of economic opportunities, breakdown of cultural identity, loosening of social and familial structures, interruption of schooling, and increased poverty levels (International Federation of Social Workers, 2002).

Although dwarfed by the movements of people within borders (internal migration), international migration is also increasing. This includes permanent migration and temporary or labor migration, as well as the movements of refugees and undocumented migrants. International migration is often associated with differences in economic opportunities, and the rate has accelerated with increasing globalization. Labor shortages and increased labor demand to support growing economies are key factors in international migration flows. International migration is projected to remain high during the twenty-first century. The United Nations Population Fund (2004) projects that the more developed regions will continue to receive international migrants, with an average net gain of about 2 million per year over the next 50 years.

International migration can cause a host of problems, ranging from fragmented communities in the countries left behind to difficulties in settling down and becoming integrated in the receiving country. Among the most important of these problems are communication difficulties (different languages, cultural beliefs, and behaviors); psychological adjustments (family and personal conflicts); and material issues (food, work, accommodation, structuring of the day, and emphasis on saving money) (International Federation of Social Workers, n.d.).

In the developed regions, two-thirds of the aged were in urban areas in 1975, and this proportion reached three-quarters by the year 2000. In the developing regions, three-quarters of the aged were to be found in rural areas. Nevertheless, the increase in the proportion of the ageing in urban areas in these countries could be considerable and exceed 40 percent within the near future (International Federation on Ageing, n.d.).

THE EMERGENCY OF SOCIAL WORK TRAINING AND EDUCATION

The United States, the United Kingdom, and Canada contributed to the early globalization of social work education and practice after the Second World War by exporting their social work expertise. The content of the exported social work curricula, however, tended to focus on an American-style, clinical, casework approach (Brigham, 1982) that did not translate well to many other parts of the world. Failing to take into account the differences in culture, social structures, economic conditions, education, social policies, and underlying community values, American social work education methodologies faced resistance from local educators and practitioners (Brigham, 1982).

The exportation of Western practice to the rest of the world has begun to change with the acknowledgment that the developed world has much to learn from those in developing countries (Caragata & Sanchez, 2002). The active social work presence in global social work practice today continues to be found more at the university level than in the practice arena. Certainly, in North America, a global social work focus is found primarily within academic social work settings. But international nongovernmental organizations (NGOs) as well as other international development agencies are more likely to employ non-social workers. This disconnect between academia and the field raises critical questions about the adequacy of social work education in adapting to global needs (Caragata & Sanchez, 2002). However, contemporary global social work culture does have many pedagogical practices in common. The universality of human issues is an overriding acknowledgment in global social work education. And schools of social work worldwide use field instruction as a major component of social work education. Field instruction has been described as the most important universal element in social work education (Raskin, Skolnik, and Wayne, 1991). Today, global social work education has significantly more consistency than is found in other closely related professions. Common global issues have supported the development of this global social work culture (Raskin, Skolnik, and Wayne, 1991).

Discussions of the Global Qualifying Standards Committee for Social Work Education and Training recognized that prescribing length of training or number of course credits can be problematic, especially given the variations of the academic year across countries and regions, and the diversities in crediting courses in different contexts. The committee recognized that quality of the educational program was to be upheld. Despite the various methods employed around the world to train and educate social workers, academization of social work is becoming the norm, with many countries opting for either a three- or four-year bachelor degree in social work, with a few countries like Chile being an exception with a five-year bachelor degree.

However social work education is designed, never before in global history has there been a greater need for social workers prepared to enter the global arena. In a world where xenophobia and racism is spreading and large groups of people, such as those with HIV and AIDS, drug abusers, migrant workers, and refugees, are excluded from normal life, social work has a critical and special calling. Social work's traditional role of advocacy for excluded groups and its emphasis on empowerment make it uniquely suited to meet today's challenge.

Recently, the United Nations World Summit for Social Development increased the importance of social issues on the global agenda. For the first time world leaders agreed to take decisive steps toward eradicating poverty. They also recognized the central role of women's empowerment as a precondition for social development. The commitment to promote social integration was a hallmark of the commitment:

We commit ourselves to promoting social integration by fostering societies that are stable, safe and just and that are based on the promotion and protection of human rights, as well as on non-discrimination, tolerance, respect of diversity, equality of opportunity, solidarity, security, and participation of all people, including disadvantaged and vulnerable groups and persons. (United Nations, 1995, p. 18).

This is the challenge for global social work and this is the time!

EMPLOYMENT IN GLOBAL SOCIAL WORK

Many interesting job opportunities exist for social workers throughout the world. The International Federation of Social Workers (IFSW) maintains an international online job bank that posts current advertisements and links to access information about interesting career possibilities (see http://www.ifsw.org/en/p38000336.html). Past advertisements have included positions as a women's rights officer in central Europe, an evaluation consultant for a children's rights advocacy organization in Switzerland, a prevention advisor in HIV/AIDS with a nonprofit international organization in Nairobi, Kenya, a youth program manager for an organization providing humanitarian assistance to children in Canada affected by war, a program manager for a civic advocacy project in Kazakhstan and Kyrgyzstan, a consultant on child protection in East Timor, a child and youth participation coordinator for a network of organizations working to eliminate the commercial sexual exploitation of children in Thailand, and a program coordinator for drought emergency preparedness in the United Kingdom. These are only some examples of the exciting and rewarding positions around the world. In addition, as Zastrow (1995) suggests, you may consider:

- Securing a position in an international organization that advances human services on a worldwide basis. The United Nations serves as the primary agency to coordinate the efforts of the various countries to overcome oppression, facilitate the delivery of health and welfare services that cross international boundaries, and promote social justice. Social work with UN agencies such as the Children's Fund (UNICEF), the Economic and Social Council, the World Health Organization (WHO), and the UN High Commission on Refugees are examples of such positions.
- Securing a U.S. government position that is concerned with global social welfare issues. The Department of Health and Human Services maintains an international affairs staff to attend to worldwide human services issues, and its Office of Refugee Settlement is actively involved in promoting the safety, welfare, and rights of refugees. The U.S. Agency for International Development (USAID) administers foreign aid programs in approximately 100 countries throughout the world, and the Peace Corps has provided developing countries with the human and technical resources to improve their physical infrastructure, health care, and human services.

- Securing a position in a government or voluntary agency in another country. These roles typically include service provision, consultation, and teaching or training activities.
- Securing a position with a multinational corporation that locates personnel in foreign countries. Social workers provide direct services to help individuals and families to deal with their social problems, assist the company in sharpening its cultural sensitivity, and represent the company as a participant in the local community, making contributions to and interfacing with the human services delivery system.

INTERNATIONAL SOCIAL WORK ORGANIZATIONS

Several international organizations provide the basic leadership for the globalization of social work. One, the International Federation of Social Workers, is structured to work through various national professional membership organizations, such as the professional social work oriented trade unions that exist in some countries. The second important international social work organization is the International Association of Schools of Social Work (IASSW), which facilitates the inclusion of global content into social work education programs (Morales & Sheafor, 2001). A third organization, the Inter-University Consortium for International Social Development (IUCISD), is designed to respond to pressing human concerns from a global, interdisciplinary perspective and seeks to develop conceptual frameworks and effective intervention strategies. A fourth organization, the International Council on Social Welfare (ICSW), represents concerns of community organizations across the world that work at the grass roots with people in poverty, hardship, or distress.

International Federation of Social Workers

A global organization, the IFSW focuses on the development of social work, best practices, and international cooperation between social workers and their professional organization. Its primary purpose is the promotion of human rights and social justice. The IFSW is a successor to the International Permanent Secretariat of Social Workers, which was founded in Paris in 1928 and was active until the outbreak of World War II. In 1950, at the time of the International Conference of Social Work in Paris, it was decided to create an international organization of professional social workers, and the concept for the International Federation of Social Workers was born. The original agreement was that the IFSW would come into being when seven national organizations agreed to become members. The Federation was finally founded in 1956 at the time of the meeting of the International Conference on Social Welfare in Munich, Germany. The International Federation of Social Workers recognizes that social work originates variously from humanitarian, religious, and democratic ideals and philosophies, and that it has universal applications to meet human needs arising from person-societal interactions, and to develop human potential. At present, national organizations in 78 countries with more than 450,000 members belong to the federation.

In 1988, IFSW established a Human Rights Commission with members appointed by each region. The Commission coordinates the work of IFSW in relation to human rights issues and works with Amnesty International and other human rights organizations to support individual social workers, social work students, and social service workers suffering a denial of their human rights. It makes representations to governments and publicizes cases of social workers, social work students, and social service workers whose rights have been violated or threatened. The Commission is also involved in human rights education for the profession. The IFSW publishes the document *The Ethics of Social Work—Principles and Standards* as an instrument to guide the development of professional ethics. A permanent committee on ethical issues, made up by members from each of the five regions, is charged with keeping ethical reflection and discussion at the forefront of the federation's agenda, reviewing the ethical instruments of the federation, and offering advice to member organizations and others on ethical matters.

Special consultative status has been granted to the federation by the Economic and Social Council of the United Nations, and by UNICEF. At the regional level the federation cooperates with the Council of Europe and the European Union by means of a formally established Permanent Committee. This official recognition provides channels and forums for expressing the viewpoints of social workers at the world level on matters of concern to the profession (http://www.ifsw.org).

International Association of Schools of Social Work

The IASSW is an international association of institutions of social work education, organizations supporting social work education, and social work educators. Its mission is:

- to develop and promote excellence in social work education, research, and scholarship globally in order to enhance human well being;
- to create and maintain a dynamic community of social work educators and their programs;
- to support and facilitate participation in mutual exchanges of information and expertise; and
- to represent social work education at the international level.

In fulfilling its mission, IASSW adheres to all United Nations Declarations and Conventions on human rights, recognizing that respect for the inalienable rights of the individual is the foundation of freedom, justice, and peace. Members of IASSW are united in their obligation to the continued pursuit of social justice and social development. In carrying out its mission, IASSW fosters cooperation, collegiality, and interdependence among its members and with others (International Association of Schools of Social Work, n.d.).

Inter-University Consortium for International Social Development

Started in the 1970s by a group of social work educators to respond to pressing human concerns from a global, interdisciplinary perspective, IUCISD seeks to develop conceptual frameworks and effective intervention strategies geared to influencing local, national, and global systems. It is committed to creating peaceful solutions to the problems of survival at the local, national, and global levels. According to IUCISD, members of the organization use a social development approach to:

- promote world peace and social justice;
- fight economic and political oppression;
- improve access to adequate health care and education;
- overcome discrimination against women and minorities; and
- create sustainable income and economic structures.

IUCISD serves as a clearinghouse for information on global social development and fosters collaboration among personnel or organizations, including the United Nations, World Bank, UNESCO, and UNICEF, as well as among professional associations in the human services and institutions of higher learning.

IUCISD maintains a technical assistance roster that links members' special expertise in global social development to agencies, governments, and organizations. IUCISD also provides mutual consultation and cooperative action on social development. It also publishes the journal *Social Development Issues: Alternative Approaches to Global Human Needs.*

International Council on Social Welfare

The ICSW, founded in Paris in 1928, is a nongovernmental organization that represents national and local organizations in more than 50 countries throughout the world. Membership also includes a number of major international organizations. Member organizations collectively represent tens of thousands of community organizations that work directly at the grass roots with people in poverty, hardship, or distress. Almost all of the organizations are independent entities working in their own communities rather than branches of organizations based in other countries. Within their own communities, the network of organizations belonging to ICSW provides help for a wide range of people who are poor, ill, disabled, unemployed, frail, or oppressed. They help young people, older people, families, indigenous peoples, migrants, refugees, and others who are experiencing special hardship or vulnerability. ICSW's activities are funded by membership fees as well as grants from private foundations and from governmental or intergovernmental sources. ICSW has the highest level of consultative status with the United Nations' Economic and Social Council and is accredited to the Food and Agriculture Organization, International Labour Organization, UNICEF, UNESCO,

WHO, and a number of regional intergovernmental organizations (The International Council on Social Welfare, n.d.).

Purpose and Mission   The mission of ICSW is to promote forms of social and economic development that aim to reduce poverty, hardship, and vulnerability throughout the world, especially amongst disadvantaged people. It strives to recognize and protect fundamental rights to food, shelter, education, health care, and security. ICSW believes that these rights are an essential foundation for freedom, justice, and peace. It also seeks to advance equality of opportunity, freedom of self-expression, and access to human services. To achieve its mission, ICSW advocates policies and programs that strike an appropriate balance between social and economic goals and that respect cultural diversity. To advance ICSW's goals, ICSW gathers and disseminates information, undertakes research and analysis, convenes seminars and conferences, draws on grass-roots experiences, strives to strengthen non-governmental organizations, develops policy proposals, engages in public advocacy, and works with policy-makers and administrators in government and elsewhere.

Communication, Development, and Advocacy   ICSW is active in a wide range of fields within the general areas of social development, social welfare, and social justice. This includes issues such as food and nutrition, welfare and health services, social security, and education and housing, as well as many issues relating to economic development, human rights, and community participation. ICSW gathers and distributes information to community groups, other civil society organizations, governments, and intergovernmental organizations.

ICSW undertakes research and organizes consultations to help analyze problems and develop policies. ICSW prepares written policy submission, lobbies governments, and organizes delegations to attend key international meetings. The organization also provides training to its members and other organizations, especially in developing countries, and supports individual organizations with specific information and advice.

ICSW has a signed Memorandum of Understanding with the United National Development Programme (UNDP), which ensures close cooperation between the two bodies. Since the memorandum was signed in July 1997, ICSW and UNDP have worked closely together on the series of ICSW regional and subregional civil society forums on the implementation of the World Summit for Social Development. ICSW's high level of consultative status within the United National Development Programme has also ensured that the organization is fully consulted and involved in important social development issues being discussed by the United Nations.

Publications   ICSW publishes a quarterly magazine entitled *Social Development Review* that contains news and views from experts in civil society organizations, universities, governments, and intergovernmental organizations. It also publishes reports on international conferences and workshops, a series entitled "Copenhagen Papers" that includes policy papers by experts, global and regional newsletters, and other material relating to the implementation of the World Summit on Social Development. The ICSW website (http://www.icsw.org) carries a wide range of information and references in relation to social development and social welfare.

Global Meetings   ICSW holds a global conference every two years that covers a wide range of social development and social welfare issues. It convenes a global social development forum every year in New York City immediately before the meeting of the UN Commission for Social Development, and other global forums periodically on special topics. Regional conferences are held every two years.

THE CAMPBELL COLLABORATION: AN INTELLECTUAL TRUST

The Campbell Collaboration is an international organization that aims to prepare, maintain, and disseminate high quality, systematic reviews of studies of effectiveness. By supporting the production of these reviews and by disseminating results in an accessible fashion, the Campbell Collaboration intends to contribute to decisions in practice, policy, and to public understanding. The Campbell Collaboration was established by 80 people from four countries at an exploratory meeting at University College London in July 1999, and then formally established at a meeting at the University of Pennsylvania on February 24–25, 2000.

The Campbell Collaboration works closely with its sibling organization, the Cochrane Collaboration, which prepares and maintains systematic reviews of the effects of interventions in health care. The systematic reviews of research evidence prepared and maintained by contributors to the Campbell Collaboration's Review Groups are designed to meet the needs of those with a strong interest in high quality evidence on "what works." These persons include members of the public who want to keep abreast of the best evidence on the effects of social and educational policies and practices, service providers, policy makers, educators and their students, and professional researchers. Campbell systematic reviews are published electronically, are updated promptly as relevant additional evidence emerges, and are amended in response to criticisms and advances in methodology (The Campbell Collaboration, n.d.).

The Campbell Collaboration Library holds two unique data bases, the C2 Social, Psychological, Education, and Criminological Trials Registry (called C2-SPECTR) and the C2 Reviews of Interventions and Policy Evaluations (called C2-RIPE). C2-SPECTR contains over 11,700 entries on randomized and possibly randomized trials. C2-SPECTR is updated regularly and its entries are potential ingredients for the Collaboration's systematic reviews. It serves as an important resource for identifying studies for inclusion in the Campbell Collaboration's systematic reviews. Access to C2-SPECTR is provided free of charge to the public via the Internet. The C2-RIPE database contains approved titles, protocols, reviews, and abstracts. It also contains refereed comments and critiques.

GLOBAL OVERVIEW OF SOCIAL ISSUES

Social workers want to make the world a better place for all people—and particularly for those who are most vulnerable to experiencing social problems. Social workers harbor universal concern for improving the social, economic, and health conditions of the most vulnerable people throughout the world, and for changing the political and social structures that have made people likely to experience hunger, violations of basic human rights, and other expressions of poverty, disease, and various forms of abuse or oppression (Morales & Sheafor, 2001). Social workers and social work organizations are concerned with such worldwide issues as achieving and preserving peace, preventing the use of landmines in wartime situations, distributing human and economic resources more equitably, protecting the rights and preventing the exploitation of children, enhancing women's status and safety, minimizing substance abuse, promoting health and mental health, and protecting the elderly. These are only some of the many concerns shared worldwide by social workers. The following provides a brief overview of some of the most pressing social problems found throughout the world today.

Collective Violence

The twentieth century was one of the most violent periods in human history. An estimated 191 million people lost their lives directly or indirectly as a result of conflict, and well over half of them were civilians. Violent conflicts between nations and groups, state and group terrorism, rape as a weapon of war, the movement of large numbers of people displaced from their homes, and gang warfare occur on a daily basis in many parts of the world. Worldwide, the highest rates of conflict-related deaths are found in Africa. In addition to the many thousands killed each year in violent conflicts, huge numbers are physically injured as a result, and some are permanently disabled or mutilated. Torture and rape are used to terrorize and undermine communities (World Health Organization, 2002).

Poverty

Despite unprecedented progress reducing poverty in the last 50 years, about 1.3 billion people in the world still live in abject poverty. Nearly half of all poor people live in South Asia. The poverty rate is increasing in sub-Saharan Africa (Seipel, 2003). Poor people not only suffer from economic hardships, but many also suffer from malnutrition, illiteracy, poor health, premature death, and hopelessness (Birdsall, 1999, Cox, 1990; Kammerman & Kahn, 1997). Extreme poverty robs people of real choices, opportunities, and basic services to improve their life situations. Due to inequality and discrimination, women suffer the most. One-fourth of all women in developing countries are adversely affected at some point in their lives by a lack of proper maternal health care. Every minute, one woman dies during pregnancy and birth because she did not receive adequate care and prompt treatment. Poverty experienced in childhood and adulthood is likely to deepen with age. Older people who have experienced a lifetime of poor diet, multiple pregnancies, inadequate reproductive health care, and arduous physical labor are likely to enter old age in ill health. The inevitable physical decline brought on by ageing reduces each person's ability to contribute to the household and to remain economically self-sufficient (Obaid, 2002).

HIV/AIDS

In 2003, 3 million people died from AIDS; in the same year, the number of AIDS orphans climbed to 14 million, 11 million of whom live in sub-Saharan Africa. Indications are that HIV infections are not leveling off. Every day, 14,000 people are newly infected, half of whom are young people under the age of 25. This accounted for more than 5 million people newly infected in 2003—half of them young people between the ages of 15 and 24. Women, too, are becoming increasingly infected. In 1997, women 15 to 49 years old accounted for 41 percent of adults living with HIV/AIDS, rising proportionately to 50 percent by 2003. Many people in the world know little about the disease and how the virus is transmitted. Among all groups, women and youth are the most vulnerable. In some African countries, teenage girls are six times more likely to be infected with HIV than are boys of the same age.

The number of people living with HIV and AIDS continues to increase, most markedly in sub-Saharan Africa but also within the expanding epidemics in Asia, the Pacific, Eastern Europe, and Central Asia. Today, approximately 40 million people are living with HIV/AIDS across the globe.

The impact of HIV/AIDS goes far beyond the statistics both in economic and social terms. Infrastructures are often stressed beyond capacities, past development gains are quickly eroded, and families and communities are destabilized. HIV/AIDS is assuredly one of the biggest challenges facing today's global community (United Nations Population Fund, 2004).

Family Planning

Women in the developing world are having half as many children today as they did in the 1960s, but fertility remains highest in the poorest countries due to a lack of social services. The last two generations of women have chosen to have smaller families and the next generation will do the same if they have access to education and reproductive health services. However, 350 million couples still do not have access to a range of effective and affordable family planning services, and demand for these services is expected to increase by 40 percent in the next 15 years.

Ageing

The elderly are a diverse group that experiences varying degrees of dependency on external support. The situation of many older persons living in less developed countries is one of extreme poverty and exclusion. They often lack access to adequate and affordable health care and other basic requirements, especially in rural areas, and some are also confronted with financial, emotional, and physical abuse (Leete, 2002). Traditional family support mechanisms are being eroded due to declining family size, rural to urban migration, urbanization, and declining co-residence, and in some countries, younger family members dying of HIV/AIDS. As a result, many older people, and particularly older women, are faced with isolation, abandonment, and loneliness.

Older persons, especially women, are increasingly at risk of violence and other serious human rights abuses and violations, particularly during times of wars and military conflicts. Wars and military conflicts force children, young women, and older persons to seek refuge in displaced persons' camps, or to stay and face danger in their own communities. Elderly persons are particularly vulnerable in Sierra Leone, Liberia, the Democratic Republic of the Congo, Afghanistan, and the Occupied Palestinian Territory (Obaid & Malloch-Brown, 2002). More and more older people are being forced to raise grandchildren left behind by parents dead from AIDS or war, or absent after migrating to urban centers in search of jobs. Grandparents, particularly those who live in poverty, struggle to care for their grandchildren (HelpAge, n.d.).

The impact of population ageing is increasingly evident in the old-age dependency ratio, the number of working-age persons (age 15–64) per older person (65 years or older) that is used as an indicator of the so-called dependency burden on potential workers. Between 2000 and 2050, the old-age dependency ratio will double in more developed regions and triple in less developed regions. The potential socioeconomic impact on society that may result from an increasing old-age dependency ratio is an area of growing concern (United Nations, n.d.).

SUMMARY

World population changes and increased social problems around the globe create an emergency for social workers prepared to intervene effectively to promote human well-being, social justice, and peace. An increasing commitment by the United Nations World Summit for Social Development and the growing recognition by national and international social work organizations of the critical needs around the world are raising the consciousness of social work educators and practitioners. Schools of social work are preparing social workers in culturally relevant and competent practice and beginning to infuse global issues and perspectives into their curricula. Employment opportunities in social work, social welfare, and social development are providing exciting avenues for innovative practice in the global arena.

Thinking About Practice: From Local to Global Perspectives

1. Compare and contrast population changes throughout the world with changes occurring in your own community, state, and nation. What are the similarities and differences?
2. How might the world population changes that are occurring affect your community?
3. Compare and contrast the critical social problems worldwide with the social problems in your community. What are the similarities and differences?

4. Peruse the international employment website at http://www.ifsw.org/en/p38000336.html. Select four positions that you find particularly interesting. What are the challenges and obstacles you face in seeking these job opportunities?
5. Peruse the international employment website at http://www.ifsw.org/en/p38000336.html. Overall, what are the differences and similarities in job readiness skills and requirements compared to social work practice jobs in your community?

Social Work Practice and Social Justice Website

Please go to the Book Companion Website at http://www.thomsonedu.com/author/sowers to find a rich collection of related articles selected by the authors from Info Trac College Edition.

References

Birdsall, N. (1999). Life is unfair: Inequality in the world. In R. J. Griffiths (Ed.), *Developing world 99/00,* pp. 25–33. Sluice Dock, CT: Dushkin/McGraw-Hill.

Brigham, T. (1982). Social work education patterns in five developing countries: Relevance of US microsystems model. *Journal of Education for Social Work, 18*(2), 68–75.

The Campbell Collaboration. (n.d.). *About the Campbell Collaboration.* Retrieved March 3, 2003, from http://www.campbellcollaboration.org

Caragata, L., & Sanchez, M. (2002). Globalization and global need: New imperatives for expanding international social work education in North America. *International Social Work 45*(2), 217–238.

Chazin, R., & Hanson, M. (2000, 29 July–2 August). *Transferring social work technology in a global village.* Paper presented at the International Association of Schools of Social Work Conference, Montreal, Canada.

Cox, D. (1990). An international overview. In H. Campfens (Ed.), *New reality of poverty and struggle for social transformation,* pp. 53–55. Vienna: International Association of Schools of Social Work.

Desjarlais, R., Eisenberg, L., Good, B., & Kleinman, A. (1995). *World mental health: Problems and priorities in low-income countries.* New York: Oxford University Press.

Dill, E., & Dill, C. (1998). Video game violence: A review of the empirical literature. *Aggression and Violent Behavior, 3*(4), 407–28.

Harpham, T., & Blue, I. (Eds). (1995). *Urbanization and mental health in developing countries.* Aldershot, UK: Avebury.

HelpAge. (n.d.). *Older people's role in mitigating child exploitation.* Retrieved June 29, 2004, from http://www.helpage.org

International Association of Schools of Social Work. (n.d.). Retrieved July 12, 2004, from http://www.iassw.soton

International Council on Social Welfare. (n.d.). *Organizational structure.* Retrieved June 24, 2004, from http://www.icsw.org

International Federation of Social Workers. (n.d.). Retrieved July 13, 2004, from http://www.ifsw.org

International Federation of Social Workers. (2002). *International policy statement on displaced persons.* Geneva: Author.

International Federation on Ageing. (n.d.). *Part of a world wide revolution.* Retrieved June 30, 2004, from http://www.ifa-fiv.org

Kammerman, S. B., & Kahn, A. J. (1997). The problem of poverty in the advanced industrialized countries and the policy and programme response. In UNDP *Poverty and human development,* pp. 81–124. New York: UNDP.

Klein, N. (1999). *No logo: Taking on the brand bullies.* New York: Picador.

Leete, R. (2002). *Poverty Issues in Old Age: Operational Challenges.* Statement presented at the Valencia Forum, United Nations Population Fund, April 2, 2002, Madrid, Spain.

Morales, A. T., & Sheafor, B. W. (2001). *Social work—A profession of many faces.* Needham Heights, MA: Allyn & Bacon.

Obaid, T. A. (2002). *Statement at the Launch of HelpAge International's State of the World's Older People.* (2002). April 8, 2002, Madrid, Spain.

Obaid, T. A., & Malloch-Brown, M. (2002). *Joint Statement to the Second World Assembly on Ageing.* April 8–12, Madrid, Spain.

Raskin, J. L., Skolnik, L., & Wayne, J. (1991). An international perspective of field instruction. *Journal of Social Work Education, 27*(3), 258–70.

Seipel, M. (2003). Global poverty—No longer an untouchable problem. *International Social Work, 46*(2), 191–207.

Stein, H. (1990). The international and the global in education for the future. In K. Kendall (Ed.), *The International in American Education.* New York: Proceedings of an International Symposium, Hunter College School of Social Work.

United Nations. (n.d.). *The ageing of the world's population.* Retrieved June 30, 2004, from http://www.un.org/esa/socdev/ageing/agewpop.htm

United Nations. (1995). *World summit for social development.* New York: Author.

United Nations. (2003). *World population prospects: The 2002 revision.* (Report ST/ESA/SER-A/222). New York: United Nations.

United Nations, Centre for Human Rights, Professional Training Series No. 1. (1994). *Human rights and social work.* New York: Author.

United Nations Population Fund. (2004). *Investing in people: National progress in implementing the ICPD Programme of Action 1994–2004.* New York: United Nations Population Fund.

World Health Organization. (2002). *Collective violence.* Retrieved July 20, 2004, from http://www.who.org

World Health Report. (2001). Retrieved July 9, 2004, from http://www.who.int/whr2001/2001/main

Zastrow, C. (1995). *The practice of social work* (5th ed.). Pacific Grove, CA: Brooks/Cole Publishing.

Going beyond the national level in social work cannot be the personal hobby of a few specialists who are dealing with migrant and refugee groups or with ethnic minorities...or of a few idealists who want to promote international exchanges to widen their horizon and to learn more about methods and practices in other countries. On the contrary, all social work is enmeshed in global processes of change.

Walter Lorenz (1997)

3 CHAPTER | Global Standards for Social Work Practice

Implications for Generalist Practice

CORE PURPOSES OF SOCIAL WORK

Social workers are involved as change agents in working with individuals, groups, families, organizations, and the larger community. The amount of time spent at these levels varies from worker to worker and from situation to situation. Almost all social workers around the world are trained in the problem-solving process to assess and intervene in problems confronting individuals, families, groups, organizations, and communities. As such, social workers should be knowledgeable and skillful in a variety of roles. Zastrow (1995, pp. 18–20) delineates the following roles and notes that role selection should be determined by what will be most effective, given the circumstances:

- **Enabler**—In this role a worker helps individuals, groups, or communities articulate their needs, clarify and identify their problems, explore resolution strategies, select and apply a strategy, and develop their capacities to deal with their problems more effectively.
- **Broker**—A broker links individuals, groups, and communities who need help accessing services and resources.
- **Advocate**—This is an active, directive role in which the social worker is an advocate for a client or a citizen's group when they need help and existing institutions are uninterested in providing services. The advocate provides leadership for collecting information, arguing the correctness of the need and request and challenging the institution's original decision.
- **Mediator**—The mediator role involves intervention in disputes between parties to help them find compromises, reconcile differences, or reach mutually satisfactory agreements.
- **Negotiator**—A negotiator brings together those who are in conflict over one or more issues and seeks to bargain and compromise in order to arrive at mutually acceptable agreements.
- **Educator**—The educator role involves giving information to clients/communities/organizations and teaching adaptive skills.
- **Initiator**—An initiator calls attention to a problem, or to potential problems.
- **Coordinator**—Coordination involves bringing components together in an organized manner. Frequently, one social worker needs to assume the role of case manager to coordinate the services to avoid duplication of efforts and conflicting objectives.
- **Researcher**—At times, every social worker is a researcher. This includes researching the literature, evaluating the outcomes of one's practice, assessing the merits and shortcomings of programs, and studying community needs.
- **Group facilitator**—A group facilitator leads a group that may be therapeutic, educational, self-help, organizational, or some other focus.
- **Public speaker**—Social workers often talk to a variety of groups to inform them of available services or to advocate developing new projects or services.

CULTURAL AND ETHNIC DIVERSITY

Social work practice does not follow the same patterns in all parts of the world. The form of social work that develops in any society is shaped by the prevailing social, economic, and cultural forces (Doel & Shardlow, 1996). But most cultures around the world are responding to the challenges of rapidly changing social and economic forces in their countries. Extreme cultural fluctuations, such as intercultural migration, interethnic marriage, reduced family size, and individual mobility, all of which are impacting family size and family structures, pose great challenges. In some countries the HIV pandemic is placing extreme strains on families and on organizational structures that support family functioning (Obaid & Malloch-Brown, 2002).

We have a responsibility to promote citizen well-being. This can be accomplished by building on and reinforcing those cultural values that promote the well-being of all citizens. But social work has been profoundly influenced by Western thought, values, and views (Sacco, 1996). From the dominant Western perspective, key assumptions are that professional acts are rational acts (Constable, 1983); that professional activity is instrumental problem solving through the application of rigorous and scientifically tested and derived methods, where the professionals are the experts (Gowdy, 1994); and that effective practice must be rooted in an established theoretical foundation, without which the quality of practice suffers (Goldstein, 1986; Shutte, 1993). Sacco (1996) contends that this paradigm results in the separation of scientific knowledge from all other forms and sources of knowledge, and a hierarchy of educators over students, researchers over practitioners, and of practitioners over clients. Social scientists and educators have questioned the validity of this approach, rooted in positivism, even for its utility in the Western world (Faver, 1986; Gowdy, 1994; Saleeby, 1994). Arising from the dominant Western cultural point of view, human needs are based on the assumption that each individual needs a decent standard of living, education, housing, medical care, and social services, and that the provision of universal services would lead to the elimination of poverty, the advancement of underprivileged groups, and the narrowing of gaps in income, education, and employment (Barretta-Herman, 1994).

But to understand and work effectively with a wide range of people, families, groups, communities, and societies, social workers need to become open to the search for truth from a variety of sources (Sacco, 1996). For instance, within the African context, traditional African thinking understands human nature and human flourishing as a network of life forces that emanate from God and end in God, who is the source of all life forces. For many Africans, personhood is attainable only in community and the single most important concept within African traditional life is the inclusion of all into the community (Senghor, 1966; Setiloane, 1986). Traditional Native American teachings hold that mental, physical, and spiritual disease is caused by disharmony within the individual, or by disconnection from the family, community, nature, or the greater universe. Working out an understanding of human beings and personal development that incorporates cultural conceptions and beliefs is critical to effective social work practice, particularly in a global context. Making professional social work services more accessible by working with informal caregiving resources can enhance culturally relevant and appropriate practice (Sherraden & Martin, 1994). Some global examples exist that can serve as a model for social work practice grounded in understanding and actions in the stories and meaning systems of those whom social workers serve (Saleeby, 1994).

Recently, social work has placed a decided emphasis on the necessity to include cultural factors in the helping process. Initially, the social work literature focused on the need for culturally sensitive practice but it has more recently moved to emphasize the importance of social workers being culturally competent in practice. Cultural competence, incorporated into the practitioners' assessments and interventions, allows the social work to integrate cultural knowledge and sensitivity with skills for a more effective and culturally appropriate helping process (Weaver, 1999). As the citizens of the United States and other parts of the world become increasingly diverse so too do the norms, beliefs, and value systems of those citizens (Manoleas, 1994; Mason, Benjamin, & Lewis, 1996; Matthews, 1996; McPhatter, 1997; Ronnau, 1994; Sowers-Hoag & Sandau-Beckler, 1996). The current National Association of Social Workers (NASW) Code of Ethics (1996) reinforces the importance of cultural competence to effective social work practice. While earlier versions of the Code of Ethics implied the relevance of cultural issues to practice, the current code is explicit in delineating the critical importance of culturally competent practice within the profession. Culturally competent practice requires that social workers become aware of their own values, biases, and beliefs (Mason, Benjamin, & Lewis, 1996; Ronnau, 1994; Sowers-Hoag & Sandau-Beckler, 1996) and must value and respect differences as well as understand the dynamics of difference (Manoleas, 1994; Mason, Benjamin, & Lewis, 1996; Ronnau, 1994; Sowers-Hoag & Sandau-Beckler, 1996).

Social and cultural realities can create both challenges and opportunities in working to advance human rights. Field experience shows that cultural sensitivity and responsiveness demonstrated by program staff, in designing programs and advocacy campaigns using local knowledge, leads to higher levels of program acceptance and ownership by the community as well as program sustainability. An examination of programming approaches by the United Nations Population Fund found that the most effective approaches embrace inclusive programming approaches that encompass culture and religion and the roles played by local power structures and institutions in mobilizing communities to become active partners in development. More specifically, the United Nations Population Fund (n.d.) has developed the following basic assumptions to be applied when working to mobilize communities:

- Cultures are realities of history and geography.
- Cultures are the context in which all development work takes place.
- Cultures are the context in which international human rights agreements are implemented.
- Cultures are dynamic, interactive, and subject to change, and no culture is immune to external stimuli.
- People are products of their cultures, but they are also active participants in shaping these cultures.

- Development paradigms have paid limited attention to cultural variables and approaches to create an enabling environment for the promotion of international human rights and gender equity and equality.
- There is need to reformulate the premises of development paradigms to include factors that contribute to ownership of development programs.
- Adopting culturally sensitive development policies and practices does not entail making positive or negative value judgments on any culture, ethnicity, or religion.
- In essence, using the "culture lens" in development programming enables policy makers and practitioners to understand the context in which programs are implemented.
- Culturally sensitive approaches can be applied to understand social practices that are harmful to people and hinder their enjoyment of human rights.
- The culture lens is an analytical tool that helps policy makers and practitioners to contextualize development approaches to fit the diversified national and local contexts in which programs are being implemented, without losing sight of the human rights that they are promoting. Thus, these approaches should facilitate an enabling environment for promoting human rights as an integral part of the development framework.
- Evidence of what works and what does not work at the country level is the most crucial input for developing more effective and holistic development approaches.

The United Nations Population Fund (n.d.) has developed the *culture lens* as a tool to help practitioners analyze and more effectively intervene in communities and to:

- understand the realities of societies in which development and humanitarian programs are delivered;
- identify influential local power structures and pressure groups (religious, cultural, political, legal, and professional) that can be potential allies or adversaries to development programming;
- identify internal cultural tensions and aspirations of the various subcultures;
- develop skills for dealing with individuals, communities, and interest groups living in a specific cultural context;
- develop culturally acceptable language and negotiation and communication tools in contexts where they work;
- achieve the goals of development programming more effectively and efficiently, with stronger community acceptance and ownership; and
- facilitate the creation of an environment in which bridges can be established between local cultural values and universally recognized human rights and gender equity and equality.

The New Zealand Example

In 1986, New Zealand restructured its social welfare department. The need for restructuring was based on increasing levels of dissatisfaction with the bureaucratic features of the Department of Social Welfare and with the continued emphasis of social work on individualized casework services, and increasing criticism regarding the ability of the Department to be responsive to local needs. Additionally, considerable pressure was being exerted by Maoris within the Department to respond more effectively to the needs of the Maori community through less reliance on state provided services and more support of extended family and tribal-based services.

The new model adopted by New Zealand allowed for joint decision making and resource sharing with communities. New Zealand particularly targeted indigenous communities for this new model of social work activity. These communities included the Maori *whanau* (extended family), *hapu* (subtribe), and *iwi* (tribe). The new process utilized community as provider within the social service delivery system. Changes in the department's social work practice included the development of culturally sensitive practice models, the establishment of Maori and Pacific Island teams, the involvement of local *iwi* in the recruitment and selection of staff, the development of strong links with the Maori community, and the promotion and funding of preventive, community-based services as determined by local communities. In recognition of the need to allow for the cultural context and community-based input, the passage of the Children, Young Persons and Their Families Act in 1989 provided for *whanau* conferences that have reduced the power of the state and professional social workers to make decisions for children, instead placing that responsibility in the hands of the *whanau*. As a result social workers now serve a more advisory, consultative, or facilitative role with clients and community groups rather than direct service provider roles (Barretta-Herman, 1994).

GLOBAL SOCIAL WORK VALUES AND ETHICAL CODES OF CONDUCT

Western social work practice began over a century ago. Democratic and humanitarian ideals guided the development of Western social work. It has incorporated the values of respect for the equality, worth, and dignity of all people and has focused on meeting human needs and developing human potential. Verschelden (1993) suggested the following as underlying social work values:

- primary importance and dignity of the individual;
- respect and appreciation for differences;
- commitment to social justice and the well-being of all in society; and
- willingness to persist despite frustration.

Findings from a recent study, however, indicate that the last three values are held commonly by social workers regardless of their country of origin, whereas the first (an individual focus) plays out differently across cultures (Rowe, et al., 2000).

Global social work practice is based on the values of human rights and social justice. A core concept is the principle of social inclusion by alleviating poverty and promoting self-determination and self-sufficiency of vulnerable and oppressed people. The underlying beliefs about the inherent value of people and the responsibility of societies to create conditions in which people can thrive are commonly held among social workers. These basic principles transcend the particular cultures and social welfare systems in various parts of the world and are the most universal beliefs that characterize social work globally (Morales & Sheafor, 2001).

Social work values are embodied in the profession's national and international codes of ethics. The IFSW and IASSW have given high priority to developing an international ethical code that includes 12 statements of the fundamental principles that underpin social work and provides a related set of guidelines for ethical practice. These principles are helpful not just in content but also as a means to generate support when advocating on local issues. Further, the purpose of the work on ethics is to promote ethical debate and reflection in the member associations and among the providers of social work in member countries. The following principles reflect social work's fundamental commitment to serving people (International Federation of Social Workers, 1996):

1. Every human being has a unique value, which justifies moral consideration for that person.
2. Each individual has the right to self-fulfillment to the extent that it does not encroach upon the same right of others, and has an obligation to contribute to the well-being of society.
3. Each society, regardless of its form, should function to provide the maximum benefits for all of its members.
4. Social workers have a commitment to principles of social justice.
5. Social workers have the responsibility to devote objective and disciplined knowledge and skill to aid individuals, groups, communities, and societies in their development and resolution of personal-societal conflicts and their consequences.
6. Social workers are expected to provide the best possible assistance to anybody seeking their help and advice, without unfair discrimination on the basis of gender, age, disability, color, social class, race, religion, language, political beliefs, or sexual orientation.
7. Social workers respect the basic human rights of individuals and groups as expressed in the United Nations Universal Declaration of Human Rights and other international conventions derived from that Declaration.
8. Social workers pay regard to the principles of privacy, confidentiality, and responsible use of information in their professional work. Social workers respect justified confidentiality even when their country's legislation is in conflict with this demand.
9. Social workers are expected to work in full collaboration with their clients, working for the best interests of the clients but paying due regard to the interests of others involved. Clients are encouraged to participate as much as possible, and should be informed of the risks and likely benefits of proposed courses of action.
10. Social workers generally expect clients to take responsibility, in collaboration with them, for determining courses of action affecting their lives. Compulsion

which might be necessary to solve one party's problems at the expense of the interests of others involved should take place only after careful explicit evaluation of the claims of the conflicting parties. Social workers should minimize the use of legal compulsion.

11. Social work is inconsistent with direct or indirect support of individuals, groups, political forces, or power structures suppressing their fellow human beings by employing terrorism, torture, or similar brutal means.

12. Social workers make ethically justified decisions, and stand by them, paying due regard to the IFSW International Declaration of Ethical Principles, and to the International Ethical Standards for Social Workers adopted by their national professional association.

Recognizing that all social problems are not universal, the IFSW encourages discussion within each national association to clarify important issues and problems particularly relevant to its country. IFSW (n.d.) identifies the following problem areas as widely recognized:

- When the loyalty of the social worker is in the middle of conflicting interests
  - between those of the social worker's own and the client's.
  - between conflicting interests of individual clients and other individuals.
  - between the conflicting interests of groups of clients.
  - between groups of clients and the rest of the population.
  - between systems/institutions and groups of clients.
  - between system/institution/employer and social workers.
  - between different groups of professionals.
- The fact that the social worker functions both as a helper and controller. The relation between these two opposite aspects of social work demands a clarification based on an explicit choice of values in order to avoid a mixing-up of motives or a lack of clarity in actions and their consequences. When social workers are expected to play a role in the state control of citizens, they are obliged to clarify the ethical implications of this role and to what extent this role is acceptable in relation to the basic ethical principles of social work.
- The duty of the social worker to protect the interests of the client will easily come into conflict with demands for efficiency and utility. This problem is becoming important with the introduction and use of information technology within the fields of social work.

The IFSW notes that social workers should always take into account the stated principles of IFSW when dealing with issues/problems within the above problem areas. Further, these principles provide the following methods for the solution of issues and problems:

- The various national associations of social workers are obliged to treat matters in such a way that ethical issues/problems may be considered and tried to be solved in collective forums within the organization. Such forums should enable the individual social worker to discuss, analyze, and consider ethical issues/problems in collaboration with colleagues, other expert groups, and/parties affected by the matter under discussion. In addition such forums should give the social worker opportunity to receive advice from colleagues and others. Ethical analysis and discussion should always seek to create possibilities and options.

- The member associations are required to produce and/or adapt ethical standards for the different fields of work, especially for those fields where there are complicated ethical issues/problems as well as areas where the ethical principles of social work may come into conflict with the respective country's legal system or the policy of the authorities.
- When ethical foundations are laid down as guidelines for actions within the practice of social work, it is the duty of the associations to aid the individual social worker in analyzing and considering ethical issues/problems on the basis of:
  - the basic principles of the Declaration.
  - the ethical/moral and political context of the actions, that is, an analysis of the values and forces constituting the framing conditions of the action.
  - the motives of the action, that is, to advocate to a higher level of consciousness of the aims and intentions the individual social worker might have regarding a course of action.
  - the nature of the action, that is, help in providing an analysis of the moral content of the action, for example, the use of compulsion as opposed to voluntary cooperation, guardianship vs. participation, etc.
  - the consequences the action might have for different groups, that is, an analysis of the consequences of different ways of action for all involved parties in both the short and long terms.

According to the IFSW, member associations are responsible for promoting debate, education, and research regarding ethical questions. The IFSW principles and policy statements are meant to act as guidelines rather than prescriptives for practitioners.

GLOBAL ETHICAL STANDARDS FOR SOCIAL WORKERS

Global Ethical Standards for Social Workers is based on the International Code of Ethics for the Professional Social Worker adopted by the IFSW in 1976. The IFSW outlines international ethical standards in five general categories: general standards of ethical conduct, social work standards relative to clients, social work standards relative to agencies and organizations, social work standards relative to colleagues, and standards relative to the profession. According to the IFSW (n.d.), on the basis of the International Declaration of Ethical Principles of Social Work (provided above), the social worker is obliged to recognize the following standards of ethical conduct:

- General Standards of Ethical Conduct
  - Seek to understand each individual client and the client system, and the elements that affect behavior and the service required.
  - Uphold and advance the values, knowledge, and methodology of the profession, refraining from any behavior that damages the functioning of the profession.
  - Recognize professional and personal limitations.
  - Encourage the utilization of all relevant knowledge and skills.
  - Apply relevant methods in the development and validation of knowledge.

- Contribute professional expertise to the development of policies and programs that improve the quality of life in society.
- Identify and interpret social needs.
- Identify and interpret the basis and nature of individual, group, community, national, and international social problems.
- Identify and interpret the work of the social work profession.
- Clarify whether public statements are made or actions performed on an individual basis or as representative of a professional association, agency or organization, or other group.
- Social Work Standards Relative to Clients
  - Accept primary responsibility to identified clients, but within limitations set by the ethical claims of others.
  - Maintain the client's right to a relationship of trust, to privacy and confidentiality, and to responsible use of information. The collection and sharing of information or data is related to the professional service function with the client informed as to its necessity and use. No information is released without prior knowledge and informed consent of the client, except where the client cannot be responsible or otherwise may be seriously jeopardized. A client has access to social work records concerning them.
  - Recognize and respect the individual goals, responsibilities, and differences of clients. Within the scope of the agency and the client's social milieu, the professional service shall assist clients to take responsibility for personal actions and help all clients with equal willingness. Where the professional service cannot be provided under such conditions the clients shall be so informed in such a way as to leave the clients free to act.
- Help the client—individual, group, community, or society—to achieve self-fulfillment and maximum potential within the limits of the respective rights of others. The service shall be based upon helping the client to understand and use the professional relationship, in furtherance of the client's legitimate desires and interests.
- Social Work Standards Relative to Agencies and Organizations
  - Work and/or cooperate with those agencies and organizations whose policies, procedures, and operations are directed toward adequate service delivery and encouragement of professional practice consistent with the ethical principles of the IFSW.
  - Responsibly execute the stated aims and functions of the agency or organizations, contributing to the development of sound policies, procedures, and practice in order to obtain the best possible standards or practice.
  - Sustain ultimate responsibility to the client, initiating desirable alterations of policies, procedures, and practice, through appropriate agency and organization channels. If necessary remedies are not achieved after channels have been exhausted, initiate appropriate appeals to higher authorities or the wider community of interest.
  - Ensure professional accountability to client and community for efficiency and effectiveness through periodic review of the process of service provision.
- Use all possible ethical means to bring unethical practice to an end when policies, procedures, and practices are in direct conflict with the ethical principles of social work.

- Social Work Standards Relative to Colleagues
  - Acknowledge the education, training, and performance of social work colleagues and professionals from other disciplines, extending all necessary cooperation that will enhance effective services.
  - Recognize differences of opinion and practice of social work colleagues and other professionals, expressing criticism through channels in a responsible manner.
  - Promote and share opportunities for knowledge, experience, and ideas with all social work colleagues, professionals from other disciplines, and volunteers for the purpose of mutual improvement.
  - Bring any violations of professional ethics and standards to the attention of the appropriate bodies inside and outside the profession, and ensure that relevant clients are properly involved.
  - Defend colleagues against unjust actions.
- Standards Relative to the Profession
  - Maintain the values, ethical principles, knowledge, and methodology of the profession and contribute to their clarification and improvement.
  - Uphold the professional standards of practice and work for their advancement.
  - Defend the profession against unjust criticism and work to increase confidence in the necessity for professional practice.
  - Present constructive criticism of the profession and its theories, methods, and practices.
  - Encourage new approaches and methodologies needed to meet new and existing needs.

The IFSW is currently working on a new ethical document that was presented at the IFSW General Meeting in Adelaide, Australia, in October 2004.

THE UNIVERSAL DECLARATION OF HUMAN RIGHTS

Soon after the events of the Second World War, members of the global community came together to adopt a body of principles and standards of behavior for all people, called the Universal Declaration of Human Rights (United Nations, 1994). Hoping to prevent many of the same types of crimes against humanity and violations of human rights evidenced during the Second World War, the Declaration delineates human rights and fundamental freedoms of all men and women in all nations, everywhere in the world. It states that

> liberty, equality, and dignity are the birthright of every person and that the rights to life, liberty, and security of persons are essential to the enjoyment of all other rights.
>
> Among the civil and political rights recognized by the Declaration are the right to freedom from slavery, from torture, from arbitrary arrest, and from interference with family; the right to recognition before the law; the right to a fair trial; the right to marry and have a family; and the right to freedom of thought and peaceful assembly. The economic, cultural, and social rights the Declaration

recognized include the right to work and the right to equal pay for equal work, the right to education, the right to a standard of living adequate for health and well-being, the right to rest and leisure, and the right to participate in the cultural life of communities.

Since 1948, the Universal Declaration of Human Rights has served as the premier standard for national and global efforts to promote and protect human rights and fundamental freedoms. It has provided the basic philosophy for the development of legally binding contracts and more recently has specifically included the rights of ethnic minorities, women, and children.

The creation of a body of international human rights law is one of the great achievements of the United Nations. Subsequent World Conferences organized by the United Nations (most notably in the 1990s) have reinforced the Declaration through specific plans of action.

In June 1993, The World Conference on Human Rights further strengthened its position on the human rights of children and declared that such rights would be a priority for action within the United Nations system. Through the setting of this priority the Conference recommended that UN agencies, such as UNICEF, periodically assess the effectiveness of their strategies and policies on children's enjoyment of human rights.

Although social work practice must always be contextualized within the culture and society in which it is located, human rights based on ideas of a common humanity and global citizenship must undergird practice (Ife, 2001). The concept of human rights implies a set of universal principles applicable to all human beings. Although appearing rather straightforward, the definition of what constitutes a "human" for the granting of human rights has been historically problematic. Examples abound throughout world history. Slaves in the United States were not afforded many fundamental human rights, children are often not given the same rights as adults, and people with intellectual disabilities, the frail or elderly, refugees, women, and prisoners are often denied common human rights. Thus, claiming that "human rights are universal" denies the reality that still today many persons are not given the same rights as others. Because the notion of "human" is a construction of society and culture, dialogue, discussion, and exchange of ideas must continue globally as we seek universal values (Ife, 2001). Ife (2001, p. 10–11) asserts that the following criteria should be met to serve as a definition of human rights:

- Realization of the claimed right is necessary for a person or group to be able to achieve their full humanity, in common with others.
- The claimed right is seen either as applying to all of humanity, and is something that the person or group claiming the right wishes to apply to all people anywhere, or as applying to people from specific disadvantaged or marginalized groups for whom realization of that right is essential to their achieving their full human potential.
- There is substantial universal consensus on the legitimacy of the claimed right; it cannot be called a 'human right' unless there is widespread support for it across cultural and other divides.

- It is possible for the claimed right to be effectively realized for all legitimate claimants. This excludes rights to things that are in limited supply, for example the right to housing with a panoramic view, the right to 'own' a TV channel, or the right to own large tracts of land.
- The claimed right does not contradict other human rights. This would disallow as human rights the 'right' to bear arms, the 'right' to hold other people in slavery, a man's 'right' to beat his wife and children, the 'right' to excessive profits resulting in poverty for others, and so on.

The following chapters throughout this book help to demonstrate the varying application of human rights around the globe and across cultures.

INTERNATIONAL FEDERATION OF SOCIAL WORKERS POLICY STATEMENT ON HUMAN RIGHTS

In 1996, the International Federation of Social Workers issued a policy statement on human rights. That policy statement recognizes the Universal Declaration of Human Rights by the General Assembly of the United Nations. Updated in 2003, the International Federation of Social Workers has adopted the following policy on human rights (pp. 5–9):

- Human rights are those fundamental entitlements that are considered to be necessary for developing each personality to the fullest. Violations of human rights are any arbitrary and selective actions that interfere with the full exercise of these fundamental entitlements.
- The social work profession, through historical and empirical evidence, is convinced that the achievement of human rights for all people is a fundamental prerequisite for a caring world and the survival of the human race. It is only through the recognition and implementation of the basic concept of the inherent dignity and worth of each person that a secure and stable world can be achieved. Consequently, social workers believe that the attainment of basic human rights requires positive action by individuals, communities, nations, and international groups, as well as a clear duty not to inhibit those rights.
- The social work profession accepts its share of responsibility for working to oppose and eliminate all violations of human rights. Social workers must exercise this responsibility in their practice with individuals, groups, and communities, in their roles as agency or organizational representatives, and as citizens of a nation and the world.
- IFSW, representing the social work profession internationally, sets forth the following human rights as a common standard and guide for the work of all professional social workers:
  - Life
    - The value of life is central to human rights work. Social workers have not only to resist violations of human rights that threaten or diminish the quality of life, but also actively to promote life enhancing and nurturing activities.
    - Physical and psychological well-being is an important aspect of the quality of life. The deterioration of the environment and the nonexistence or curtailment of health programs threaten life.

- Social workers assert the right of individuals and communities to have protection from preventable disease and disability.
- Freedom and Liberty
  - All human beings are born free. The fundamental freedoms include the right to liberty, to freedom from slavery, to freedom from arbitrary arrest, torture, and cruel or inhuman or degrading treatment, and freedom of thought and speech.
  - Next to life itself, freedom and liberty are the most precious human values asserting the worth of human existence.
- Equality and Non-Discrimination
  - The fundamental principle of equality is closely linked to principles of justice. Every person regardless of birth, gender, age, disability, race, color, language, religious or political beliefs, property, sexual orientation, status, or social class has a right to equal treatment and protection under the law.
  - Social workers have to ensure equal access to public services and social welfare provision in accordance with the resources of national and local governments, and have a particular responsibility to combat discrimination of any kind in their own practice.
- Justice
  - Every person has a right to protection against arbitrary arrest or interference with privacy, and to equal protection under the law. Where laws have been violated, every person has a right to a prompt and fair trial by an objective judicial authority. Those convicted are entitled to humane treatment whose purpose is to secure the reform and social readaptation of the individual.
  - The impartial operation of the law is a crucial safeguard for the citizen in the administration of justice. Social justice, however, requires more than a legal system untainted by interference by the executive. It requires the satisfaction of basic human needs and the equitable distribution of resources. It requires universal access to health care and education, thus enabling the achievement of human potential. It underpins concepts of social development. In the pursuit of social justice workers may have to face conflict with powerful elite groups in any given society.
- Solidarity
  - Every person whose fundamental freedoms are infringed has a right to support from fellow citizens. The concept of solidarity recognizes the fraternity ideal of the French Revolution, and the importance of mutual support. Social workers give expression to this through the Human Rights Commission in relation to social workers whose political freedoms are infringed. In their daily practice they express solidarity with the poor and oppressed. Poverty, hunger, and homelessness are violations of human rights. Social workers stand with the disadvantaged in campaigning for social justice.
- Social Responsibility
  - Social responsibility is the recognition that each of us has a responsibility to family, to community, to nation, and to the world community to contribute personal talents, energy, and commitment to the advancement of human rights. Those with intellectual and physical resources

should utilize them to assist those less well equipped. Social work's engagement with the disadvantaged is a reflection of that responsibility. No person or collective body has the right to engage in any activity, including propaganda, to incite war, hostility, hatred, bigotry, or violence, contrary to the institution and maintenance of human rights.

- Peace and Nonviolence
  - Peace is more than the absence of organized conflict. It is the goal of achieving harmony with self and with others. Social workers are committed to the pursuit of nonviolence. Their experience in conflict resolution teaches that mediation and arbitration are effective instruments to overcome seemingly irreconcilable differences. Nonviolence does not mean passivity in the face of injustice. Social workers will resist and exercise nonviolent pressure for change, but will not engage in acts of violence in the course of their professional activity. Social workers devote their energies to constructive efforts to achieve social justice.
- The Environment
  - Humankind has trusteeship responsibility for the care of the planet. Environmental degradation poses a threat to life itself in some areas, and to the quality of life in many countries. False development models based on industrialization, the unequal distribution of resources, excessive consumerism, and ignorance of the pernicious consequences of pollution have all contributed to this global plight. Social workers need to work with community groups in tackling the consequences of environmental decline and destruction.

SUMMARY

Human rights are dynamic rather than static in nature. Not all rights claimed by people can be regarded as human rights. The conflicts between human rights and individual rights, and conflicts between the globalization of human rights and the locality of human rights, challenge all of us to continue the dialogue on the universality of human rights. Social work is uniquely poised to engage in the unfolding discussion. Human rights should be the framework for guiding social work practice.

Global standards for social work practice are consistent with local, regional, and national standards throughout the world. Differences, however, lie in the emphasis placed on the method of practice, with social workers in developing countries more likely to employ community organization and social development strategies. Cultural differences demand that social workers be culturally sensitive, responsive, and competent in working with specific populations. Because societies and cultures are increasingly complex and changing, social workers must be willing to view themselves as lifelong learners—willing to change, adapt, and utilize strategies that are relevant and specific to differing situations. This is one of the most demanding elements of domestic social work practice and is even more challenging in the global arena. It is also one of the most exciting and dynamic elements of social work practice.

Thinking About Practice: From Local to Global Perspectives

1. What are the most frequently used roles of social workers where you live? You may want to interview several practicing social workers in your community who work with different types of problems and populations. How do they see their practice role?

2. How might the roles of social workers in your community differ from social workers in other communities, regions, or nations?
3. Compare the Universal Declaration of Human Rights and the IFSW policy statement on human rights. How are they similar/different?

4. Apply the Universal Declaration of Human Rights and the IFSW policy statement on human rights to at least one client population in your community. In what ways is the protection of human rights of clients upheld or violated?

Social Work Practice and Social Justice Website

Please go to the Book Companion Website at http://www.thomsonedu.com/author/sowers to find a rich collection of related articles selected by the authors from Info Trac College Edition.

References

Barretta-Herman, A. (1994). Revisioning the community as provider: Restructuring New Zealand's social services. *International Social Work, 37*(1), 7–21.

Constable, T. T. (1983). Values, religion, and social work practice. *Social Thought, 9,* 29–41.

Doel, M., & Shardlow, S. (1996). Introduction to the context of practice learning: An overview of key themes. In M. Does & S. Shardlow (Eds). *Social work in a changing world: An international perspective on practice learning.* Brookfield: VT: Arena Ashgate Publishing.

Faver, C. A. (1986). Religion, research and social work. *Social Thought, 18,* 20–29.

Goldstein, H. (1986). Toward the integration of theory and practice: A humanistic approach. *Social Work, 5,* 352–357.

Gowdy, B. A. (1994). From technical rationality to participating consciousness. *Social Work, 4,* 362–370.

Ife, J. (2001). *Human rights and social work: Towards rights-based practice.* New York: The Cambridge Press.

International Federation of Social Workers. (n.d.) *The ethics of social work principles and standards.* Retrieved March 10, 2003, from http://www.ifsw.org/Publications/4.4.pub.html

International Federation of Social Workers. (1996). *International policy on human rights.* Hong Kong: Author.

Lorenz, W. (1997, August 24). *Social work in a changing Europe.* Paper presented to the Joint European Regional Seminar of IFSW and IASSW on Culture and Identity, Dublin, Ireland.

Manoleas, P. (1994). An outcome approach to assessing the cultural competence of MSW students. *Journal of Multicultural Social Work, 3*(1), 43–57.

Mason, H. R. C., Benjamin, M. P., & Lewis, S. (1996). The cultural competence model: Implications for child and family mental health services. In C. A. Heflinger & C. T. Nixon (Eds.), *Families and the mental health system for children and adolescents* (pp. 165–190). Thousand Oaks, CA: Sage Publications.

Matthews, L. (1996). Culturally competent models in human service organizations. *Journal of Multicultural Social Work, 4*(4), 131–135.

McPhatter, A. R. (1997). Cultural competence in child welfare: What is it? How do we achieve it? What happens without it? *Child Welfare, 76,* 255–278.

Morales, A. T., & Sheafor, B. W. (2001). *Social work: A profession of many faces* (9th ed.). Boston: Allyn & Bacon.

National Association of Social Workers. (1996). *Code of ethics.* Washington, DC: Author.

Obaid, T. A., & Malloch-Brown, M. (2002). *Joint statement to the Second World Assembly on Ageing*, April 8–12, 2002, Madrid, Spain.

Ronnau, J. P. (1994). Teaching cultural competence: Practical ideas for social work educators. *Journal of Multicultural Social Work, 3*(1), 29–42.

Rowe, W., Hanley, J., Moreno, E. R., & Mould, J. (2000). Voices of social work practice: International reflections on the effects of globalization. *Canadian Social Work, 2*(1), 65–87.

Sacco, T. (1996). Towards an inclusive paradigm for social work. In M. Doel & S. Shardlow (Eds.), *Social work in a changing world: An international perspective on practice learning.* Brookfield, VT: Arena Ashgate Publishing.

Saleeby, D. (1994). Culture, theory, and narrative: The intersection of meanings in practice. *Social Work, 39*(4), 351–359.

Senghor, L. S. (1966). Negritude. *Optima, 16,* 1–8.

Setiloane, G. M. (1986). *African theology: An introduction.* Johannesburg: Skotaville.

Sherraden, M. S., & Martin, J. J. (1994). Social work with immigrants: International issues in service delivery. *International Social Work, 37*(4), 369–84.

Shutte, A. (1993). *Philosophy for Africa.* Cape Town: UCT Press.

Sowers-Hoag, K. M., & Sandau-Beckler, P. (1996). Educating for cultural competence in the generalist curriculum. *Journal of Multicultural Social Work, 4*(3), 37–56.

United Nations. (1994). *Human rights: A compilation of international instruments* (Vols. 1 & 2). New York: Author.

United Nations Population Fund. (n.d.). *Culture matters—Working with communities and faith-based organizations: Case studies from country programmes.* Retrieved July 10, 2004, from http://www.unfpa.org

Weaver, H. N. (1999). Indigenous people and the social work profession: Defining culturally competent services. *Social Work, 44*(3), 217–225.

Zastrow, C. (1995). *The practice of social work* (5th ed.). Pacific Grove, CA: Brooks/Cole.

Verschelden, C. (1993). Social work values and pacifism: Opposition to war as a professional responsibility. *Social Work, 38*(6), 765–769.

A Global Perspective Is a Human Perspective

PART 2

Sample Populations

Globally, all societies have portions of their population that are fragile and vulnerable. Social workers strive to create conditions that empower, support, and sustain disadvantaged and oppressed people who cannot advocate for themselves. Historically and currently children, women, and the elderly are among the most vulnerable and at risk peoples in every country of the world. This section of the text focuses on their plight and provides both extreme and diverse examples of their oppression. This section also provides some solutions—exemplars from around the world that have proven effective in promoting the safety, well-being, and advancement of children, women, and the elderly.

We make a living by what we get, we make a life by what we give.
Sir Winston Churchill

4 CHAPTER | Social Work Practice with Children and Youth

CORE ELEMENTS OF GLOBAL CHILD WELFARE

The emergence of a global women's movement brings worldwide issues of social services and supports for women and children to the fore (Popple & Leighninger, 2002). Today's generation of 1.2 billion adolescents, the largest in global history, will be entering adulthood during a period of rapid global change. Despite having their youth in common, these adolescents have a wide variance of life experiences and face very different political, economic, social, and cultural realities in their communities (United Nations Population Fund, n.d.). Nearly half of the world's population is under the age of 25, constituting the largest generation of youth in history. Their success as adults will largely depend upon supportive networks of family, community, and government. And the success and future of various countries will be largely determined by their youth's educational and health status, as well as their readiness to take on adult roles and responsibilities. Early marriage and childbearing, incomplete education, and HIV/AIDS are threats to millions of today's adolescents and young people. In order to ensure that young people will be able to lead healthy and productive lives and contribute fully to their communities, emphasis must be placed on increasing the knowledge, opportunities, choices, and participation of young people.

The global community has established and accepted specific human rights for all people. These rights include ones that are particularly relevant to adolescents and youth, and that specifically address the opportunities and risks they face. Among these are gender equality and the rights to education, health (including reproductive and sexual health information), and services appropriate to a person's age, capacities, and circumstances. Tremendous benefits can be derived by ensuring these rights for youth by facilitating individual empowerment and well-being, the reduction of poverty, the improvement of prospects for social and economic progress and stability, and the reduction of the spread of HIV disease. Taking action to ensure these rights must become a development priority.

Positive dialogue and greater understanding among parents, families, communities, and governments about the critically complex and sensitive situations facing adolescents and young people can lead to a solution-focused response that develops the supportive relationships and institutions needed by young people. This need exists in every region throughout the world.

The terms *adolescents, youths,* and *young people* are used differently in various parts of the world. Some societies do not recognize these terms at all. Where they are recognized, however, the different roles, responsibilities, and ages associated with these categories are dependent upon the context of the local region. The key life events of young people such as marriage, sexual debut (first sexual intercourse), employment, childbearing, acceptance into adult organizations, and political participation often occur at differing times between and within societies. The most commonly used definitions in different demographic, policy, and social contexts are as follows:

- Adolescents: 10–19 years of age (early adolescence, 10–14; late adolescence, 15–19).
- Youth: 15–24 years of age.
- Young people: 10–24 years of age.

Different distinctions are often made by national programs. In India, for example, the policy affecting youth includes people up to age 35. Programs in Jamaica base their goals and strategies for youth upon various age increments. Recognizing that the interests, skills, and needs of younger adolescents are different from those of older adolescents, Jamaica tailors its programs and policies to fit the need of specific age groups. And, in many countries, health education materials are tailored to different grade levels.

In almost all societies adolescence is viewed as a growth process and most societies attempt to help children as they grow into adulthood. In traditional rural communities, the extended family and established systems of hierarchy and respect guide young people's transition into adulthood. But in all developing countries, the rural traditions of the past are being lost to urbanization. This transition to urban life brings a different set of opportunities and risks, as well as an increasingly complex set of social demands and frameworks of support. In the rapidly changing urban environment, young people are more likely to derive most of their information and understanding about the world, what to expect and how to behave, from their peers, and increasingly from mass media. There is a growing tension between parents, who tend to see children as needing protection, and the outside world, which makes demands upon them as adults. This tension of expectations produces serious dilemmas and internal conflicts for modern adolescents (United Nations Population Fund, 2004).

From age 10–19 young people are faced with many life transition challenges. Cultural and societal circumstances influence how and when young people will experience these transitions. Most societies expect that children at age 10 live at home, go to school, have not yet gone through puberty, are unmarried, and have never worked. But, within 10 years (by the time they reach the age of 20) many adolescents have left school and home. Many of these young people have become sexually active, married, and entered the labor force (Cohen, 2003).

Despite the differing views of adolescence from one society, culture, or community to the next, the psychosocial, emotional, and biological changes that characterize this stage of life are widely shared. During this stage of life, the personality and self-identity of the young person becomes more defined. It is during this stage that youth begin to expand their relationships and friendships to persons outside of the immediate and expanded family. They begin to establish greater autonomy as individuals and develop greater interpersonal and social skills. The developmental process, which influences their understanding of the biological, emotional, and social changes they experience, is strongly influenced by their sense of social identity and purpose, self-perception and self-esteem, thoughts and feelings, and capacity to establish caring relationships and intimacy with others.

Worldwide, adolescence is a time when many people become sexually active. This may occur within or outside of marriage. Guidance and support during this developmental stage is critical, particularly since this is a time when adolescents are at high risk of physical and sexual abuse, exploitation, and violence. Their striving for greater autonomy and self-definition often results in a reduced reliance on parents or other adults as trusted sources of guidance and support, leaving them more vulnerable. This is especially true when it comes to sensitive areas such as sexual and reproductive health and gender relations. Without support and guidance, young people are vulnerable to situations that may result in exploitation, violence, or abuse. They are also particularly vulnerable to becoming sexually active without the knowledge and means they need to avoid unintended consequences.

The onset of puberty often results in a change in the way girls and boys are perceived and treated by their parents. Peers, extended family, and the community may also treat them differently. For many boys and girls, these changes often result in marked differences in the opportunities and constraints girls and boys face, based on their gender. This change and imposition of strict gender norms can be especially dramatic and harmful for girls. Girls may find increased restrictions on their freedom of movement, educational and personal development, security, and life choices. Girls in many parts of the world are taught during this stage of their development to be submissive to male authority. They begin to recognize that their social worth will be defined by if and whom they marry, and the children they have. Boys face maturational pressures different from girls, often having to prove their masculinity and virility.

Adolescents and Globalization

Historically, adolescents have not been given serious consideration by public sector programs and budgets. In fact, until recently, the focus has been on children under 10, and then on adults. However, since the 1990s, many international agreements and forums have focused their attention on the development of policies and programs to address the needs of adolescents and young people.

Young people today face a longer period between sexual maturity and marriage. They are entering puberty at a younger age but getting married later than in the past. As a result, many young people now are dependent upon outside sources for their information and guidance. Influenced by a growing network of global telecommunication and youth culture, young people today rely increasingly on the mass media. Whereas they once depended upon the family for imparting social norms, they are now much more likely to get their information, including information about sexuality and health, from outside of the family.

Overall, young people tend to have higher levels of educational attainment than in the past. The complexity of rapidly changing societies means that young people today need a better education and more skills to compete in today's world, and overcome social exclusion and poverty. Despite the progress that has occurred across the globe in increasing school enrollment, millions of adolescents still do not have access to continuing education, or are forced to abandon their schooling due to poverty or HIV/AIDS, among other reasons. Access to relevant information, skills, and opportunities is critical to young people being able to act on their own and claim their human rights. This aspect of empowerment is a critical global issue to ensure the promotion and safeguarding of human rights for the younger generation. Global efforts must be made to recognize the needs and realities of adolescents. There must be an increased emphasis on the promotion of the rights and capacities of young people, which will facilitate their participation in decisions affecting their lives.

Universal Rights of the Child

The rights of young people are established by national laws and international agreements. However, these rights are often neglected and largely go unrecognized. National laws and international agreements explicate the human rights that governments, families, and society at large are responsible for fulfilling. The Convention on the Rights of the Child is the one international human rights treaty that fully articulates the standards to which all governments must aspire in realizing rights for all children. It is the most universally accepted human rights instrument in history. The Convention on the Rights of the Child was unanimously adopted by the United Nations General Assembly on November 20, 1989. It has been ratified by every country in the world except two (the United States and Somalia, both which have signaled their intention to ratify by formally signing the Convention). The ratification of the Convention on the Rights of the Child has placed children at the forefront of the universal application of human rights. By ratifying the Convention on the Rights of the Child, each national government agreed to protect and ensure children's rights. By their ratification, each national government also agreed to be accountable to the global community for upholding the rights of children as specified in the Convention (United Nation's Children's Fund, n.d.; Youth Advocate Program International, n.d.).

The Convention on the Rights of the Child was built upon varied legal systems and cultural traditions. It is a set of nonnegotiable standards and obligations for children that is universally agreed upon. It spells out the basic human rights that children everywhere have without discrimination.

> The Convention offers a vision of the child as an individual and a member of a family and a community, with rights and responsibilities appropriate to his or her age and stage of development. Basic human rights for children include the right to survival; to develop to the fullest; to protection from harmful influences, abuse, and exploitation; and to participate fully in family, cultural, and social life. Every right spelled out in the Convention is inherent to the human dignity and harmonious development of every child. The Convention protects children's rights by setting standards in health care, education, and legal, civil, and social services. These standards are benchmarks against which progress can be assessed.

The Convention on the Rights of the Child requires that governments report their compliance status to the United Nations Committee on the Rights of the Child. A report is required two years after initial ratification and every five years thereafter. The Committee consists of an internationally elected body of independent experts in Geneva. This Committee monitors continuing implementation of the Convention and requires governments that have ratified the Convention to submit their reports on the status of children's rights in their countries. The Committee reviews and comments on these reports. The Committee recommends and promotes the development of special institutions for the protection of children's rights to member nations. The Committee promotes the utilization of international assistance from member governments and technical assistance from many international organizations like the United Nations Children's Fund. Member nation-states are required and expected to promote the best interests of the child through undertaking actions and developing policies that promote child protection and well-being (United Nations Children's Fund, n.d.; Youth Advocate Program International, n.d.).

The first legally binding international agreement to address the full range of human rights, the Convention on the Rights of the Child incorporates civil and political rights as well as economic, social, and cultural rights. The Convention on the Rights of the Child adopted two optional protocols in 2002. These protocols addressed the involvement of children in armed conflict and the sale of children, child prostitution, and child pornography. The optional protocols were adopted to strengthen the provisions of the Convention in these areas (United Nations Children's Fund, n.d.; Youth Advocate Program International, n.d.).

The Changing Global Context of Home and Family Life

Traditionally, in most parts of the world the nuclear family relied heavily upon extended family relations. The child-parent relationship was augmented and enhanced by aunts, uncles, grandparents, and cousins. Because of migration, particularly to the cities, and the development of new values and understandings there has been a drastic reduction in extended family support. This has been exacerbated, particularly in cities, by poverty, drug abuse, and the impact of HIV/AIDS. As a result, parents are often finding increased demands placed upon them, in conjunction with fewer extended family supports. In addition to the reduction of extended family supports, many young people are living without one or both of their parents, and may not be able to rely on their families for support (United Nations Population Fund, n.d.).

Homelessness and Street Children

The loss of one or both parents dramatically changes adolescents' lives, forcing them to become heads of households or onto the streets. Poverty and political and ethnic conflict exacerbate the situation. The true extent of the numbers of children living on the streets is difficult to ascertain because of the hidden and isolated nature of street children. UNICEF (n.d.) estimates, however, that there are approximately 100 million street children worldwide, with that number constantly growing. Latin America has approximately 40 million street children and at least 18 million street children are in India. Those studies which do exist estimate that street children are most often boys aged 10 to 14, with increasingly younger children being affected (Beasley, 1999). Although many girls also live on the streets, it is believed that they are fewer in number because they are considered useful at home caring for younger siblings and the household (Beasley, 1999).

Street children are highly vulnerable and are often the victims of extreme social and economic distress, natural disaster, disease, armed conflict, and exploitation (USAID, n.d.). AIDS has so far orphaned at least 13 million children currently under the age of 15. The total number of children orphaned by AIDS since it began is estimated to more than double by 2010 (USAID, UNICEF, & UNAIDS, 2002). Another reason that children become homeless or take to the streets is the disintegration of homes and families due to war or civil emergency (United Nations Children's Fund, 2001). Children may be driven from their homes due to extreme poverty, violence or substance abuse in the family, or conflicts with relatives. Some children may be escaping physical or mental abuse, failure at school, mental health or behavioral problems, boredom, lack of opportunity, or unsatisfactory peer relations (National Center for Missing and Exploited Children, n.d.; ChildLine, n.d.; Centre for Addiction and Mental Health, n.d.).

Many orphaned adolescents are involved in crime, drug use, and street life. Girls and young women are often forced into early marriage or turn to sex work due to economic or parental pressure, further subjecting them to physical, mental, and sexual trauma. The risk of contracting sexually transmitted diseases including HIV/AIDS is high for these youth (United Nations Population Fund, n.d.).

Article 27 of the Convention on the Rights of the Child asserts that "States Parties recognize the right of every child to a standard of living adequate for the child's physical, mental, spiritual, moral and social development." Homelessness denies each of those rights. A street child is "any girl or boy who has not reached adulthood, for whom the street (in the widest sense of the word, including unoccupied dwellings, wasteland, etc.) has become his or her habitual abode and/or source of livelihood, and who is inadequately protected, directed, and supervised by responsible adults" (Youth Advocate Program International, n.d.).

USAID has divided street children into four categories:

- Children who have no home but the streets, and no family support. They move from place to place, living in shelters and abandoned buildings.
- Children who visit their families regularly and might even return every night to sleep at home, but spend most days and some nights on the street because of poverty, overcrowding, or sexual or physical abuse at home.

- Children who live on sidewalks or city squares with the rest of their families. They may be displaced due to poverty, wars, or natural disasters. The families often live a nomadic life, carrying their possessions with them. Children in this case often work on the streets with other members of their families.
- Children who live in institutionalized care and come from a situation of homelessness and are at risk of returning to a life on the street.

Although there are children who are homeless and living on the streets in all parts of the world, child homelessness is largely an urban phenomenon. Street children are evident in developing countries and some of the most affluent countries. Latin America and India have large populations of street children despite the efforts of government agencies and nongovernmental organizations in those countries (Beasley, 1999). A large number of street children are homeless due to the AIDS epidemic and civil wars in Africa. Many of these children have been abandoned as a result of parents dying from AIDS or armed conflict. Failing economies and falling currencies in parts of Asia force the poorest families onto the street, often leaving children abandoned and homeless. Unstable political transitions, such as the end of Communism in Eastern Europe, caused unprecedented numbers of street children due to inadequate social security for the poor and those who were formerly state-supported. Children often experience the effects of political, economic, and social crises within their countries more severely than adults, and many lack the adequate institutional support to address their special needs (Youth Advocate Program International, n.d.).

In 1996, the United States had 5.5 million children living in extreme poverty, approximately 1 million of whom were on the streets (Alston, 1998). Research conducted by the Luxembourg Income Study shows that poor children in the United States are poorer than children in most Western industrialized countries. The United States has less generous social programs, the widest gap between rich and poor, and high numbers of poor immigrants as well as unwed teen mothers (*New York Times,* 1999). The poverty and social conditions many American children face lead to large numbers of homeless and street children (Department of Health and Human Services, 2003).

Homelessness and street life have extremely detrimental effects on children. Because of their unstable lifestyles, inadequate living conditions, and lack of medical care, young people are increasingly susceptible to many chronic illnesses, including sexually transmitted diseases, gastrointestinal disorders, and respiratory and ear infections (Alston, 1998). Children who are without family, community, or organizational support often must scavenge for food or engage in exploitive physical work to support themselves. Often, adults or older youth are instrumental in enticing homeless children into selling drugs, stealing, and prostitution (Youth Advocate Program International, n.d.). Drug use by children on the streets is common. Studies have found that up to 90 percent of street children use psychoactive substances, including medicines, alcohol, cigarettes, heroin, cannabis, and readily available industrial and household products, which can produce serious side effects and addictions (Youth Program International, n.d.).

Children's mental, social, and emotional growth are affected by their transitory lifestyles. The manner in which they are treated by authorities, who often expel them from such temporary homes as doorways, park benches, and railway platforms, also negatively affects these children. Police officers or death squads in countries in Latin America, particularly Colombia, Guatemala, Honduras, and Brazil, have been known to inflict torture and violence on street children (Youth Advocate Program International, n.d.). Lacking security, protection, and hope, street children continuously face the deep-rooted and negative stigma associated with homelessness.

As this vulnerable population continues to grow, many governments, nongovernmental organizations, and members of civil society around the world have increased their attention on homeless and street children. Recognizing the increasing populations of children living in the streets, and how societies marginalize or act violently against them, the United Nations issued a Resolution on the Plight of Street Children. The resolution called for international cooperation to address the needs of homeless children and for enforcement of international child rights laws. As a result of this resolution, some European nations have taken effective steps toward combating child homelessness. These nations include Belgium, Finland, the Netherlands, Portugal, and Spain. And, in many countries, a right to housing has been included (Alston, 1998). In 1987 the Finnish government implemented a plan that included house-building, social welfare, health care service, and a duty to provide a decent home for every homeless person. Implementing this plan reduced by half the number of homeless people in Finland over 10 years (Alston, 1998). Locally and regionally shelters have been established to assist street children. Shelter programs are designed to provide safety, healthcare, counseling, education, vocational training, legal aid, and other social services (Youth Advocate Program International, n.d.).

Children and War

War can have devastating effects upon children. Children may be the victims of combat or may be forced into war as child soldiers. Such effects are a clear violation of the Convention on the Rights of the Child, which seeks to protect the rights of every child. Despite international humanitarian law, which asserts that children's rights must be respected during armed conflict, children are often taken from their families, forced into serving as soldiers, held in captivity, or simply killed (International Committee of the Red Cross, n.d.). During the 1990s nearly 2 million children were killed in armed conflicts and an additional 6 million were seriously injured or permanently disabled. Twelve million children have become homeless around the world due to war (United Nations Children's Fund, 1995). In 2000, an estimated 300,000 child soldiers, some as young as seven years old, were involved in 30 armed conflicts around the world (United Nations Children's Fund, 2001). Each day, 5,000 children become refugees, and one in every

230 persons in the world is a child or adolescent who has been forced to flee his or her home (United Nations High Commission for Refugees, 1999). A child soldier, as defined by the United Nations Children's Fund, is "any child—girl or boy—under the age of 18, who is part of any kind of regular or irregular armed force or armed group, including but not limited to combatants, cooks, porters, messengers, and anyone accompanying such groups other than as family members. It includes girls and boys recruited for sexual purposes or forced marriage" (United Nations Children's Fund, 2002, p. 35).

Government forces, rebel groups and guerilla armies use child soldiers to bolster their forces. Because of their psychological and physical immaturity, and because they are easily manipulated, obedient, and cheap, children are attractive as recruits. Because of their age, children also appear to be nonthreatening and are used to confuse the adversary or to serve as informants. Long lasting conflicts resulting in a lack of available adult soldiers and the proliferation of easily operated small arms can lead to the use of child soldiers as well.

Child soldiers are often poor, illiterate, and from rural zones. Children who are most at risk live in combat zones, are separated from their parents, or are displaced from their homes. Orphans and refugee children are particularly vulnerable to recruitment.

Key factors contributing to the growing involvement of children in many conflict areas include poverty, lack of access to education, unemployment, domestic violence, exploitation, and abuse. Some children enlist because they view enlistment as their only means of survival in war-torn regions; others enroll after seeing family members tortured or killed by government forces or armed opposition groups (United Nations, 2003).

Although some children volunteer, most child soldiers are recruited forcibly. Children of different ages have been abducted from their homes, schools, or refugee camps in order to be made soldiers. Recently there has been a significant increase in the kidnapping of boys and girls by government or opposition forces (Youth Advocate Program International, n.d.).

After more than 20 years of war, hundreds of thousands of adolescents from Afghanistan are refugees in Pakistan. Family poverty and a lack of access to education have led young people to work in menial, dangerous, and sometimes illegal jobs, often as carpet weavers, garbage pickers, brick makers, house servants, and drug sellers (Women's Commission for Refugee Women and Children, 2002). In 1998 children as young as 13 were forcibly recruited by military units in the Democratic Republic of Congo and in Afghanistan (United Nations Children's Fund, 2001). In 1999, Angolan armed forces rounded up young men from street markets to force them into the military. In Myanmar, the army is reported to have kidnapped underage children from schools. In El Salvador, Ethiopia, and Uganda, a third of all child soldiers were girls (United Nations Children's Fund, n.d.).

Some progress has been made in recent years in the development of a legal and policy framework for protecting children involved in armed conflict. Today the three key regulations that prohibit the use of child soldiers are:

- the Optional Protocol on the Involvement of Children in Armed Conflict to the Convention of the Rights of the Child passed in February 2002;
- the Rome Stature of the International Criminal Court passed in 1998;
- and the Convention 182 of the International Labor Organization passed in 1999.

Stateless Children

Nationality establishes what rights and responsibilities are provided to a person, and grant him/her citizenship. But many people do not have a nationality or are denied the rights of citizenship because they lack official proof of birth. An estimated 50 million births per year are unregistered. Sub-Saharan Africa is the region with the highest percentage of unregistered births. South Asia, however, has the largest number of unregistered children in any one region. Many countries, such as Afghanistan, Cambodia, Eritrea, Ethiopia, Namibia, and Oman, have no mandatory birth registration system (Aird, Harnett, & Shah, 2002).

The Universal Declaration of Human Rights (Article 15) asserts that "everyone has the right to a nationality and that no child should be arbitrarily deprived of his or her nationality" (United Nations Human Rights Commission, n.d.). The United Nations Convention on the Rights of the Child (Article 7.1) states that "national governments must register children immediately after birth and that children should enjoy the right from birth to acquire a nationality" (United Nations Human Rights Commission, n.d.). The Convention on the Rights of the Child expects that all member states and nations put into practice policies and programs that guarantee that families and national authorities can secure citizenship for every child in that nation. Every country in the world, except the United States and Somalia, has ratified the Convention on the Rights of the Child.

Child Labor

Estimates indicate that one in every six children in the world today aged between 5 and 17 years is working instead of attending school (HelpAge, n.d.). About 100 million children under 16 years of age are exploited as a source of cheap labor in many parts of the developing world (U.N. Chronicle, 1989). Although the International Labor Organization (ILO) lacks figures on full-time child employment, children comprise approximately 11 percent of the work force in Asia, 17 percent in Africa, and 25 percent in Latin America (United Nations Children's Fund, 1995). The population of economically active children is 30 percent in India, 20 percent in Africa, and 10–25 percent in Latin America (Kawewe & Dibie, 1999).

In many parts of Asia, poor children work in factories, make bricks, become prostitutes, beg, or do menial domestic labor for wealthy families. In India, many children make carpets and clothes for export to the West. Many Latin American children pan for gold in sweltering, malaria-ridden jungles or suffer eardrum damage from diving for fish. And in Africa, many children work long hours in subsistence farming or tend domestic animals (U.N. Chronicle, 1989).

The Convention on the Rights of the Child (Article 32) recognizes the right of the child "to be protected from economic exploitation and from performing any work that is likely to be hazardous or to interfere with the child's education, or to be harmful to the child's health or physical, mental, spiritual, moral, or social development" (Convention on the Rights of the Child, n.d.). In addition, the Convention requires the appropriate regulation of the hours and conditions of employment and appropriate penalties or other sanctions to ensure the effective enforcement. However, the U.N. has limited international enforcement capability over governments that ignore or condone child labor. This significantly complicates the issue of child labor. Further complicating the issue is that many of the developed countries continually buy the goods made by exploited children overseas.

Child Protection

The United Nations Convention on the Rights of the Child (Article 19) "seeks to protect children from all forms of physical or mental violence, injury or abuse, neglect or negligent treatment, maltreatment or exploitation" (Convention on the Rights of the Child, n.d.). Despite these efforts, reports of infanticide, mutilation, abandonment, and other forms of physical and sexual violence against children are widespread. Deeply rooted in cultural, social, and economic practices, child abuse is a significant global problem. For example, an estimated 57,000 children worldwide were victims of homicide in the year 2000 (World Health Organization, n.d.). But it is difficult to know the true extent of the problem because many child deaths are not routinely investigated or autopsied. The highest rates of fatal child abuse are found among children aged 0–4 years old. The most common cause of child death is head injury, followed by abdominal injuries and intentional suffocation. Millions of children are victims of nonfatal abuse and neglect. In some studies, between one-quarter and one-half of children report severe and frequent physical abuse. Frequently cited forms of abuse include being beaten, kicked, or tied up by parents. Available data also suggest that about 20 percent of women and 5–10 percent of men suffered sexual abuse as children. A substantial amount of harsh punishment in the form of hitting, punching, kicking, or beating is perpetrated upon children in schools and other institutions. Additionally, many children are subjected to psychological or emotional abuse as well as neglect, although the exact extent of the frequency and severity of these problems is not known (United Nations Children's Fund, n.d.).

Ill health caused by child abuse forms a significant portion of the global burden of disease. According to the World Health Organization (n.d.) and the United Nations Children's Fund (n.d.), apart from physical injuries such as bruises and welts, burns and scalds, and lacerations and fractures, child maltreatment is associated with a number of other consequences, including:

- alcohol and drug abuse;
- cognitive impairment and developmental delays;
- delinquent, violent, and other risk-taking behaviors;
- eating and sleep disorders;
- poor school performance;
- poor relationships;
- reproductive health problems;
- post-traumatic stress disorder;
- depression and anxiety; and
- suicidal behavior and self-harm.

Research has linked certain characteristics of the child and caregiver, as well as features of the family environment, to child abuse and neglect. Risk factors associated with child abuse have been delineated by the World Health Organization (n.d.) and include:

- The age and sex of the child. Young children are most at risk of physical abuse. The highest rates of sexual abuse are found among children who have reached puberty or adolescence. In most cases, boys are the victims of beatings and physical punishment more often than girls. Girls are at higher risk of infanticide, sexual abuse, forced prostitution, and educational and nutritional neglect.
- Being raised by a single parent or by very young parents without the support of an extended family.
- Household overcrowding.
- A lack of income to meet the family's needs.
- The presence of other violent relationships in the home.

Communities with high rates of poverty and few social networks and neighborhood support systems are more likely to experience child maltreatment. In fact, research indicates that low poverty rates, and the availability of strong social networks and neighborhood support systems, are protective factors for vulnerable children (World Health Organization, n.d.). Parents who have low self-esteem, poor impulse control, mental health problems, and antisocial behavior are more likely to abuse their children. These parents tend to be uninformed and have unrealistic expectations about child development. Social networks and neighborhood support systems can provide the parental education and oversight to prevent child abuse or provide early intervention to stop child maltreatment.

The United Nations Children's Fund (n.d.) has identified eight key aspects to a protective environment for children:

- **Attitudes, traditions, customs, behavior, and practices:** In societies where attitudes or traditions facilitate abuse—for example, regarding sex with minors, the appropriateness of severe corporal punishment, the application of harmful traditional practices or differences in the perceived status and value of boys and girls—the environment will not be protective. In societies where all forms of violence against children are taboo, and where the rights of children are broadly respected by custom and tradition, children are more likely to be protected.
- **Governmental commitment to fulfilling protection rights:** Government interest in, recognition of, and commitment to child protection is an essential element for a protective environment.

- **Open discussion of, and engagement with, child protection issues:** At the most immediate level, children need to be free to speak up about child protection concerns affecting them or other children. At the national level, both media attention and civil society engagement with the issue contribute to child protection. Partnerships among actors at all levels are essential for an effective and coordinated response.

- **Legislation and enforcement:** An adequate legislative framework, its consistent implementation, accountability, and a lack of impunity are essential elements of a protective environment.

- **Capacity:** Health workers, teachers, police, social workers, and many others who deal with children need to be equipped with the skills, knowledge, authority, and motivation to identify and respond to child protection problems. The capacity of families and communities to protect their children is essential. Other broader types of capacity that relate to the protective environment include the provision of education and safe areas for play.

- **Children's life skills, knowledge, and participation:** If children are unaware of their right not to be abused, or are not warned of the dangers of, for example, trafficking, they are more vulnerable to abuse. Children need information and knowledge to be equipped to protect themselves. Children also need to be provided with safe and protective channels for participation and self-expression.

- **Monitoring and reporting:** A protective environment for children requires an effective monitoring system that records the incidence and nature of child protection abuses and allows for informed and strategic responses. Such systems can be more effective when they are participatory and locally base.

- **Services for recovery and reintegration:** Child victims of any form of neglect, exploitation, or abuse are entitled to care and nondiscriminatory access to basic social services. These services must be provided in an environment that fosters the health, self-respect, and dignity of the child.

Globally, 36–58 percent of rapes are committed by adult men against girls 15 years old and younger. The highest incidence of rape of young girls is among those who are 10 or younger. Empirical studies show that an overwhelming majority of perpetrators of rape are known by their victims (Heise, 1995). For example, in Lima, Peru, 90 percent of the young mothers in a maternity hospital aged 12 to 16 were raped by their father, stepfather, or another close relative (Heise, 1995). In some countries child sexual abuse does not receive stiff penalties. For instance, in South Africa when an 11-year-old girl died of AIDS after contracting HIV from two rapists, the rapists received only minor jail sentences (Heise, 1995). In some parts of India, sexual abuse is institutionalized in the practice of offering teenage girls as *devdasis*—girls, usually from poor families, who are officially dedicated to Hindu gods and goddesses and then sexually exploited (Kawewe & Dibie, 1999).

Child abuse and neglect still exist in virtually all cultures and societies despite worldwide articulation of concern for children (Kawewe & Dibie, 1999). Every society has values that could potentially protect children from child abuse and neglect. All too often, however, these values conflict with other cultural norms and practices that place children at risk of abuse. In parts of the Third World and in other regions across the globe, widespread abusive practices inflicted on children have been largely neglected because they are protected under the rubric of family privacy at the state and global levels (Kawewe & Dibie, 1999). Although UN international instruments along with regional jurisprudence define and acknowledge that political and civil rights violations fall within the domain of state responsibility, little emphasis is put on the affirmative responsibilities to ensure the rights of children (Kawewe & Dibie, 1999).

Foster Care

At any given time, numerous children around the world are without a primary caregiver. Although the reasons vary greatly for child separation from parents, that separation is usually detrimental to the overall well-being and development of the child (International Federation of Social Workers, 2002). Children without the guidance and protection of their primary caregivers are often more likely to become victims of violence, exploitation, trafficking, or discrimination. Institutional care has long been a major means of providing for children who lack a primary caregiver. Recently, however, there is an increasing emphasis worldwide on a child's right to grow up in the care and protection of a family (UNICEF, n.d.).

In the United States, 568,000 children live in foster families (U.S. Department of Health and Human Services, 2001). One and a half million children live in public care in Central and Eastern Europe. In Russia, the annual number of children without parental care nearly doubled between 1989 and 1999. It is projected that by the year 2010 orphans will compose at least 15 percent of all children under 15 years of age (UNICEF, n.d.).

In recognition of the importance of children growing up with the care and protection of a family, nations are embracing a family-based alternative care model. Foster homes are intended to provide a safe, stable living environment that simulates a family as closely as possible (Ellis, Dulmus, & Wodarski, 2003). But across the globe many foster care systems are replete with problems. In many countries, including the United States, children are placed in foster homes that are inadequate and overcrowded. Other children in the system bounce from home to home and never experience the stability of family life. In some countries, governments refuse to admit that there is a problem with the growing numbers of orphaned children. This denial places those countries in a poor position to respond to the needs of displaced children (UNICEF, n.d.).

One of the major keys to success lies in identifying an appropriate placement for the child and providing the needed supports to both the child and the foster parents. Successful identification and support requires a good assessment, a carefully developed case plan, and a thorough understanding of the foster care system (Ellis, Dulmus, & Wodarski, 2003). Equally important is the successful recruitment and retention of foster parents and the provision of psychosocial and economic resources necessary to support successful foster parenting (Rhodes et al., 2003).

Kinship care is an alternate form of foster care and is the "full-time nurturing and protection of children by relatives, members of their tribes or clans, godparents, stepparents, or other adults to whom a child, the child's parents, and family members ascribe a family relationship" (Child Welfare League of America, 1994, p. 2). In the United States, kinship care is being increasingly used in response to the profound increase in the incidence of child abuse, neglect, and maltreatment and the insufficient number of foster families (Liederman, 1995). This unique approach promotes family ties as a means of preserving families and avoiding the unnecessary placement of children in the custody of the state. Similar to foster care, providing psychosocial and economic supports is critical to the successful placement and retention of children in kinship homes.

Out of its growing concern for the large numbers of children worldwide growing up without the benefit of a supportive family environment, UNICEF is attempting to influence governments to promote family-based alternatives to institutional care through appropriate policies and legislation. To support this effort, UNICEF (n.d.) supports the following guidelines:

- Staff in social services, institutions, and civil servants dealing with children need to be aware of alternatives to institutional care and how to pursue them. Social and health workers, as well as staff in institutions and civil servants dealing with children without primary caregivers and in institutional care, need to be familiar with a range of approaches to ensure that children are provided with a family environment in which to grow up.
- Families need to be strengthened. By supporting the caring and coping capacities of families, for example by providing free basic education and expanding social welfare and income-generating programs, many children who might otherwise be separated from their families can remain with them.
- Children who have been deprived of a family environment need assistance to be returned to one. This may mean the provision of domestic adoption or different types of foster care. In such situations, children and those who care for them may require assistance to ensure these arrangements work out in the best interest of the child.

Child Adoption

Adoption is not a new phenomenon but rather a process that has existed in one form or another since ancient times all around the world (Kadushin & Martin, 1988; MacDonald, 1984). However, the reasons for adoption are significantly different across the globe (Durst, 1992). The practices regarding child adoption in Western societies, based on legal procedures and structures, are in contrast to many cultures around the world. Reasons for adoption practices are often rooted in history and culture. For some cultures, the major reason for childless couples to adopt was to provide them an heir in order to perpetuate the family name and continue building the family estate (Durst, 1992). In ancient Rome and traditional Japan, child adoption permitted the formal alliance between families (Brown, 1990). In many societies adoption processes and customs are framed on the basis of community survival (Morrow, 1984). In Botswana, for example, children were viewed by the family as a source of security for the future (Brown, 1990). As the parents aged, the young adults assumed the responsibility of providing the necessities for the family and the community. Because child rearing was expensive, it was shared by all members of the community (Durst, 1992). In Inuit families, a childless couple may assume the major responsibility of a child of a mother or family who were having difficulty due to illness or death (Henriksen, 1973). Such adoptions are permanent but not secret. The child may have regular contact and full knowledge about his or her natural parents and siblings (Durst, 1992). According to Durst (1992), in these societies there is little stigma to adoption or childlessness. Clearly, Western adoption processes and procedures, which rest on principles of secrecy and separation, are inappropriate for such native cultures and undermine the cultural values of the community.

Research indicates that many of the adoption principles governed by Western thought are inappropriate, and perhaps harmful, to all children from all backgrounds and cultures (Brown, 1990; Johnston, 1983; Hudson & MacKenzie, 1981; MacKenzie, 1985; Morrow, 1984; Ryant, 1984). For example, current research indicates that birth mothers long for knowledge about their natural children and would like to have information about their well-being (Sachdev, 1989). Most adopted adults are curious about and have a need to discover their roots and backgrounds (Durst, 1992). The practice of permanent secrecy has been challenged by some, arguing that it violates one's personal rights to information relevant to one's life (Sachdev, 1989, p. 11). Social welfare agencies rooted in Western philosophy, however, have been slow to implement change or respond to research indicating that many current adoption policies are harmful to adopted children, biological parents, and native communities (Durst, 1992).

The need for adoptive and foster homes and for new social welfare policies in many countries is of critical importance. In South Africa, for example, as in other African countries as well, there is a growing need for the care of AIDS orphans and children infected with AIDS who are left behind by parents who died of AIDS. The conventional forms of substitute care are not adequate to accommodate the swelling numbers of AIDS orphans (Rankin, 2000). Recruitment of a sufficient number of homes for these children is a huge problem. Adjustment of the traditional substitute care paradigms for these children should be considered as a viable solution to this problem (Harber, 1999).

Children in Conflict with the Law

Millions of children throughout the world are held in jails, prisons, and detention centers. Many are brought to trial and sentenced in ways that violate their human rights and ignore international principles that recognize the deprivation of liberty to be a measure of last resort for children. The UN Convention on the Rights of the Child (Article 37) clearly articulates that "no child should be subjected to torture or other cruel, inhuman, or degrading treatment or punishment." The Convention outlines other safeguards for children, including the exclusion of capital punishment or life imprisonment without possibility of release.

A number of societal factors contribute to the development of delinquent behavior in children. Left-behind children, runaways and street children, and children living in poverty are at the greatest risk. Other specific risk factors are child abuse and family disintegration, low neighborhood attachment, parental attitudes condoning illegal behavior, academic failure, truancy, school drop-out, and antisocial behaviors early on in life (Ellis & Sowers, 2001). The reasons for incarceration of children in conflict with the law vary not only from country to country but from jurisdiction to jurisdiction within a country. Children who commit crimes, from petty theft to murder, often face harsh sentences. Incarceration in adult systems rather than traditional youth justice practices, such as rehabilitation, counseling, and restorative justice programs, are common in many countries (Youth Advocate Program International, n.d.).

In some countries children are jailed on false charges or no charges at all. In Kenya, for example, street children are routinely picked up individually by police or rounded up in groups. They may be assaulted and arrested simply because they are living on the streets or because a theft has occurred in the area (Human Rights Watch, n.d.). There is also clear and statistically proven evidence of racial and socioeconomic bias in police arrest of juveniles (Snyder et al., 1993). African Americans, for example, make up only 15 percent of all U.S. youth between the ages of 10 and 17, yet they comprise 30 percent of youth arrested from that age group, and 50 percent of the cases transferred to the criminal court (Youth Advocate Program International, n.d.). The double standard existing in many court systems often results in more severe sentences for ethnic minority youth than those given to whites who committed similar crimes (National Council of Juvenile and Family Court Judges, 1990; Pope & Feyerherm, 1993; Roscoe & Morton, 1994).

A report issued in November 1998 by Amnesty International takes the United States to task for its high levels of juvenile incarceration and for the treatment of those children under the imposed supervision of the state. In fact, the United States leads the world in child incarceration (Amnesty International, 1998). Among Amnesty's findings are that 200,000 children per year are prosecuted in general criminal courts, with an estimated 7,000 of those children held in jails before trial. Over 11,000 children are currently being housed in prisons and other adult correctional facilities. In the United States there has been an effort to have more and more children tried as adults. In 1995, more than half of children whose cases were transferred out of the juvenile courts and into the adult courts were charged with nonviolent offenses (Amnesty International, 1998).

Execution of youthful offenders is prohibited almost everywhere in the world. Since 2000 only three countries (The Democratic Republic of Congo, Iran, and the United States) have resorted to capital punishment for those offenders who committed crimes before reaching the age of 18 (Youth Advocate Program International, n.d.). The United States is the world leader in execution of youthful offenders. Between 1990 and January 2000, the United States executed more juvenile offenders than all other countries combined.

Research indicates that in most cases the incarceration of young offenders is more harmful than beneficial. Incarceration often results in grave psychological trauma and deteriorating emotional and physical health of the detained youth. This makes their successful reintegration back into society more difficult and unlikely. In fact, children in conflict with the law who are not given proper counseling and rehabilitation programs not only find reintegration into society difficult but also face high rates of return to the prison system.

International Federation of Social Workers Policy Statement on Youth

In 2000, the International Federation of Social Workers endorsed the general development and implementation of policies aimed at strengthening young peoples' participation in policy formulation, the development of programs of action, and implementation and assessment of such programs. It issued the following policy statement (pp. 2–5) in support of strengthening policy and programs for youths:

- IFSW believes that it is important for governments and agencies to systematically review the position of young people, as of other groups, at periodic intervals in order to identify problems, evaluate the results of previous policies and activities, and select logical points on which to concentrate. A general model could include assessment of the content of programs (in relation to the problems tackled); the methods of service delivery and implementation (in relation to reaching the target groups, and whether strategies and approaches are appropriate); and resource utilization, considered in terms of cost efficiency and cost effectiveness (including the mobilization of local and indigenous resources and people).
- IFSW suggests that principles to be fostered by such programs and subsequently appraised, include:
  - Ensuring that young people are active participants in formulating programs, rather than passive recipients. This requires the use of a "bottom up" and "top down" model of planning.
  - Decision making should be geared towards planned social change, which will include enhancing the power of those currently powerless.
  - Co-ordination efforts should be made among agencies, from the planning stages right through to the evaluation of the programs, and with a focus upon the needs of young people themselves.
- It is recommended by IFSW that youth services should be provided as a special part of mainstream services whenever possible, recognizing that particular groups require additional specific services. Young people receiving services should receive the same guarantees of confidentiality as adults. Workers in services for young people should recognize the importance of linkage with other services, for example, with teachers, school counselors, refugee workers etc. IFSW suggests that objectives of programs aiming to meet the needs of youth should include:
  - Strengthening family life and relationships, and encouraging parental participation in programs; promoting productive employment opportunities and self-employment; improving general education and specific education on youth issues; maintaining services and facilities that cater for youth, and reappraising their effectiveness.
- IFSW believes that the above programs should be geared towards the needs of emotionally disturbed, physically handicapped, socially and economically deprived youth, including those discharged from psychiatric or other health

facilities, young offenders, those at risk of delinquency, mendicants, street boys and girls, and those dependent on drugs or other addictive substances.

- IFSW proposes that an appraisal of programs and their effectiveness be undertaken in respect of the following types of activity in the social services sector: Family support activities; preventive, habilitative, interceptive, and rehabilitative facilities; youth participation activities; social services in occupational settings; preventive, youth placement, and youth advocacy schemes; substitute family care provision; detention and rehabilitation centers; lodging facilities; and the use of volunteers.
- IFSW recommends in the employment sector the establishment and appraisal of resources such as: Centers for working youth; "schools in factories" and "schools in farms;" working youth co-operatives; and self employment for youth.
- IFSW recommends in the justice and penal system that: The numbers of juveniles going through the formal system should be identified, and reduced by diversion or interception; the number of special juvenile units in police organizations should be evaluated, and appropriately increased; detention facilities which cater exclusively for youth should be developed; measures to integrate the juvenile/minor offender with the rest of society should be strengthened; proposals should be formulated for decriminalizing certain prohibited acts such as vagrancy and the violations of local laws, where no victims are involved.
- IFSW observes that against a background that includes lack of formal education and unemployment for a substantial minority of youth, all young people are exposed to values, lifestyles, and culture which may be harmful to their development. Mobilization and organization of young people should be encouraged in order to help achieve their potential. This could include: Promoting nonformal education programs, based on the needs of young people, rather than commercial considerations; and working to enhance the preservation and promotion of indigenous culture and values where these are regarded as positive for young people.
- IFSW notes that as the group of people we have called "youth" or "young people" is necessarily transitory in its identity, it is important to bear in mind that today's policies for youth represent policies not just for today but for the future.

INTERNATIONAL ORGANIZATIONS FOR CHILDREN AND YOUTH

United Nations Children's Fund (UNICEF)

The World Conference on Human Rights, held in June 1993 in Vienna, recognized that the human rights of children constitute a priority for action with the United Nations system. The Conference also recommended that UN agencies, such as UNICEF, periodically assess the impact of their strategies and policies on children's enjoyment of human rights. UNICEF's work in the area of child rights is informed by the World Summit for Children (1990), as well as by the World Conference on Education for All (1990), the World Conference on Human Rights (1993), the World Summit for Social Development (1995), and the Fourth World Conference on Women (1995).

Box 4.1   Exemplars from Around the World

India

Infant mortality and child ill health have only recently been recognized as a serious social problem in the West (Combs-Orme, 1987). But social workers could learn much from the experiences of social workers in India. Of particular use is the success of social work in impoverished urban communities where young children face additional problems of malnutrition, health, and social problems. In India, conventional approaches to child welfare have been modified because the most pressing manifestations of child need are not abuse or neglect but malnutrition and ill health. Each year, millions of children in India and other developing countries die of medical conditions associated with malnutrition and poverty, and Indian social workers have rightly focused their attention on the problem. India's Integrated Child Services Development Scheme, established in the 1970s on an experimental basis, seeks to provide integrated social work, education, health care, and nutritional services to needy children. The local community is enlisted to establish day care centers, which are staffed by volunteers and supported by medical, nutritional, and educational professionals. Social workers usually are responsible for administering these programs at the local level, and they use their training to mobilize community involvement, coordinate services, and meet other social needs as they arise (Ministry of Social Welfare, 1980).

Cotonou, Benin

One of the biggest challenges facing poor developing countries in sub-Saharan Africa is providing youths with education, health services, and job opportunities. Cotonou, a small coastal city with a population of over 500,000, is a chief seaport and a commercial, transportation, and communications hub of Benin. The average family income is approximately $400 per year. Close to half of Benin's population is under 15. In Cotonou, only 7 percent of girls and 17 percent of boys go on to secondary school. As a result, close to three-quarters of all females and half of the males over 15 remain illiterate, with few prospects for jobs

or independent income other than the informal sector. Preventing unwanted teenage pregnancies and combating HIV/AIDS are also major social problems. Close to half of all adolescent girls have their first sexual encounter before age 15. Many young girls are forced into early marriages, which contributes to the country's high birth rate. Because of a lack of information about disease prevention and limited access to appropriate services, including condoms, HIV/AIDS and sexually transmitted infections are on the increase among young people.

However, a new innovative program, the Multi-Media Centre complex, funded by the United Nations Foundation in cooperation with the government, integrates job training with education about preventing HIV/AIDS and unwanted pregnancies, so trainees can also become local advocates for healthier behavior. The Centre, next to the football stadium in Cotonou, has its own television and FM radio stations offering programs produced by and for youths. It is training youths to be print journalists, photographers, radio and TV broadcasters, magazine writers, layout artists, computer graphics experts, web designers, videographers, and digital videotape editors. The TV station has an audience of 1 million and the radio station broadcasts 24 hours per day, seven days a week, and reaches over 300,000 listeners every day. All aspects of production are done by young people. The program at the Multi-Media Centre is two-pronged: young people not only develop a variety of media skills, they also learn about substantive adolescent health and development issues. They then become recognized focal points for these issues in their communities as well as effective advocates on radio, TV, and in print. The radio and TV programs written, produced, and broadcast by youth are having a real impact on Cotonou and its surrounding areas (United Nations Population Fund, n.d.). The radio programs pull the audience in with music but wrapped inside the music programs are short, informative segments dealing with current events and issues important to young people. According to United Nations Population Fund country representative Philippe Delanne, the latest professional equipment is used to "teach by doing." After six months at the Centre, young people have real skills and are ready to work in any number of media professions—from computer graphic designers and editors to radio broadcasters and TV talk show hosts. Most of the graduates also become a valuable community resource for information affecting young people.

Canada

The National Arts and Youth Demonstration Project was a three-year study initiated in 2001 and implemented in five sites across Canada. The objectives of the project were three-fold:

- to evaluate the extent to which community-based organizations can successfully recruit, engage, and maintain children and youth 10–15 years of age from lower-income communities, in artistic endeavors;
- to determine whether involvement in art programs demonstrates positive outcomes with respect to child and youth psychosocial functioning; and
- to determine if there were any spillover effects in the home, school, and community.

Analysis of the project found improvement in prosocial skills and behavior, task completion, and participation levels, as well as improvement in conduct, emotional problems, and hyperactivity (Wright et al., 2004).

Mexico

The group El Caracol (meaning *the snail*) works with street youth in Mexico aged 15–23. Street educators build relationships with the young people; make presentations on HIV/AIDS, drug use, and other health and social issues; and then work with the young people to identify their own needs. El Caracol runs a restaurant, a print shop, and a rabbit farm, where street youth work as interns and apprentices. A transitional living program provides considerable freedom and responsibility. Staff members work with young people to construct new identities, helping them to shed the self-definition as "street kids" (Volpi, 2002).

Angola

In Angola, UNICEF has worked with NGOs to demobilize children through a program for the reintegration of underage soldiers. Children returning from war received assistance to trace their relatives, and were transferred back to their home villages to be reunited. The program also identified appropriate school and job training opportunities. Work in the communities was conducted by *catequistas*, trained local church members who provided psychosocial assistance. The group drew upon traditional beliefs and practices to aid local communities to accept former child soldiers and to facilitate their reintegration (United Nations Children's Fund, n.d.).

Kosovo

In Kosovo, UNICEF is supporting the establishment of a range of services for children temporarily or permanently deprived of family care, including short-term placement into small group homes, professional short-term foster care, and national adoption and reunification with birth parents. UNICEF is also providing technical assistance for needs assessment and analysis; development, implementation, and monitoring of a pilot foster care program for abandoned babies under two years of age; training of social workers and foster parents; financial assistance to start up the payment of foster allowances to cover the basic needs of children in care; and an intensive media campaign on foster care and adoption to promote the basic right of all children to grow up in a family (United Nations Children's Fund, n.d.).

Ukraine

In Kiev, a project to transform the state child-care system is pushing for a change in policy that will support foster family care for orphaned children instead of institutionalizing them. This UNICEF-supported project has trained potential foster families and has successfully convinced public officials and other decision makers to draft new national legislation on foster care (UNICEF, n.d.).

Box 4.2 | Research Evidence Driving the Future Agenda
Challenges for the Future

The involvement of adolescents in social development is a task most countries have yet to address. Because broad social changes are increasing the time between physical maturity and acceptance into adult social roles, social institutions must adjust to offer adolescents full participation. In many settings, adolescents have proven to be dynamic agents of change. Ensuring that they will enter adulthood in good health depends in part on empowering them to negotiate effectively with others to achieve a healthy lifestyle. Awareness has increased about addressing the diversity of the adolescent and youth populations. The needs of younger and older adolescents, boy and girls, married and unmarried adolescents, and those living in urban and rural areas need to be addressed. A recent study conducted by the Women's Commission for Refugee Women and Children recommends changes in national policies and legal frameworks to better protect children, adolescents, and youth, while involving young people in policy making, implementation, and enforcement. The report calls for "more attention to education and vocational training." The report emphasizes that gender equality is essential and urges that action be taken to reduce sexual and physical violence (Women's Commission for Refugee Women and Children, 2002).

The Convention on the Rights of the Child, which addresses the rights of children, including adolescents up to the age of 18, is the most widely ratified of all human rights instruments. As a result, many countries have introduced and implemented legislative measures to ensure the Rights of the Child are implemented in their respective countries. Also, countries have learned from experience that, before laws are adopted, lawmakers need to consult fully with those affected, including young people and teachers (United Nations Population Fund, 2004; United Nations Children's Fund, n.d.).

Some of the most effective responses for combating child abuse and neglect focus on child-rearing, parent-child relationships, and the family environment. The World Health Organization (n.d.) has identified two effective interventions for child abuse and neglect: training in parenting (providing parents with information about child development as well as attachment and bonding, and teaching them how to use consistent child-rearing methods and how to manage family conflict) and home visitation programs. The latter may involve regular visits from a nurse or other health professional to the homes of families in special need of support with childcare, or to those where there is an identified risk of child maltreatment. Interventions may include counseling, training, and referrals to specialists or other agencies. WHO further suggests that programs must include high levels of participant involvement, use of an approach that builds on strengths of the family, and an element of social support.

International Labor Organization

The ILO has gained a renewed interest recently in the issue of child labor and has now finalized the drafting of a new convention—the Convention Concerning the Prohibition and Immediate Action for the Elimination of the Worst Forms of Child Labour.

Coalition to Stop the Use of Child Soldiers

Founded in 1998, the Coalition to Stop the Use of Child Soldiers (CSC) unites national, regional, and international organizations and networks in Africa, Asia, Europe, Latin America, and the Middle East. Its founding organizations are Amnesty International, Defence for Children International, Human Rights Watch, International Federation Terre des Hommes, International Save the Children Alliance, Jesuit Refugee Service, the Quaker United Nations Office–Geneva, and World Vision International. It maintains active links with UNICEF, the International Red Cross and Red Crescent Movement, and the Special Representative of the Secretary-General for Children and Armed Conflict. The CSC is the leading network for monitoring the reporting on the use of child soldiers worldwide. It promotes universal ratification and implementation of international legal standards prohibiting the recruitment and use of children as soldiers, and campaigns against child soldiering by armed forces and groups. The CSC promotes and coordinates training, information sharing, and capacity building activities for NGOs in priority countries, and facilitates documentation and dissemination of experience and promising practices.

Office of the United Nations High Commissioner for Refugees

The UNHCR has adopted guidelines for refugee children informed by the Convention's guiding principles—namely nondiscrimination, the best interests of the child, and child survival, development, and participation.

United Nations Educational, Scientific, and Cultural Organization

UNESCO is working in the field of human rights education for children, using the Convention as a guide.

United Nations Development Programme

The UNDP is considering the impact of the Declaration on the Right to Development, issued in 1986, on its work.

Youth Advocate Program International

The YAPI is a registered 501(c)(3) nonprofit organization founded in 1994. The organization works to promote and protect the rights and well-being of the world's youth, with particular attention to children victimized by conflict, exploitation, and state and personal violence. It works to prevent and eliminate the worst forms of child labor, the use of children in armed conflict, commercial sexual exploitation of children, and the practice of incarcerating children as adults.

Free The Children

Free The Children is an international network of children helping children at a local, national, and global level through representation, leadership, and action. It was founded in 1995. The primary goal of the organization is to "free children from poverty and exploitation and to free children and young people from the idea that they are powerless to bring about positive social change and to improve the lives of peers." Free The Children is an organization by and for children that fully embodies the notion that children and young people themselves can be leaders today in creating a more just, equitable, and sustainable world.

International Society for Prevention of Child Abuse and Neglect

Founded in 1977, ISPCAN is the only multidisciplinary international organization that brings together a worldwide cross-section of committed professionals to work towards the prevention and treatment of child abuse, neglect, and exploitation globally. ISPCAN's mission is to "prevent cruelty to children in every nation, in every form: physical abuse, sexual abuse, neglect, street children, child fatalities, child prostitution, children of war, emotional abuse, and child labor." (For more information see http://www.ispcan.org.)

War Affected Children

In September 1997, a United Nations Special Representative of the Secretary-General for Children and Armed Conflict was appointed to promote humanitarian, diplomatic, and advocacy initiatives to help war-affected children all over the world. Many international, governmental, and nongovernmental organizations, such as the United Nations Children's Fund, Human Rights Watch, Amnesty International, the Coalition to Stop the Use of Child Soldiers, Women's Commission for Refugee Women and Children, and others have been active in the humanitarian and advocacy efforts to stop the use of child soldiers, and in developing the effective disarmament, demobilization, and reintegration programs for the former child soldiers. (For more information see http://www.un.org/special-rep/children-armed-conflict.)

SUMMARY

No place in the world is free of incidents of child maltreatment and exploitation. As violence escalates children become increasingly vulnerable. Recent efforts by the United Nations and the World Health Organization to bring this critical issue to the forefront, to protect the rights of the child, and to insist on laws and policies that protect children are quite promising. Various organizations throughout the world are rallying to raise consciousness and mobilize forces to intervene on behalf of the world's children. Many programs are beginning to successfully make a positive difference in children's lives. Social work has a unique opportunity to provide effective interventions at the micro, meso, and macro levels to support these efforts.

Thinking About Practice: From Local to Global Perspectives

1. What are the most pressing social problems affecting children in your community? How do these differ from those affecting children in other parts of the world?
2. What do you see as the primary obstacles to promoting safety and a stable family environment to children who live in your community?

3. What opportunities are available in your community to change services to children that would promote family stability and child safety?
4. Identify at least one strategy, utilized in a community other than yours, which might be useful in promoting child well-being in your own community.

Social Work Practice and Social Justice Website

Please go to the Book Companion Website at http://www.thomsonedu.com/author/sowers to find a rich collection of related articles selected by the authors from Info Trac College Edition.

References

Aird, S., Harnett, H., & Shah, P. (2002). *Stateless children: Youth who are without citizenship.* Washington, DC: Master Print.

Alston, P. (1998). Hardship in the midst of plenty. *The progress of nations.* United Nations Children's Fund. Retrieved July 2, 2004, from http://www.unicef.org

Amnesty International. (1998). *U.S. leads world in child incarceration.* Retrieved July 21, 2004, from http://www.injusticeline.com

Beasley, R. (1999, April). *On the streets.* Amnesty Magazine. Retrieved July 18, 2004, from http://www.amnesty.org

Brown, H. A. F. (1990). Child care practice in Botswana with particular reference to adoption practice. *Social Work and Social Science Review, 1*(1), 45–58.

Centre for Addiction and Mental Health. (n.d.). Retrieved July 7, 2004, from http://www.camh.net

ChildLine. (n.d.). *Why children and young people run away, or become homeless.* Retrieved July 7, 2004, from http://www.childline.org

Child Welfare League of America. (1994). *Kinship care: A natural bridge.* Washington, DC: Author.

Cohen, B. (2003). *Youth in cities: An overview of key demographic shifts.* Power-Point presentation at the meeting, Youth Explosion in Developing World Cities: Approaches to Reducing Poverty and Conflict in an Urban Age, Woodrow Wilson Center for International Scholars, Washington, DC, February 20, 2003.

Combs-Orme, T. (1987). Infant mortality: Priority for social work. *Social Work, 32,* 507–511.

Convention on the Rights of the Child. (n.d.). Retrieved May 13, 2005, from http://www.unhchr.ch/html/menu3/b/k2crc.htm

Department of Health and Human Services. (2003). *Trends in the well-being of America's children and youth: 2003.* Retrieved July 18, 2004, from http://aspe.hhs.gov/hsp/hspinddb.htm

Durst, D. (1992). The road to poverty is paved with good intentions: Social interventions and indigenous peoples. *International Social Work, 35*(2), 191–202.

Ellis, R., Dulmus, C. N., & Wodarski, J. S. (2003). *Essentials of child welfare.* Hoboken, NJ: John Wiley & Sons.

Ellis, R., & Sowers, K. M. (2001). *Juvenile justice practice: A cross disciplinary approach to intervention.* Belmont, CA: Brooks/Cole.

Harber, M. (1999). Transforming adoption in the "new" South Africa in response to the HIV/AIDS epidemic. *Adoption and Fostering, 23*(1), 6–15.

Heise, L. E. (1995). Freedom close to home: The impact of violence against women on rights. In J. Peters & A. Wolper (Eds.), *Women's rights, human rights: International feminist perspective* (pp. 238–255). New York: Routledge.

HelpAge. (n.d.). Retrieved July 14, 2004, from http://www.helpage.org

Henriksen, G. (1973). *Hunters in the Barrens: The Naskapi on the edge of the White man's world.* St. John's, Canada: Institute of Social and

Economic Research, Memorial University of Newfoundland.

Hudson, P., & MacKenzie, B. (1981). Child welfare and native people: The extension of colonialism. *The Social Worker, 49*(2), 63–88.

Human Rights Watch. (n.d.). Retrieved July 20, 2004, from http://www.hrw.org

International Committee of the Red Cross. (n.d.). *Children in war.* Retrieved May 13, 2005, from http://www.icrc.org/eng/children

International Federation of Social Workers. (2000). *International statement on youth.* Retrieved July 20, 2004, from http://www.ifsw.org

International Federation of Social Workers. (2002). *Social work and the rights of the child: A professional training manual on the UN Convention.* Berne, Switzerland: Author.

Johnston, P. (1983). *Native children and the child welfare system.* Toronto: Canadian Council on Social Development.

Kadushin, A., & Martin, J. A. (1988). *Child welfare services* (4th ed.). New York: MacMillan.

Kawewe, S., & Dibie, R. (1999). United Nations and the problem of women and children abuse in Third World nations. *Social Justice, 26*(1), 78–98.

Liederman, D. S. (1995). Child welfare overview. In R. L. Edwards & J. G. Hopps, *Encyclopedia of social work* (19th ed.). Washington, DC: NASW Press.

MacDonald, J. A. (1984). Canadian adoption legislation: An overview. In P. Sachdev (Ed.), *Adoption, current issues and trends* (pp. 43–61). Toronto: Butterworths.

MacKenzie, B. (1985). Social work practice with native people. In S. Yelaja (Ed.), *Introduction to social welfare* (pp. 272–278). Scarborough, Canada: Prentice Hall.

Ministry of Social Welfare. (1980). Integrated Child Development Service Scheme. New Delhi, India: Author.

Morrow, J. W. G. (1984). Custom adoption law. In P. Sachdev (Ed.), *Adoption, current issues and trends* (pp. 245–251). Toronto: Butterworths.

National Center for Missing and Exploited Children. (n.d.). *Why children run away.* Retrieved July 7, 2004, from www.operationlookout.org

National Council of Juvenile and Family Court Judges. (1990). Minority youth in the juvenile justice system: A judicial response. *Juvenile and Family Court Journal, 41*(3A, special issue), 1–71.

New York Times. (1999, August 14). *U.S. poor are among world's poorest.* New York: Author.

Pope, C. E., & Feyerherm, W. (1993). *Minorities and the juvenile justice system: Research summary.* Washington, DC: U.S. Department of Justice, Office of Juvenile Justice and Delinquency Prevention.

Popple, P. R., & Leighninger, L. (2002). *Social work, social welfare, and American society* (5th ed.). Boston: Allyn & Bacon.

Rankin, P. (2000, 29 July–2 August). *Protecting the best interests of the child: Some issues and solutions.* Paper presented at the International Association of Schools of Social Work Conference, Montreal, Canada.

Rhodes, K. W., Orme, J. G., Cox, M. E., & Buehler, C. (2003). Foster family resources, psychosocial functioning, and retention. *Social Work Research, 27*(3), 129–192.

Roscoe, M., & Morton, R. (1994). *Disproportionate minority confinement.* Retrieved July 20, 2004, from http://www.ncjrs.org

Ryant, J. C. (1984). Some issues in the adoption of native children. In P. Sachdev (Ed.), *Adoption, current issues and trends* (pp. 169–180). Toronto: Butterworths.

Sachdev, P. (1989). *Unlocking the adoption files.* Toronto: Lexington Books.

Snyder, H. N., Butts, J. A., Finnegan, T. A., Nimick, E. H., Tierney, N. J., Sullivan, D. P., Poole, R. S., & Sickmund, M. H. (1993). *Juvenile court statistics: 1990.* Washington, DC: U.S. Department of Justice, Office of Juvenile Justice and Delinquency Prevention.

United Nations. (2003). *Child soldiers use 2003: A briefing for the 4th UN Security Council open debate on children and armed conflict.* Coalition to Stop the Use of Child Soldiers. New York: Author.

United Nations Children's Fund. (n.d.). *Convention on the Rights of the Child.* Retrieved July 7, 2004, from http://www.unicef.org/crc

United Nations Children's Fund. (1995). *Introduction: Children and war.* Retrieved July 13, 2004, from http://www.unicef.org/sowc96/intro.htm

United Nations Children's Fund. (2001). *The state of the world's children 2001: Early childhood.* New York: Author.

United Nations Children's Fund. (2002). *Children affected by armed conflict: UNICEF actions.* New York: Author.

United Nations Chronicle. (1989). Retrieved July 17, 2004, from http://www.un.org/Pubs/chronicle

United Nations High Commission for Refugees. (1999). *Global appeal: Programme overview.* Retrieved July 15, 2004, from http://www.unhchr.ch.fdrs/ga99/children.htm

United Nations Human Rights Commission. (n.d.). *Convention on the rights of the child.* Retrieved July 20, 2004, from http://www.unhcr.ch

United Nations Population Fund. (n.d.). *State of world population 2003.* Retrieved June 25, 2004, from http://www.unfpa.org

United Nations Population Fund. (2004). *Investing in people: National progress in implementing the ICPD program of action 1994–2004.* New York: Author.

USAID. (n.d.). *Global health: Confronting the challenges.* Retrieved July 12, 2004, from http://www.usaid.gov/our_work/global_health/home/confrontingfactsheet.html

USAID, UNICEF, & UNAIDS. (2002). *Children on the brink 2002: A joint report on orphan estimates and programme strategies.* Washington, DC: The Synergy Project.

U.S. Department of Health and Human Services. (2001). *Well-being of children in foster care.* Retrieved July 14, 2004, from http://cbexpress.acf.hhs.gov/articles.cfm?issue_id=2004-03&article_id=780&

Volpi, E. (2002). *Street children: Promising practices and approaches.* WBI Working Papers. Washington, DC: The World Bank Institute, The World Bank.

Women's Commission for Refugee Women and Children. (2002). *Fending for themselves: Afghan refugee children and adolescents working in urban Pakistan.* New York: Author.

World Health Organization. (n.d.). *Child abuse and neglect.* Retrieved July 7, 2004, from http:www.who.org

Wright, R., John, L., Rowe, W., Morton, T., & Sheel, J. (2004, September 20). *National arts and youth demonstration project: Interim report.* Paper presented at the National Arts & Youth Demonstration Project Symposium, Montreal, Canada.

Youth Advocate Program International. (n.d.). Retrieved July 7, 2004, from http://www.yapi.org

It is about time that we all realize that investment in women is the single most important path to higher productivity for society as a whole—in industrial as well as in developing countries.

Gro Harlem Brundtland (1995)

5 CHAPTER | Social Work Practice with Women and Girls

From birth to death, in times of peace as well as war, women across the globe are vulnerable to violence and discrimination, often perpetrated by the state, the community, and the family. At least one out of every three women has been beaten, coerced into sex, or abused in her lifetime. More than 60 million women are "missing" from the world today as a result of sex-selective abortions and female infanticide. Millions of women are raped every year by partners, relatives, friends, and strangers, by employers and colleagues, soldiers and members of armed groups. Family violence is perpetrated all over the world and the overwhelming majority of victims are women and girls (Amnesty International, n.d.). In the United States, for example, women account for around 85 percent of the victims of domestic violence. The World Health Organization has reported that up to 70 percent of female murder victims are killed by their male partners (World Health Organization, n.d.).

Across socioeconomic levels, the multiple roles that women fulfill in society put them at greater risk of experiencing mental and behavioral disorders than others in the community. Women bear the burden of multiple roles and responsibilities associated with being wives, mothers, educators, and caregivers. They are also increasingly becoming an essential part of the labor force. In fact, in one-quarter to one-third of households they are the prime source of income. In addition to the pressures placed on women because of their expanding and often conflicting roles, they face significant sex discrimination and associated poverty, hunger, malnutrition, overwork, and domestic and sexual violence. Because of these life stressors, women are more likely than men to be prescribed psychotropic drugs for depression and bipolar illnesses. And in some populations of women throughout the world, such factors as age, socioeconomic conditions, political pressures, geography, and minority status increase their vulnerability (Wetzel, 1992). Violence against women constitutes a major social and public health problem, affecting women of all ages, cultural backgrounds, and income levels (World Health Report, 2001).

VIOLENCE AGAINST WOMEN

According to Maslow (1970), safety is one of the most basic needs of humankind. A lack of safety, stability, or consistency in their chaotic world prevents many women from reaching their full potential. In recognition of the devastating effects of violence against women, the UN adopted the Declaration on the Elimination of Violence against Women in December 1993. This document defined what constitutes violence against women and outlined actions governments and communities should take to prevent such acts. One of the outcomes of the Conference was the appointment of a "Special Rapporteur" on violence against women. The Rapporteur, who seeks and receives information on violence against women, its causes and consequences, and recommends means and ways to eliminate them, reports to the UN Commission on Human Rights. The

UN Declaration on the Elimination of Violence against Women defines violence against women as:

> any act of gender-based violence that results in, or is likely to result in, physical, sexual, or psychological harm or suffering to women, including threats of such acts, coercion, or arbitrary deprivation of liberty, whether occurring in public or in private life (United Nations, 1994).

Progressive interpretations of this definition include acts of omission, such as neglect or deprivation, which can constitute violence against women. Structural violence (harm arising from the organization of the economy) is also considered by some to be part of violence against women (Amnesty International, n.d.). Three broad categories characterize violence against women:

- violence in the family
  - battering by intimate partners, fathers, or brothers
  - sexual abuse of female children and young women in the household by family members
  - dowry-related violence
  - marital rape
  - female genital mutilation and other traditional practices harmful to women
- violence in the community
  - involuntary confinement
  - physical brutality
  - slavery-like conditions
  - sexual assault
- violence by the state
  - acts of violence committed or condoned by police, prison guards, soldiers, border guards, or immigration officials
  - rape by government forces during armed conflict
  - torture in custody
  - violence by officials against refugee women

Most studies on violence against women indicate that "the perpetrators of violence against women are almost exclusively men; women are at greatest risk of violence from men they know; women and girls are the most frequent victims of violence within the family and between intimate partners; physical abuse in intimate relationships is almost always accompanied by severe psychological and verbal abuse; and social institutions put in place to protect citizens too often blame or ignore battered women" (World Health Organization, n.d.).

In every country where reliable, large-scale studies have been conducted, results indicate that 10 to 50 percent of women report they have been physically abused by an intimate partner in their lifetime. Population-based studies report that 12 to 25 percent of women have experienced attempted or completed forced sex by an intimate partner or ex-partner at some time in their lives. Interpersonal violence was the tenth leading cause of death for women 15–44 years of age in 1998 (World Health Organization, n.d.).

DISCRIMINATION AGAINST THE GIRL CHILD

Many children around the world face great adversity but girl children are especially subjected to multiple forms of oppression, exploitation, and discrimination because of their gender. United Nations statistics, national reports, and studies by nongovernmental organizations repeatedly show that girls, as a group, have lower literacy rates, receive less health care, and grow up more often in poverty than boys (United Nations Children's Fund, n.d.). Unfortunately these conditions, more often than not, do not improve as girls grow to become women (Youth Advocate Program International, n.d.). Certain social problems affecting girls across the globe are particularly life-threatening and impact the lives of millions of girl children. These include female genital cutting, female infanticide and sex-selective abortion, and honor killing.

Female Genital Cutting

Female genital cutting involves the removal of part or all of the female genitalia (otherwise known as the clitoris). The most severe form is infibulation, also known as *pharaonic circumcision. Female genital mutilation* is a recently coined term for a custom going back to the ancient Egyptians. It has been reported to exist as far as South America and Malaysia. Its main locus, however, is Africa, where female circumcision (removal of all or part of the clitoris) is practiced in Chad, Niger, Nigeria, Togo, Burkina Faso, Ghana, Cote d'Ivoire, Liberia, Sierra Leone, Guinea, Guinea Bissau, Senegal, The Gambia, Mauritania, Egypt, Sudan, Djibouti, Ethiopia, Somalia, Kenya, and Tanzania. Infibulation is found chiefly in Sudan, parts of Ethiopia, Djibouti, Somalia, and Mali.

An estimated 15 percent of all mutilations in Africa are infibulations. The procedure consists of clitoridectomy (where all or part of the clitoris is removed), excision (removal of all or part of the labia minora), and cutting of the labia majora to create raw surfaces, which are then stitched or held together to form a cover over the vagina when they heal. A small hole is left to allow urine and menstrual blood to escape. In some less conventional forms of infibulation, less tissue is removed and a larger opening is left.

The age and variation of female cutting is largely dictated by culture and region. Ages at which the procedure takes place vary from shortly after birth to some time during the first pregnancy. Most commonly, however, the procedure is carried out between the ages of four and eight. According to the World Health Organization (n.d.), the average age is falling. This would indicate that the practice of female genital cutting is becoming less associated with the initiation into adulthood. This is believed to be particularly the case in urban areas. An estimated 135 million of the world's girls and women have undergone genital mutilation—approximately 6,000 per day. Infibulation is practiced extensively in Africa and is common in some countries in the Middle East. It also occurs, mainly among immigrant communities, in parts of Asia and the Pacific, North and Latin America, and Europe.

The effects of genital mutilation can lead to death. At the time the mutilation is carried out, pain, shock, hemorrhage, and damage to the organs surrounding the clitoris and labia can occur. Afterwards urine may be retained and serious infection can develop. Use of the same instrument on several girls without sterilization can cause the spread of HIV and other diseases. Infibulation can have other serious long-term effects including chronic urinary tract infections, stones in the bladder and urethra, kidney damage, reproductive tract infections resulting from obstructed menstrual flow, pelvic infections, infertility, excessive scar tissue, keloids (raised, irregularly shaped, progressively enlarging scars), and dermoid cysts. During childbirth, existing scar tissue on excised women may tear. Infibulated women, whose genitals have been tightly closed, have to be cut to allow the baby to emerge during birth (Daw, 1970; Lightfoot-Klein, 1989). If no attendant is present to do this, perineal tears or obstructed labor can occur. After giving birth, women are often reinfibulated to make them "tight" for their husbands (Pieters & Lowenfels, 1977). The constant cutting and restitching of a woman's genitals with each birth can result in tough scar tissue in the genital area (Lightfoot-Klein, 1989).

Custom and tradition are by far the most frequently cited reasons for female genital mutilation. Along with other physical or behavioral characteristics, female genital mutilation defines who is in the group (Kenyatta, 1938). This is most obvious where mutilation is carried out as part of the initiation into adulthood. Many people in female genital mutilation practicing societies, especially traditional rural communities, regard female genital mutilation as normal and cannot imagine a woman who has not undergone mutilation (Kenyatta, 1938). In fact, a girl cannot be considered an adult in a female genital mutilation society unless she has undergone the procedure.

Female genital mutilation predates Islam and is not practiced by the majority of Muslims, although it has acquired a religious dimension. Where it is practiced by Muslims, religion is frequently cited as a reason. However, there is much debate over the link between the practice and religion. Other than religious reasons, some societies practice female genital mutilation because of a belief that it reduces a woman's desire for sex, therefore reducing the chance of sex outside of marriage. In these societies, the ability of a woman to be faithful through her own choice is doubted. In many such societies, it is extremely difficult for a woman to marry if she has not undergone mutilation. In the case of infibulation, a woman is "sewn up" and "opened" only for her husband (Peiters & Lowenfels, 1977). The societies that practice infibulation are strongly patriarchal. They believe that preventing women from indulging in "illegitimate" sex, and protecting them from unwilling sexual relations, are vital to protect the honor of the family.

Certain cultures believe that a woman's genitals can grow and become unwieldy, hanging down between her legs, unless the clitoris is excised. Some groups believe that a woman's clitoris is dangerous and that if it touches a man's penis he will die. Others believe that if the baby's head touches the clitoris during childbirth, the baby will die.

Health benefits are not the most frequently cited reason for mutilation in societies where it is still practiced. It is more likely to be said that mutilation is part of an initiation in which women are taught to be strong and uncomplaining about illness. Some societies where female genital mutilation is practiced claim that it enhances fertility, with the more extreme believing that an unmutilated woman cannot conceive. In some it is believed that clitoridectomy makes childbirth safer.

Campaigns to end female genital mutilation have faced enormous obstacles, the greatest of which is the tenacity of tradition. In the 1940s Sudan attempted unsuccessfully to eradicate infibulation. Many have questioned why—despite the wishes of international agencies, national governments, and men—infibulation continues to flourish, even to proliferate. But Hicks (1993) notes that although the outside world may see the practice as a social problem, the vast majority of the female population in infibulation-practicing regions insist on initiating girls in this fashion. She asserts that they do so because women's collective social identity is based on all women being infibulated and that, in fact, a woman's very existence is recognized through the act of being infibulated. Given this very large function, Hicks suggests that external attempts to eradicate infibulation will be both futile and counterproductive. She purports that in order to eradicate the practice successfully, it will require changing "nothing less than whole ways of life."

Nevertheless, some positive steps are underway. For instance, in Kenya, Diduyu girls are undergoing rites of passage that mimic the old ways but do not include circumcision. Among the Bambara/Manding and Fulani communities of Malicounda, Senegal, in the months from May to July 1997, the traditional period for genital cutting, no such operations were performed for the first time in their history. In December 1998, the Senegal government passed laws prohibiting the practice of female circumcision. However, it has become clear that abolishing a people's social custom by force of law has not led to change. Deeply entrenched customs and traditions generally represent great psychological importance and bonding within the community—far beyond the actual ritual act. It is critical to understand the history and meaning of the culture and how a practice is entrenched in the community. For many cultures, female genital mutilation identifies age groups within the communities and promotes the spirit of collectivism and national solidarity (Kenyatta, 1938). Only from respecting the customs and traditions and working within the culture can change be achieved.

Female Infanticide and Sex-Selective Abortion (Feticide)

Female infanticide is the murder of a young girl child. Female infanticide may occur as a deliberate murder of a girl infant or young girl child, or as the result of neglect. Feticide, or gender-selective abortion, is the abortion of a fetus because it is a female. No overall statistics exist on the number of girls who die annually from infanticide. Gendercide Watch reports that a minimum estimate places the casualties in the hundreds of thousands. Feticide is most prevalent in China and India, the world's two most populous countries. Sex-selective abortions probably account for an even higher number of deaths than infanticide (Gendercide Watch, n.d.).

Infanticide and feticide are believed to occur most frequently in societies where a girl child is viewed as culturally and economically less advantageous than a boy child. These two practices are most often found in poor and over-populated regions. In some cultures boys are valued more than girls because boys preserve the family lineage and name. Also, in many cultures boys are much more likely to be able to provide economically for aging parents. However, in some cultures dominated by men, where daughters are objectified and subjugated, mothers resort to infanticide and feticide to protect their daughters from a life of oppression (Youth Advocate Program International, n.d.).

Honor Killing

In various countries throughout the world, particularly in the Middle East and parts of South Asia, women who bring dishonor to their families are subject to honor killing (Muslim Women's League, n.d.). Girls and women who are suspected of having defiled a family's honor by engaging in sexual activity before marriage, having an affair while married, or engaging in other improprieties are killed to restore the honor of the family. Some transgressions, however, which result in honor killings are not initiated by the girl. Transgressions for which a girl may be subject to death include rape, incest, sexual abuse, or sexual rumor. In honor killings, a girl or woman is most often killed by male relatives such as a father, husband, brother, uncle, or cousin. In those countries where this practice is prevalent the criminal penalties are quite lenient.

It is almost impossible to determine the number of women and girls who are the victims of honor killing. The United Nations Population Fund (n.d.) estimates as many as 5,000 females are honor killed each year. Honor killings have been reported in Bangladesh, Britain, Brazil, Ecuador, Egypt, India, Israel, Italy, Norway, Jordan, Pakistan, Peru, Morocco, Sweden, Turkey, Uganda, and Venezuela (Youth Advocate Program International, n.d.).

THE FEMINIZATION OF HIV/AIDS

Currently, women between the ages of 15 to 49 years account for 50 percent of adults living with HIV/AIDS (United Nations Population Fund, 2004). The United Nations Population Fund predicts that this number will continue to rise. Across the world, less than 1 in 20 pregnant women presenting for antenatal care are able to access services to prevent mother-to-child transmission of the virus, and less than 5 percent of those who could benefit from antiretroviral treatment are currently able to access such treatment. This rise in HIV infection among women, and the inability of many women across the globe to access testing and treatment, has been referred to as the "feminization" of the HIV epidemic. Women's difficulty accessing testing and treatment is further exacerbated by the burden on women as primary caregivers and maintainers of the household, and by the legal and social inequalities they often face in the areas of education, health care, livelihood opportunities, legal protection, and decision making (United Nations Population Fund, 2004).

THE UNITED NATIONS, THE STATUS OF WOMEN, AND THE RIGHTS OF WOMEN

Sixty years ago, in October 1945, the United Nations was formally organized and the advancement of women began with the signing of the founding charter. In its preamble, the members of the UN declared their faith "in fundamental human rights, in the dignity and worth of the human person, in the equal rights of men and women and of nations large and small" (United Nations, n.d.). Since then, the UN has been at the center of a growing global movement for women's rights (Wetzel, 1993). Legally binding international treaties and conventions adopted by the UN include:

- The Convention on the Political Rights of Women (1952)
- The Convention on the Nationality of Married Women (1957)
- The Convention on Recovery Abroad of Maintenance (1956)
- The Convention on the Consent to Marriage (1962)
- The Convention on the Elimination of All Forms of Discrimination Against Women (1979).

In 1975 the United Nations proclaimed a Decade of Women. At the initial conference on the Decade of Women, a document called "The Declaration of Mexico, 1975" mandated the elimination of violence against women. The Declaration called for the elimination of rape, incest, forced prostitution, physical assault, mental cruelty, and coercive and commercial marital transactions. The Declaration was adopted together with a "World Plan of Action" to be implemented by each nation (Wetzel, 1993). In 1980 the United Nations endorsed the Convention on the Elimination of All Forms of Discrimination Against Women (1980). The Convention on the Elimination of All Forms of Discrimination Against Women is often described as an international bill of rights for women. Consisting of a preamble and 30 articles, it defines what constitutes discrimination against women and sets up an agenda for national action to end such discrimination. The Convention has been accepted by 139 UN member states. According to the Convention, discrimination against women is "any distinction, exclusion or restriction made on the basis of sex which has the effect or purpose of impairing or nullifying the recognition, enjoyment or exercise by women, irrespective of their marital status, on a basis of equality of men and women, of human rights and fundamental freedoms in the political, economic, social, cultural, civil or any other field." By recognizing the Convention, nations commit themselves to undertake a series of measures to end discrimination against women in all its forms, including efforts:

- to incorporate the principle of equality of men and women in their legal systems, abolish all discriminatory laws, and adopt appropriate ones prohibiting discrimination against women;
- to establish tribunals and other public institutions to ensure the effective protection of women against discrimination; and
- to ensure elimination of all acts of discrimination against women by persons, organizations, or enterprises.

The Convention is the only human rights treaty that affirms the reproductive rights of women. It targets culture and tradition as the major forces shaping gender roles and family relations. It affirms women's right to "acquire, change, or retain their nationality and the nationality of their children." Member states agree to take appropriate measures against all forms of traffic in women and exploitation of women.

The strongest international statement about women's rights emerged from the United Nations Fourth World Conference on Women held in September 1995 in Beijing. At this conference a statement was developed representing an agenda to empower women in economic, social, and political areas (United Nations, 1996). The statement, referred to as the Platform for Action and supported by women from all over the world, decreed that the rights of women and the girl child are an inalienable, integral, and indivisible part of universal human rights (Reichert, 1998). Adopted by consensus at the official meeting of 5,000 delegates and 4,000 nongovernmental organization representatives, the statement set an agenda for national and global action well into the twenty-first century (Wetzel, 1996).

INTERNATIONAL FEDERATION OF SOCIAL WORKERS INTERNATIONAL POLICY ON WOMEN

In 1999, in recognition of the importance of social workers enhancing the well-being of women and girls as an essential aspect of the profession's ethical and practice commitment to human rights, the IFSW issued the following statement:

> Social workers are involved in the broadest range of professional activities that are critical to the well-being of women and girls. Specific antipoverty efforts include the delivery of health and mental health care services and public health programs; prevention and early intervention efforts addressing both interpersonal and community-based violence; education, employment, and training programs; and activities to increase the participation of people traditionally excluded from political, economic, and community decision making (pp. 1–2).

In that same year, the IFSW issued the following policy statement (pp. 6–8):

- IFSW endorses the platform statement adopted by the United Nations Fourth World Conference on Women. IFSW recognizes that global progress toward gender equality, gender-sensitive development, and peace requires attention to all the areas of critical concern described in the platform statement.

- IFSW stresses and affirms the core commitment of the social work profession to human rights, human welfare, peace, and the enhancement of the human potential and well-being of all people as well as from its mission of service to those from vulnerable, oppressed, and disadvantaged groups.
- IFSW and its member organizations will work to advocate for development of policies, implementation of programs, and social action to improve the well-being of women of all ages. This work can be effective only if the special needs and contributions of indigenous, migrant, displaced, and poor women are emphasized.
- Women's rights are human rights. To the extent that women and girls do not enjoy equal rights, their common human needs, and those of their families, will not be fully met and their human potential will not be fully realized. Therefore, the social work profession's core commitment to human rights must involve a commitment to protecting and preserving the basic rights of all women and girls. Women of all ages and at all stages of the life cycle deserve protection from discrimination in all forms, including the elimination of all forms of gender-specific violence.
- IFSW recognizes that policies and programs designed to eliminate poverty and to promote the economic well-being of all people will not succeed without attention to gender discrimination in economic arrangements, in the workplace, in the household, and to social and economic policies and programs themselves.
- IFSW will work to improve the health status of women of all ages. Social workers are involved greatly in the delivery of women's health care, including maternal and child health, mental and behavioral health care services, and sexual and reproductive health care, including the care and prevention of HIV/AIDS and other sexually transmitted diseases. Improving the health and well-being of women requires attention to physical, mental, emotional, and social well-being, and the provision of gender-sensitive prevention, intervention, and long-term care services.
- In addition, IFSW endorses women's self-determination in all health care decisions as a core professional value, including all decisions regarding sexual activity and reproduction. Social workers understand that women have the right to receive competent and safe reproductive and sexual health care services free from government, institutional, professional, familial, or other interpersonal coercion.
- IFSW recognizes that social workers involved in schools and in adult education and training and literacy efforts must attend to gender issues as they affect the education and training of women and girls of all ages.
- IFSW affirms that social work's commitment to children and youths and their families must include attention to the risks associated with being a girl.
- IFSW supports the full participation of women in all decision-making bodies and processes that affect the political, economic, social, educational, and health concerns of women and girls. This commitment includes full participation in the profession, education for the profession, social agencies, and other social services delivery systems.
- Finally, IFSW recognizes the need to expand the social work knowledge base and improve the skills of professional social workers as they relate to the needs of women and girls, especially those from indigenous, poor, migrant, or displaced groups.

Box 5.1   Exemplars from Around the World

Mexico

Mexico began to monitor the incidence of HIV in 1985. Since 1986 it has taken action to ensure blood safety through education and filtering out donors at high risk. This action has resulted in a fall in the blood supply infection rate to 0.02 percent, and a decrease in perinatal transmission to only 14 cases in 2000. Since 90 percent of virus transmission is through sexual contact in Mexico, women are particularly vulnerable to infection and need to be included in prevention programs. The Latin American Women's Working Group and the National Institute of Public Health brought together 140 NGOs working with women in the region to promote policies and programs targeting particular groups of women, including sex workers; prepubescent girls; adolescents and young women; rural or urban marginalized groups; migrant workers or wives of migrants; women living with HIV; and housewives who are in relationships where they may be at risk (United Nations Population Fund, 2004).

Eritrea

Eritrea, located in Eastern Africa bordering the Red Sea between Djibouti and Sudan, has a population of almost 4.5 million. Eritrea recently initiated a range of social and economic development actions tied to the reduction and elimination of female genital cutting. Specific actions focused on women's empowerment and included emphasis on girls' education, women's literacy, and women's right to own and inherit land and other property. Programs were also implemented to address harmful traditional practices (United Nations Population Fund, 2004).

India

The tribals in India are a nomadic people living apart and outside the mainstream of the general population. They live in remote or forested areas and generally in clusters in hamlets. They have their own sociocultural life, which is male-dominated and patriarchal. Their health status is poor, they are uneducated, their life expectancy is low, and their main economic activity centers around casual labor for both men and women. Despite more than 50 years of efforts by the government to raise their standard of living, not much has been achieved. Recently a community development project focused on using women as catalysts for community development work was initiated to promote health and wellness among tribal communities. Indigenous women were recruited from the local tribal villages. The women were provided education and skills training in health promotion and care. As they gained knowledge and skills, the women eventually became part-time paid employees. They became responsible for identifying the needs of the villages and implementing the day-to-day services and programs. Program elements included development of primary, secondary, and vocational education, as well as adult education and the promotion of good nutrition for the children. Use of indigenous women proved very successful. A primary school was established. This school provided education to the girls of the village and surrounding villages who would never have otherwise had access to education. Newly established community centers provided vocation education for the women, which proved useful for securing jobs. As a result of the Community Development Project, quality and utilization of health care has improved, children are being educated in the schools, and tribal women have received vocational training. A large number of women are now employed (Miranda, 2000).

INTERNATIONAL ORGANIZATIONS SUPPORTING WOMEN

Gendercide Watch

Gendercide Watch is a project of the Gender Issues Education Foundation (GIEF), a registered charitable foundation based in Edmonton, Alberta. Gendercide Watch seeks to confront acts of gender-selective mass killing around the world. Gendercide Watch is working to raise awareness, conduct research, and produce educational resources on gendercide. In particular, they seek to

Box 5.2	**Research Evidence Driving the Future Agenda** Challenges for the Future

Long-term social intervention strategies that enhance women's status, carried out both by government and NGOs, are most likely to succeed in reducing and eventually eradicating female infanticide. These have a better chance of success if the social, cultural, and political leaders of Indian society take a public position against it and put forward actions that will lead to social transformation in favor of gender equality. Consciousness-raising and gender sensitization of women and families should aim for better care for girls who are the most vulnerable to neglect. Unless the community is involved it will be difficult to ascertain the actual effectiveness of intervention efforts. Success in a few regions would provide hope and perhaps motivate some change in high-incidence communities. In addition to these steps, it appears that it is critical to implement policies and programs for the promotion of equality for women in political, legal, economic, educational, and social spheres (Batliwala, 1994). The principle of equality between men and women should also be more widely promoted through the news media to change the attitude of son preference and improve the awareness of the general public. Family planning programs should focus on effective public education, good counseling and service delivery, and the fully voluntary participation of the community and individuals (Gendercide Watch, n.d.).

dispel stereotypes that blame victims and survivors for their own suffering. (For more information see http://www.gendercide.org.)

Equality Now

Equality Now was founded in 1992 to work for the protection and promotion of the human rights of women around the world. Working with national human rights organizations and individual activists, Equality Now documents violence and discrimination against women and adds a global action overlay to support their efforts to advance equality rights and defend individual women who are suffering abuse. (For more information see http://www. equalitynow.org.)

International Council of Jewish Women

The ICJW is made up of 52 Jewish women's organizations in 47 countries. Its core purpose is to bring together Jewish women from all walks of life in order to become a driving force for social justice for all races and creeds. (For more information see http://www.icjw.org.)

The United Nations Commission on the Status of Women

The United Nations Commission on the Status of Women is the international governmental advocate for equality between men and women. It is a subsidiary body of the United Nations Economic and Social Council. The Commission actively monitors the situation of women worldwide and promotes women's rights in all societies. It makes recommendations on issues affecting women and suggests policy goals for UN member states. The Commission is also empowered to receive complaints on violations of the rights of individual women or groups of women. Founded in 1946, the Commission has 45 members representing governments. Supported in its work by the UN Division for the Advancement of Women, the Commission reports to the General Assembly through the Economic and Social Council. Nongovernmental organizations and specialized agencies of the United Nations contribute actively to its work. (For more information see http://www.un.org.)

The United Nations Development Fund for Women

UNIFEM is the women's fund at the United Nations. It provides financial and technical assistance to innovative programs and strategies that promote women's human rights, political participation, and economic security. Within the UN system, UNIFEM promotes gender equality and links women's issues and concerns to national, regional, and global agendas by fostering collaboration and providing technical expertise on gender mainstreaming and women's empowerment strategies. UNIFEMS's mandate is to:

- support innovative and experimental activities benefiting women in line with national and regional priorities;
- serve as a catalyst, with the goal of ensuring the appropriate involvement of women in mainstream development activities, as often as possible at the preinvestment stage; and
- play an innovative and catalytic role in relation to the United Nations system of development cooperation.

Created in 1976 in response to a call from women's organizations attending the 1975 UN First World Conference on Women in Mexico City, UNIFEM today works in over 100 countries and has 14 regional program directors and a growing network of affiliated gender advisors and specialists in Africa, the Arab States, Asia and the Pacific, Central and Eastern Europe, the Commonwealth of Independent States, Latin America, and the Caribbean.

SUMMARY

Often women have no knowledge of their rights and they hold out little hope that their lives can change in their lifetime. Social workers throughout the world can help to shape the direction that the future holds for women and the world. Comprehensive efforts at multiple levels are needed to overcome the vast problems facing women around the world (Wetzel, 1992). Violence against women is a global problem. From sexual harassment to physical and sexual abuse, women throughout the ages have experienced discrimination and violence, preventing them from actualizing their worth and potential and jeopardizing their children and families. Recent efforts by the World Health Organization, the United Nations, and international women's organizations are beginning to improve the plight of women across the globe. Many social programs have shown promising results in the support of women.

Thinking About Practice: From Local to Global Perspectives

1. Apply the Declaration on the Elimination of Violence against Women to the rights and protections of women in your own community. How well are women protected and supported? What are the barriers women face, and what facilitating conditions present in your community protect and support women?

2. What organizations exist in your community to protect and support women? Are additional resources or services needed?

3. What micro, meso, or macro interventions used in other countries would be useful in your own community?

Social Work Practice and Social Justice Website

Please go to the Book Companion Website at http://www.thomsonedu.com/author/sowers to find a rich collection of related articles selected by the authors from Info Trac College Edition.

References

Amnesty International. (n.d.). *STOP violence against women.* Retrieved July 12, 2004, from http://web.amnesty.org/actforwomen

Batliwala, S. (1994). The meaning of women's empowerment: New concepts from action. In G. Sen, A. Germain, & L. C. Chen (Eds.), *Population policies reconsidered.* Boston: Harvard University Press.

Brundtland, Gro Harlem. (1995). United Nations Development Programme. *Human development report,* p. 110. New York: Oxford University Press.

Convention. (1980). *The elimination of all forms of discrimination against women.* New York: United Nations.

Daw, E. (1970). Female circumcision and infibulation complicating delivery. *Practitioner, 204,* 559.

Gendercide Watch. (n.d.). *Case study: Female infanticide.* Retrieved July 8, 2004, from http://www.gendercide.org/case_infanticide.html

Hicks, E. K. (1993). *Infibulation: Female mutilation in Islamic Northeastern Africa.* New Brunswick, NJ: Transaction Books.

International Federation of Social Workers. (1999). *International policy on women.* Helsinki: Author.

Kenyatta, J. (1938). *Facing Mount Kenya: The tribal life of the Gikuyu.* New York: Vintage Books.

Lightfoot-Klein. (1989). The sexual experience and marital adjustment of genitally circumcised and infibulated females in the Sudan. *Journal of Sex Research, 26*(3), 375–392.

Maslow, A. (1970). *Motivation and personality* (2nd ed.). New York: Harper & Row.

Miranda, M. (2000, July 29–August 2). *Role of tribal women in the development process.* Paper presented at the Conference of the International Association of Schools of Social Work, Montreal, Canada.

Muslim Women's League. (n.d.). *Position paper on "honor killings."* Retrieved July 10, 2004, from http://www.mwlusa.org/publications/positionpapers/hk.html

Pieters, G., & Lowenfels, A. B. (1977). Infibulation in the horn of Africa. *New York State Journal of Medicine, 77*(5), 729–731.

Reichert, E. (1998). Women's rights are human rights: Platform for action. *International Social Work, 41*(3), 371–384.

United Nations. (n.d.). Retrieved July 7, 2004, from http://www.un.org/aboutun/charter

United Nations. (1994). *Declaration on the elimination of violence against women.* (Resolution No. A/RES/48/104). New York: Author.

United Nations. (1996). *Platform for action and the Beijing Declaration: Fourth World Conference on Women: Beijing, China, 4–15 September 1995.* New York: Department of Public Information, United Nations.

United Nations Children's Fund. (n.d.). Retrieved July 8, 2004, from http://www.unicef.org

United Nations Development Programme. (1995). Retrieved July 14, 2004, from http://www.undp.org

United Nations Population Fund. (n.d.). Retrieved July 10, 2004, from http://www.womensissues.about.com/cs/honorkillings/a/honorkillings.htm

United Nations Population Fund. (2004). *Investing in people: National progress in implementing the ICPD programme of action 1994–2004.* New York: United Nations Population Fund.

Wetzel, J. W. (1992). Profiles on women. *Social work in health care, 16*(3), 13–27.

Wetzel, J. W. (1993). *The world of women: In pursuit of human rights.* London: MacMillan Press.

Wetzel, J. W. (1996). On the road to Beijing: The evolution of the international women's movement. *Affilia, 11*(2), 221–232.

World Health Organization. (n.d.). Retrieved July 9, 2004, from http://www.who.org

World Health Report. (2001). Retrieved July 9, 2001 from http://www.who.int/whr2001/2001/main/en/chapter1

Youth Advocate Program International. (n.d.). Retrieved July 8, 2004, from http://www.yapi.org/girlchild/index.htm

Of all the self-fulfilling prophecies in our culture, the assumption that aging means decline and poor health is probably the deadliest.

Marilyn Ferguson

Social Work Practice with the Elderly

CURRENT DEMOGRAPHICS ON AGEING AROUND THE WORLD

According to the United Nations definition, persons 60 years and over are considered elderly (United Nations, n.d.). In 2000, about 600 million persons (10 percent of the world's population) was 60 years old or over. The majority of older persons are women. About two-thirds of older persons live in developing countries. Most live in rural areas. By 2050, 21 percent of the world's population is expected to be 60 years old or over. The fastest growing age group is the oldest-old, those aged 80 years and over. They are growing at a rate of 3.8 percent per year, compared to the age group 60 years and over that is growing at 2 percent per year. Globally, the total population is growing at a rate of 1.2 percent annually. Developed regions have a much larger percentage of older persons than developing regions. For example, in 2000, the percentage of older persons was as follows (United Nations, n.d.):

Africa	5%	Europe	20%
Asia	9%	North America	16%
Latin America & Caribbean	8%	Oceania	13%

The graying of the planet represents the most significant population shift in recent history (Obaid & Malloch-Brown, 2002). Although population ageing is one of humanity's major achievements, it is also a major challenge. Many developing countries are not prepared to meet all the needs of the growing numbers of older persons in their populations. Older persons living in developing countries tend to live at lower economic levels. Older persons, especially widows and the childless, are consistently among the poorest and most vulnerable (Apt, 2002). Poverty is the main threat to the well-being of older persons. Today, many of the 400 million older persons in developing countries are living below the poverty line.

Population Trends in the United States

The United States is also faced with major challenges associated with dramatic increases in the numbers of people living to an advanced old age. Rapidly expanding numbers of very old people represent a social phenomenon without historical precedent in the United States (Administration on Aging, n.d.). Minority Americans often are at greater risk of poor health, social isolation, and poverty. Currently, minority elders comprise over 16.1 percent of all older Americans who are 65 years of age and older. In the future, it is expected that their numbers will increase dramatically. Between 1999 and 2030, the minority population 65 and older is projected to increase by 217 percent, compared with 81 percent for the older white population. The number of African-American elders is expected to increase by 128 percent. The population of Asian-American elders will increase by 301 percent and the number of Hispanic-American elders will grow by 322 percent. The number of Native-American and Alaska-Native elders will increase roughly by 193 percent by 2030 if current demographic trends continue (Administration on Ageing, n.d.).

Developmental Aspects of Ageing

Individuals begin their ageing process at the moment of birth, and go through the life course accumulating a range of experiences that affect their capabilities and well-being in later years. Most persons around the globe (although not all) experience a long childhood and a long old age. Throughout history this has enabled older persons to educate the younger and pass on values to them. The presence of the elderly in the family home, the neighborhood, and in all forms of social life provides opportunity for the young to learn from the old (International Federation on Ageing, n.d.). Substantial evidence from around the world indicates that many older people can and do lead productive lives, including contributing financially, caring for children, and supporting the family.

There are important gender differences in the way people age. Throughout the world, women live longer than men. The largest differences in the life spans of men and women are in Eastern Europe, the Baltic States, and in central Asia. Although women may live longer, they tend to be affected by more disabling diseases in later life than are men. Reasons for the differences between men and women in life expectancy and relative health during the ageing process are still poorly understood (World Health Organization, 1998a).

CORE ELEMENTS OF GLOBAL GERONTOLOGICAL PRACTICE
Elder Maltreatment

It was not until well after the recognition of incidences of child abuse and domestic violence in the last quarter of the twentieth century that elderly abuse was also seen as an important problem. The World Health Organization expects that elder abuse will continue to grow as many countries experience rapidly ageing populations. Older men are at risk of abuse in about the same proportion as women. But elderly women are at high risk of abuse, neglect, and exploitation in cultures where women are devalued. In these cultures women are at high risk of being abandoned when they are widowed and having their property seized.

Similar to other types of violence, abuse of the elderly includes physical, sexual, and psychological abuse, as well as neglect. Little information exists on the extent of abuse in elderly populations. However, the World Health Organization estimates that between 4 to 6 percent of elderly people have experienced some form of abuse in the home (World Health Organization, n.d.). In addition to being at risk of abuse at home, the elderly are at risk of abuse in institutions such as hospitals, nursing homes, and other long-term care facilities. Abusive acts within institutions for the elderly include physically restraining patients, depriving them of dignity and choice over daily affairs, and providing insufficient care. Within institutions, abuse is more likely to occur where care standards are low, staff are poorly trained or overworked, interactions between staff and residents are difficult, the physical environment is deficient, and policies operate in the interests of the institution rather than of the residents (Ngan, 2004). For older people, even a minor injury can cause serious and permanent damage. The effects of abuse of the elderly can have permanent damage because their bones are more brittle and the rehabilitation process is much longer. A number of situations appear to put the elderly at risk of violence and many different factors may cause a single incident. According to Pillemar and Moore (1989) four causal theories of elder abuse appear particularly salient:

1. stress of caregivers;
2. cycle of violence;
3. personal problems of abusers; and
4. impairment of dependent elders.

In addition to these theories, the World Health Organization suggests that a caregiver's dependence on an older person for accommodation or financial support, which is a potential source of conflict and social isolation, may be an important factor in abuse and neglect of the elderly (World Health Organization Centre for Health Development, n.d.).

Cultural and socioeconomic factors may also play an important role in elder abuse. These include:

- the depiction of older people as frail, weak, and dependent;
- erosion of the bonds between generations of a family;
- restructuring of the basic support networks for the elderly;
- systems of inheritance and land rights, affecting the distribution of power and material goods within families; and
- migration of young couples to other areas, leaving elderly parents alone, in societies where older people were traditionally cared for by their offspring (World Health Organization Centre for Health Development, n.d.).

In some countries, the medical profession has played a leading role in raising public concern about elder abuse. However, there are few intervention programs for abused elders in hospital settings and many doctors do not diagnose abuse because it is not part of their training. Some of the signs and symptoms of abuse include:

- delays between injuries or illness and seeking medical attention;
- implausible or vague explanations for injuries or ill health, from either patient or caregiver;
- differing case histories from patient and caregiver;
- frequent visits to emergency departments because a chronic condition has worsened, despite a care plan and resources to deal with this in the home;

- functionally impaired older patients who arrive without their main caregiver; and
- laboratory findings that are inconsistent with the history provided (World Health Organization Centre for Health Development, n.d.)

Social Services

Social integration and support tend to provide people with emotional and practical resources that positively impact the ageing process. Those older people who are more socially integrated—for example, those who are members of social clubs or religious organizations, or those involved in family activities—enjoy better health. These involvements have been shown to increase their self-esteem, and improve their physical mobility and mental agility (World Health Organization, 1998b).

In general, countries that deliver services to abused, neglected, or exploited older people have done so through the existing health and social services network. Such services typically include medical, legal, psychological, and financial help, as well as help with housing and other environmental issues. Other interventions include emergency shelters, support groups specifically aimed at older people, and telephone help lines. In some low-income countries, local projects have been established to help older people plan programs and develop their own services.

Economic Services

Many Asian countries have only recently begun addressing a social security system to provide financial protection and assistance in old age. In general, Thailand, Malaysia, Indonesia, the Philippines, and Hong Kong have not adequately developed formal, cradle-to-grave social security safety nets. Because of a lack of a system of benefit supports or a contributory social insurance program, the East Asian welfare systems appear to be unable to meet the needs of the poor elderly. With the exception of Japan, most East Asian countries have no contributory insurance programs for long-term care to meet the rising costs of institutional placements and hospitalization of the growing numbers of frail elderly (Ngan, 2004).

Health Services

Chronic and infectious diseases, many of which are direct results of life course events, influence the quality of life in older age. The types of conditions older people experience vary by economic status, gender, race, and ethnicity. Older people with higher incomes report their health as being much better than do older people with less income (Dunkle & Norgard, 1995). Disease may affect biological structures, thus accelerating the ageing process and also possibly leading to disabilities. Diseases in adult life may hasten decline in old age.

Noncommunicable Diseases   Noncommunicable diseases tend to be established over long periods of time during the life course and may not be apparent until complications arise in later life. The most common noncommunicable diseases in old age include coronary heart disease, high blood pressure, stroke, diabetes, emphysema, cancer, musculoskeletal disorder, urinary incontinence, and mental illness (World Health Organization, 1998c). Coronary heart disease, high blood pressure, and stroke contribute to a faster decline in functional capacity, because they can reduce a person's exercise tolerance, mobility, and mental functioning. Diabetes can have a negative effect on organs, especially during later life. Diabetes associated health problems include increased lens opacity (cataract), decline in kidney function, and impaired arterial circulation. These, in turn, may lead to other health complications including circulatory diseases. Most cancers arise in later life, and the risk for many forms of cancer increases with age. The World Health Organization estimates that one-third of cancers may be preventable and a further third curable, if diagnosed early. Musculoskeletal disorders, including osteoporosis, can reduce mobility. This may affect a person's ability to function independently and care for oneself. Urinary incontinence is a common condition among older people. It can lead to social isolation, dependence, and even institutionalization. It is estimated that 12 percent of the total population aged 75 or above in developed countries are affected by incontinence. Worldwide the most common causes are thought to be dementia and stroke, the effects of childbirth, female circumcision, and diseases of the prostate gland (World Health Organization, 1998c). Mental illness contributes relatively little to life expectancy but it can contribute to major health problems and disability. Worldwide there are an estimated 400 million cases of anxiety disorder, 340 million of mood disorders, 45 million of schizophrenia, and 29 million of dementia (World Health Organization, 1998c). Depression, often a result of social exclusion and isolation, is common among older people. It can negatively impact the ability to engage in routine daily functions. It is particularly prevalent in industrialized countries.

Alzheimer's Disease   Alzheimer's disease is a degenerative brain syndrome characterized by a progressive decline in memory, thinking, comprehension, calculation, language, learning capacity, and judgment (World Health Organization, 2002). An estimated 37 million people worldwide live with dementia, with Alzheimer's disease causing the majority of cases. Two out of three people with dementia live in developing countries (Graham, 2001). About 5 percent of men and 6 percent of women over 60 years of age are affected with Alzheimer's. As the population of the elderly continues to increase, the World Health Organization projects that this figure will increase rapidly over the next 20 years (World Health Organization, 2002; World Health Organization, 2001). The cost of Alzheimer's disease to society is substantial (Rice et al.,

1993) and will continue to increase (Brookmeyer & Gray, 2000). The direct and total costs of the disorder in the United States have been estimated to be $536 million and $1.75 billion, respectively, for the year 2000 (World Health Organization, 2001).

During the course of Alzheimer's disease, nerve cells die in particular regions of the brain. The brain shrinks as gaps develop in the temporal lobe and hippocampus, which are responsible for storing and retrieving new information. This in turn affects people's ability to remember, speak, think, and make decisions. The production of certain chemicals in the brain, such as acetylcholine, is also affected. It is not known what causes nerve cells to die but there are characteristic appearances of the brain after death. In particular, tangles and plaques made from protein fragments are observed under the microscope in damaged areas of the brain. These conditions are used to confirm a diagnosis of Alzheimer's disease (Alzheimer's Disease International, 2002; World Health Organization, 2002).

Dementia affects people differently. An individual's personality, general health, and social situation are all important factors in determining the impact of dementia. Alzheimer's Disease International (2002) notes that the beginning of the condition is often characterized by:

- lapses of memory;
- difficulty in finding the right words for everyday objects; and
- mood swings.

As Alzheimer's progresses, the person may typically exhibit the following:

- routinely forget recent events, names, and faces
- have difficulty in understanding what is being said
- become confused when handling money or driving a car
- undergo personality changes
- appear to no longer care about those around them
- experience mood swings and burst into tears for no apparent reason
- become convinced that someone is trying to harm them (Alzheimer's Disease International, 2002)

In advanced cases people may also adopt unsettling or unsuitable behavior, such as getting up in the middle of the night and wandering off, undressing in public, or making inappropriate sexual advances (Alzheimer's Disease International, 2002).

There is no simple test to make a diagnosis of dementia. It can be diagnosed with certainty only by examining the brain at post mortem. However, a complete history of the person's problems taken from a close relative, and a complete physical and mental status exam, can support the diagnosis of dementia. It is important to exclude other treatable conditions that cause memory loss such as depression, urinary infection, vitamin deficiency, and brain tumor (Alzheimer's Disease International, 2002). An early diagnosis is critical in helping the family and caregivers prepare to cope with the effects of the disease as it progresses. It can also provide people with dementia an opportunity to make decisions about their financial and legal affairs before they lose the ability to do so. Early diagnosis also gives people with dementia a better chance to benefit from existing treatments.

Scientists have conducted an immense amount of research into new drug treatments for Alzheimer's disease and other dementia.

> The recently developed drugs known as cholinesterase inhibitors or anti-cholinesterase drugs work by reducing the breakdown of acetylcholine in the brain. Acetylcholine is a chemical substance that occurs naturally in the brain and enables nerve cells in the brain to pass messages to each other. Research has shown that many people with Alzheimer's disease have a reduced amount of acetylcholine, and it is thought that the loss of this chemical may result in deterioration of memory. These drugs include Reminyl (galantamine), Aricept (donepezil hydrochloride), and Exelon (rivastigmine). Side effects of the drugs may include diarrhea, nausea, insomnia, fatigue, and loss of appetite (Alzheimer's Disease International, 2002; World Health Organization, 2002).

There is no cure yet for Alzheimer's disease. The use of drugs may merely stabilize some of the symptoms of early- to mid-stage Alzheimer's disease for a limited period of time (Alzheimer's Disease International, 2002). Psychosocial interventions, including education, support, counseling, and respite care, are extremely important in Alzheimer's disease, both for patients and family givers. According to the World Health Organization (2002), the goals of care are to:

- maintain the functioning of the individual;
- reduce disability due to lost mental functions;
- reorganize routines so as to maximize use of the retained functions;
- minimize symptoms such as depression, agitation, and suspiciousness; and
- provide support to families.

Communicable Diseases   Although infectious diseases may be of short duration, they can lead to chronic problems. This is due to the infection's impact on the body's organ structure and physiology. The effects may produce permanent damage and disability in later life. The most common communicable diseases throughout the world include tuberculosis, leprosy, malaria, schistosomiasis, and HIV/AIDS (World Health Organization, 1998c). Even though tuberculosis is being controlled in many parts of the world, over 7 million new cases of tuberculosis were recorded in 1997. In the same year it caused 3 million deaths, making it the leading infectious killer of adults (World Health Organization, 1998c). Tuberculosis may cause permanent lung and other organ damage for those who survive the disease. This frequently leads to a reduced ability to function in older age. A World Health Organization eradication program has led to a substantial decline in leprosy worldwide, but residual numbers of cases remain in India, Bangladesh, Brazil, and some African countries. Leprosy that is untreated can cause obvious and sometimes disabling deformities. Vector-borne diseases, including malaria and schistosomiasis, may result from inadequate housing. They may also result from employment in agriculture, mining, and construction. Each year some 2.7 million people die from the

300–500 million clinical cases of malaria worldwide (World Health Organization, 1998c). The new health threat of HIV/AIDS, which currently affects about 31 million people, has far-reaching implications for the older generation that is left to care for orphaned grandchildren.

In all developed nations, including the United States, the overwhelming majority of long-term care received by persons with disabilities of all ages is provided by informal caregivers, family members, or a combination of caregivers and family members. Families often need support, especially when care needs are extensive. There is an enormous cost associated with caregiving of the elderly. Indirect costs include such things as increased stress on the family members and informal caregivers. Direct costs may be evident in lost wages and lost productivity. Individual caregivers and society share in these costs.

The United States does not have a comprehensive long-term care system. In general, the nation relies upon Medicaid, a state-administered safety net as the primary source of financing for long-term care. The Medicaid program is designed for persons with low incomes and few assets. Benefits vary from state to state but in general are far more generous for nursing home care than for care in home or in community-based settings. As a result, these policies often inadvertently encourage long-term dependence rather than the long-term independence that, researchers say, persons with disabilities want (American Association of Retired Persons, n.d.).

Twenty-nine nations have older populations than the United States. Although many of these countries do not have strong or effective long-term care systems, some do. For example, Germany and Japan have implemented comprehensive social insurance systems for long-term care. They cover a wide range of benefits in the home and community in addition to nursing home care Benefits typically include personal assistance services, adult day services, and respite care for family caregivers. To determine eligibility for services, these countries base their assessment on need for assistance with everyday tasks, rather than on income and assets (American Association of Retired Persons, n.d.). The United States has some model programs, such as the Program of All-Inclusive Care for the Elderly (PACE) and state Medicaid programs that permit consumers to direct their home care services. But these programs still reach only a small fraction of persons who need long-term care. Many Scandinavian nations as well as Austria, Japan, and Germany have universal long-term care programs. These programs reach large numbers of their older populations and persons with disabilities. It may be useful to look to these countries that can serve as "natural laboratories" for tracking the impact of long-term care policy changes on coverage, cost, quality of care, and quality of life (Gibson, 2003).

Long-term health care for the aged is problematic even in those countries that culturally place a high value on the elderly. Most East Asian governments promote family responsibility to care for the aged. Because many of these governments place responsibility on families to care for their elderly, they have not developed a sufficient number of long-term care facilities for frail older people to meet the need of those suffering from dementia and paraplegic strokes (Choi, 2002; Ngan, 2004; Phillips, 1999). In China there is a long time tradition of children supporting their elderly parents. As a result, many families experience undue stress and financial strain. In fact, the deep rooted attitude that families should care for their older members may be hindering the development of formal, institutional care (Choi, 2002), and family caregivers often find that they are unable to cope with the complexities of family care for elderly dependents who are in poor health (MacKenzie & Beck, 1991). Because of the rising incidence of suicide among the elderly as well as other family problems, many Asian governments are now exploring the need to introduce national policies on ageing and long-term care to augment the traditional system (Howe & Phillips, 2001; Ngan, 2004). Japan, South Korea, Hong Kong, Singapore, and Taiwan are now starting to plan for a major increase in long-term care services (Ngan, 2004).

COMMUNITY-BASED SOCIAL SERVICE AND HEALTH CARE

Most countries have moved toward community-based care to meet the needs of older people (Higgins, 1989). In many places families face increasing pressure to provide care. Filial support legislation exists in several countries, including some states in the United States (George, 1997). In China, filial support is mandated in the Marriage Laws of 1982 (Barusch, 1995), and the government of Singapore offers incentives for families to care for elderly parents (Teo, 1994).

In recent years, the quest for adequate and cost-effective care for the growing number of older persons has received increased attention from national and local governments, international organizations, NGOs, the scientific and service communities, and the general public. Major issues focus around an integrated and more comprehensive approach to the special needs of older persons, their families, and the community. The model for community-based care involves and requires interorganizational collaboration and interdisciplinary cooperation. Community-based social service and health care is a strategic approach to meet the mounting demands for integrated health and social services for older persons, their families, and their communities (Zimmerman et al., 2001). Community health care includes both the health and social services sectors. Health and social services typically provide self care, informal care, and formal care. Provisions for care encompass prevention, curative care, rehabilitation, palliative care, and terminal care. Levels of care may include individual, family, and community care. These integrated services may be delivered in various settings including home or residential care settings (World Health Organization Centre for Health Development, n.d.).

AGEING AND THE RIGHTS OF OLDER PERSONS

Although many documents over the past sixty years, including the 1948 Universal Declaration of Human Rights, have sought to address the rights of all persons, it was not until the Declaration on Social Progress and Development in 1969 that old age was specifically mentioned (Office of the United Nations

High Commissioner for Human Rights, n.d.). In 1982 the United Nations adopted the first International Plan of Action on Ageing and in 1991 the General Assembly of the United Nations adopted the Principles for Older Persons. The four main themes of the latter were independence, participation, care, and self-fulfillment and dignity [MM1]. In 1995 the Committee on Economic, Social and Cultural Rights adopted General Comment No. 6 on the economic, social, and cultural rights of older persons. The UN declared 1999 to be the International Year of Older Persons and developed a conceptual framework based on the four priority areas of 1) the situation of older persons, 2) individual lifelong development, 3) the relationship between generations, and 4) the interrelationship of populations, ageing, and development. In 2002 the Madrid Plan of Action seriously addressed the situation of older persons and the Commission for Social Development was given the charge to implement the plan (International Association of Gerontology, 2005).

Believing that these precedents were not enough to give older persons their rights or to recognize their contribution to society, the International Association of Gerontology and other nongovernmental organizations called upon the Commission on Human Rights to adopt a Declaration on the Rights of Older Persons. In their appeal to the commission they called for a declaration recognizing that older persons have rights, including intergenerational rights, and that elders need protection but also make an important contribution to social peace and cohesion. They further urged that a Declaration on the Rights of Older Persons be based on the situation of older persons, individual lifelong development, the relationship between generations, and the interrelationship of population, ageing, and development (International Association of Gerontology, 2005).

THE INTERNATIONAL FEDERATION OF SOCIAL WORKERS' INTERNATIONAL POLICY ON OLDER PERSONS

According to the IFSW (1999), recent research suggests that the current cohort of older persons is more attuned to prevention and is experiencing ageing in a more healthy manner. With many medical advances and increasing longevity, research is also beginning to reflect that the period of disability and debilitating illness is being shortened in the last stages of life. IFSW (1999) believes that meeting the needs of this population is essential to older persons' social and emotional well-being. In its statement on International Policy on Older Persons (1999), the IFSW states that "an important ingredient for this state of well-being is a group of caring professionals who show respect and honor the principle of self-determination" (p. 2). As a result, the IFSW suggests that the following principles should underpin social policy on older persons:

- A comprehensive social policy statement should be in place for older persons and should take into account the differential needs of older persons as they move through the ageing process.

- There is a similarity in the ageing process, which is universal, and thus ageing is a social issue and a global concern. In most countries it is conventional to define older people as those who have reached the age of retirement, as accepted by the particular country and culture.
- Each policy should reflect the right of older persons to continue to work if they so desire. However, the opportunity is necessary for paid and/or volunteer work to enhance a better sense of well-being for the individual and to make a major contribution to society.
- Any social policy statement should safeguard the rights of older people to exercise their freedom to live in their own way, at their own pace and in different lifestyles.
- Options and choices should be preserved for the physically dependent, respecting the rights of individuals to accept or alter the services.

IFSW (1999) supports social and economic policies for older persons that:

- ensure the delivery of coordinated and comprehensive services to sustain and enhance the well-being and quality of life of older people in the community as well as in residential settings;
- support the specific housing needs of older people in the community, in congregate care, and in institutional settings; and
- provide a level of income that ensures that older persons are able to satisfy their personal needs and maintain a standard of living appropriate to the society in which they live, in order to:
  - facilitate access to transportation, health services, adult education, and cultural and leisure activities; and
  - address the disadvantages experienced by women in particular who are now widows or living on their own, disabled, and experiencing the effects of poverty.

IFSW also endorses:

- the promotion of the rights of older people to full access to preventative and comprehensive health care including hospital and long-term care, and other services received in the community and at home;
- the right of older people to remain in their own homes and to have access to other housing options adapted to their specific condition and needs;
- policies that ensure that older persons in long-term housing must at all times be treated with respect and in so far as is possible supported to exercise the right of self-determination and choice. Further those older persons with Alzheimer's disease and other dementia should be given every opportunity for special care and services; and
- the protection, empowerment, initiation, and support of social legislation to promote and protect the rights of older people and to protect them against abuse, exploitation, and neglect.

Advocacy for the Elderly

The International Plan of Action on Ageing is the first international instrument on ageing. It influences the development and implementation of policies

Box 6.1 | Exemplars from Around the World

Republic of Seychelles

The Republic of Seychelles in Eastern Africa is a group of islands in the Indian Ocean, northeast of Madagascar. Since 1979, it has been the government's policy to address the needs of the elderly via a universal pension scheme for persons aged 63 years and older. Beginning in 1997, a home-care service provision program has been available to help meet the needs of elderly people whose families are unable to assist them due to economic limitations. The government is also providing home-care assistance through the Ministry of Social Affairs and Employment and is providing houses for the elderly who have no immediate family support. Additionally, the government is setting up a "council for the elderly" to provide information related to ageing and to offer support for the elderly (United Nations Population Fund, 2004).

The United States Targeted Capacity Expansion Program to Improve Older Adult Mental Health Services

Launched by the federal Substance Abuse and Mental Health Services Administration's Center for Mental Health Services, the Targeted Capacity Expansion (TCE) program is a three-year project designed to increase both the quantity and quality of mental health services offered to people age 65 and older. Nine sites in the United States are expanding or enhancing their programs using methods that have a proven track record of success. Using evidence-based practices, they will become model sites for other organizations. Some sites focus on screening. The City of El Paso's Project FOCUS (For the Optimal Care of Underserved Seniors), for example, has developed a mental health screening instrument that nutrition staffers incorporate into their annual assessments. Depending on client scores,

they are referred to a prevention-oriented case management program, a community mental health center, or a more intensive program that uses lay community workers to address medical and social needs of homebound elders.

Other sites focus on treatment. In Madison, Wisconsin, for instance, language barriers, transportation difficulties, and stigma kept many older Hmong refugees from seeking help for the depression, anxiety, and posttraumatic stress disorder they've developed in response to war, refugee camps, and resettlement. A psychiatrist, psychologist, and Hmong staff members assist as "culture brokers" to provide therapy and other services in the homes of elders who can't or won't come to the center. The center incorporates Hmong cultural beliefs (for example, diagnoses are often made by a shaman) with Western concepts (Substance Abuse and Mental Health Services Administration, 2004).

Malta's International Institute on Ageing in Partnership with the United Nations Population Fund

The International Institute on Ageing in Malta was established in 1988 and is largely supported by the government of Malta. The Institute is providing gerontological training and acts as a practical bridge between and among developed and developing countries. It also conducts onsite training programs in various countries that are tailored to the specific needs of the particular country. The training programs address poverty and exclusion, which remain major threats to the well-being of older persons throughout the world. The Institute enters into collaborative agreements with various organizations to enable countries to build their capacity to meet the challenges of their rapidly increasing elderly population (United Nations Population Fund, n.d.).

and programs affecting the elderly. It was endorsed by the United Nations General Assembly in 1982, having been adopted earlier the same year at the World Assembly on Ageing at Vienna, Austria. It is often referred to as the "Vienna Plan" or the "International Plan." It aims to "strengthen the capacities of governments and civil society to deal effectively with the ageing of popula-

Box 6.2	**Research Evidence Driving the Future Agenda** Challenges for the Future

With high life expectancy, older people increasingly want to remain economically active and make a contribution to society. Societies need to recognize the strengths of older persons and empower them. Human rights, sustainable human development, and poverty eradication programs must be developed, designed, and monitored at all levels, with older people playing an active role (Obaid, 2002). A number of significant challenges require the introduction of policies and programs that respond to older peoples' needs. These challenges include:

- promoting lifelong education and training, and healthy and active ageing;
- recognizing and supporting the caregiving services provided by older persons, especially women, to grandchildren orphaned by the effects of HIV/AIDS;
- eliminating violence and other crimes against older persons who are caught in conflict and other complex humanitarian situations;
- supporting gender-sensitive research on population ageing; and
- strengthening social protection schemes for older persons, particularly the long-term care of the frail and poor (Obaid & Malloch-Brown, 2002).

Research commissioned by UNFPA in India and South Africa last year found that the main concerns of older people include inadequate living conditions, lack of access to social services, and intergenerational violence and abuse. Poverty among older people is also linked to low levels of literacy, especially for women. Only one-third of women in the developing world age 60 or over can read and write. Poverty among older people

is also linked to low levels of health, lack of awareness and access to information, and a lack of participation. This leads to social exclusion and isolation, and reinforces the cycle of poverty between generations. In responding to interviews, older people identified their priority needs as food security, clean water, good health, adequate accommodation, and support in caring for families. Due to the impact of HIV/AIDS, older people, and particularly older women, are increasingly acting as caregivers for their adult children as well as for orphaned grandchildren. This is despite the fact that their own situations are characterized by extreme poverty, and they themselves often need help and support. Their concerns with growing older include fear of isolation, exclusion, illness, a sense of helplessness, violence and abuse, and confusion over the escalation of HIV/AIDS. There is a critical need to facilitate positive action by nongovernmental organizations, communities, and the private sector for the welfare of older people. Policy dialogue can help bring different stakeholders together and provide a basis for joint action. The needs and voices of the older poor need to be reflected in programs implemented at the country level (United Nations Population Fund, n.d.).

Most old age policies were designed with a youthful society in mind. From this point onward, policies for older persons, younger persons, and those in between should be designed with an ageing society in mind—a society in which every third individual will soon be over the age of 60. Global, national, and local communities must begin to adjust and design their infrastructures, policies, plans, and resources accordingly (United Nations, n.d.).

---

tions and to address the developmental potential and dependency needs of older persons. It promotes regional and global cooperation. The plan also seeks to ensure that people everywhere will age with security and dignity, and continue to participate in their societies as citizens with full rights" (United Nations, n.d.). The top priorities include:

- involving older persons in the development process;
- advancing health and well-being into old age; and
- ensuring supportive environments that enable older persons to have choices.

Core themes of the Plan include:

- the recognition of the needs of older women;
- the desire of older people to stay active and engaged; and
- the need to create intergenerational solidarity.

These themes demonstrate how the global community shares a common vision of a better future for older persons (United Nations, n.d.). It includes 62 recommendations for action addressing research, data collection and analysis, training, and education as well as the following:

- health and nutrition;
- protection of elderly consumers;
- housing and the environment;
- family;
- social welfare;
- income security and employment; and
- education.

The Plan is part of an international framework of standards and strategies developed by the global community in the last few decades (International Federation on Ageing, n.d.).

The United Nations Principles for Older Persons encourage governments to incorporate the following principles into their national programs:

- Independence
  - Older persons should have access to adequate food, water, shelter, clothing, and health care through the provision of income, family and community support, and self-help.
  - Older persons should have the opportunity to work or to have access to other income-generating opportunities.
  - Older persons should be able to participate in determining when and at what pace withdrawal from the labor force takes place.
  - Older persons should have access to appropriate educational and training programs.
  - Older persons should be able to live in environments that are safe and adaptable to personal preferences and changing capacities.
  - Older persons should be able to reside at home for as long as possible.
  - Older persons should remain integrated in society, participate actively in the formulation and implementation of policies that directly affect their well-being, and share their knowledge and skills with younger generations.
  - Older persons should be able to seek and develop opportunities for service to the community and to serve as volunteers in positions appropriate to their interests and capabilities.
  - Older persons should be able to form movements or associations of older persons.
- Care
  - Older persons should benefit from family and community care and protection in accordance with each society's system of cultural values.

- Older persons should have access to health care to help them to maintain or regain the optimum level of physical, mental, and emotional well-being and to prevent or delay the onset of illness.
- Older persons should have access to social and legal services to enhance their autonomy, protection, and care.
- Older persons should be able to utilize appropriate levels of institutional care providing protection, rehabilitation, and social and mental stimulation in a humane and secure environment.
- Older persons should be able to enjoy human rights and fundamental freedoms when residing in any shelter, care, or treatment facility, including full respect for their dignity, beliefs, needs, and privacy, and for the right to make decisions about their care and the quality of their lives.
- Self-fulfillment
  - Older persons should be able to pursue opportunities for the full development of their potential.
  - Older persons should have access to the educational, cultural, spiritual, and recreational resources of society.
- Dignity
  - Older persons should be able to live in dignity and security and be free from exploitation and physical or mental abuse.
  - Older persons should be treated fairly regardless of age, gender, racial, or ethnic background, disability, or other status, and be valued independently of their economic contribution.

INTERNATIONAL ORGANIZATIONS ON AGEING

Alzheimer's Disease International

Alzheimer's Disease International is the umbrella organization of Alzheimer associations around the world, which offer support and information to people with dementia and to their caregivers (for more information see http://www.alz.co.uk).

American Association of Retired Persons

Founded in 1958, AARP provides global resources for information and advocacy on major issues affecting ageing populations. Through its Office of International Affairs, AARP works with numerous governmental and nongovernmental organizations, promotes communication and the exchange of ideas, and establishes and communicates best practices in ageing concerns worldwide. The AARP has consultative status as a nongovernmental organization at the UN Economic and Social Council. With this status, AARP is able to submit statements and make recommendations to ensure that the interests of people over 50 are addressed in major international initiatives and documents. AARP's International Visitor Program provides informational briefings and reports to government officials, business leaders, NGO representatives, and researchers who visit AARP from around the world to learn more about policies, programs, and activities. In the United States and abroad, AARP seeks to lead positive social change and enhance the quality of life for people over 50. They seek to promote the concerns of the elderly through social policy, communications, advocacy, community service, and group buying arrangements. AARP is dedicated to bettering the situation for ageing people so they can live longer, healthier, more financially secure, and more productive lives (for more information see http://www.aarp.org).

International Federation on Ageing

The International Federation on Ageing informs, educates, and promotes policies, programs, and practices to improve the quality of life of older persons around the world. Their mission includes:

- building, facilitating, and strengthening bridges between governments, service providers, practitioners, and individuals concerned with improving the quality of life of older people around the world; and
- strengthening nongovernment organizations across the regions of the world through linking together for a common purpose.

The International Federation on Ageing focuses on three key areas:

- Policy—working with and disseminating information from governments across the world committed to developing policies for an ageing society and today's older people;
- Practice—sharing best practice from organizations committed to providing quality programs and services for older people; and
- Impact—working with older people to understand the impact that policies, programs, and practices has on the lives of older people.

The International Federation on Ageing also advocates for member organizations and older people globally within the UN, WHO, UNESCO, the United Nations Economic and Social Commission for Asia and the Pacific (UNESCAP), and the Council of Europe, though consultative status.

The IFA maintains a knowledge bank on ageing issues and best practices to influence, advocate, and promote change that affects the lives of older people (for more information see http://www.ifa-fiv.org).

HelpAge International

HelpAge International is a global network of members and partner organizations working in over 80 countries on practical and policy issues. Its mission is to improve the lives of disadvantaged older people (for more information see http://www.helpage.org).

SUMMARY

The graying of the planet represents the most significant population shift in recent history. While it is a major achievement of medical science, it is also a major challenge. With fewer young people to provide economic and social support for the burgeoning elder population, our elders across the globe are now the poorest and most vulnerable. Every nation in the world is struggling with the challenges of providing supports to the elderly, and particularly to the frail elderly. Advocacy for the elderly is taking root across the globe and the United Nations and the World Health Organization have placed a high priority on finding solutions for the well-being of the ageing population. Pilot programs to promote the health, safety, and well-being of the elderly are showing great promise, especially in the areas of health and mental health promotion.

Thinking About Practice: From Local to Global Perspectives

1. What are the population trends pertaining to the elderly in your community? Is the elder population increasing? How does this compare to the population trends in other countries?
2. What programs and services are available in your community for the protection of the elderly? How do these compare to programs and services in other communities and in other nations?
3. What are the obstacles to promoting the safety and well-being of elders in your community? What opportunities are available?
4. Apply the International Federation of Social Workers International Policy on Older Persons to the elderly in your community. Where are the gaps and how well does your community conform to the International Policy?

Social Work Practice and Social Justice Website

Please go to the Book Companion Website at http://www.thomsonedu.com/author/sowers to find a rich collection of related articles selected by the authors from Info Trac College Edition.

References

Administration on Aging. (n.d.). *International Aging.* Retrieved June 30, 2004, from http://www.aoa.gov/prof/international/international.asp

Alzheimer's Disease International. (2002). *About Alzheimer's.* Retrieved July 22, 2004, from http://www.alz.co.uk/

American Association for Retired Persons. (n.d.). *Perspectives on ageing.* Retrieved June 30, 2004, from http://www.aarp.org/international/Articles/a2002-10-17-international_ perspectives. html

Apt, N. A. (2002). Ageing and the changing role of the family and the community: An African perspective. *International Social Security Review,* 55(1), 39–47.

Barusch, A. (1995). Programming for family care of elderly dependents: Mandates, incentives and service rationing. *Social Work,* 40, 315–322.

Brookmeyer, R., & Gray, S. (2000). Methods for projecting the incidence and prevalence of chronic diseases in aging populations: Application to Alzheimer's disease. *Statistics in Medicine,* 19(11–12), 1481–1493.

Choi, S. J. (2002). National policies on aging in Korea. In D. R. Phillips & A. Chan (Eds.), *Aging and long term care: National policies in the Asia-Pacific* (pp. 68–106). Singapore: Institute of Southeast Asian Studies.

Dunkle, R. E., & Norgard, T. (1995). Aging Overview. In R. L. Edwards & J. G. Hopps (Eds.), *Encyclopedia of social work* (19th ed.). Washington, DC: NASW Press.

George, J. (1997). Global graying: What role for social work? In M. C. Hokenstad & J. Midgley (Eds.), *Issues in international social work: Global challenges for a new century.* Washington, DC: NASW Press.

Gibson, M. J. (2003, October). *Long-term care in developed nations: A brief overview.* Issue Paper #2003-13, AARP Public Policy Institute. Washington, DC: AARP.

Graham, N. (2001). *Statement of Nori Graham, Chairman of Alzheimer's Disease International for World Health Day.* Retrieved July 22, 2004, from http://www.alz.co.uk/

Higgins, J. (1989). Defining community care: Realities and myths. *Social Policy and Administration, 23*(1), 3–16.

Howe, A., & Phillips, D. R. (2001). *National policies on aging: Why have them?* Paper presented at the World Congress of Gerontology, a meeting of the International Association of Gerontology, Vancouver, British Columbia, Canada.

International Association of Gerontology, et al. (2005). *Ageing and the rights of older persons: Statement for the Human Rights Commission.* Retrieved May 13, 2005, from http://ngo.fawco.org/whi/ageing_older-persons.html

International Federation of Social Workers. (1999). *International policy on older persons.* NY: Author.

International Federation on Ageing. (n.d.). *Part of a world wide revolution.* Retrieved June 30, 2004, from http://www.ifa-fiv.org

MacKenzie, P. A., & Beck, I. (1991). Social work practice with dementia patients in adult day care. In M. Holosko & M. D. Feit (Eds.), *Social work practice with the elderly* (pp. 191–217). Toronto: Canadian Scholars Press.

Ngan, R. (2004). Long-term care for older people and the social welfare system in East Asia: Is the East Asian welfare model a myth? *Social Development Issues: Alternative Approaches to Global Human Needs, 25*(3), 74–86.

Obaid, T. A. (2002). *Statement at the Launch of HelpAge International's State of the World's Older People.* April 8, 2002, Madrid, Spain.

Obaid, T. A., & Malloch-Brown, M. (2002). *Joint statement to the Second World Assembly on Ageing.* April 8–12, 2002, Madrid, Spain.

Office of the United Nations High Commissioner for Human Rights. *Declaration on social progress and development, 1969.* Retrieved May 13, 2005, from http://www.ohchr.org.english/law/progress.htm

Phillips, D. R. (1999). Aging in the Asia-Pacific region: The impact of the aging and development report. *Hong Kong Journal of Gerontology, 13*(2), 44–53.

Pillemer, K., & Moore, D. W. (1989). Abuse of patients in nursing homes: Findings from a survey of staff. *The Gerontologist, 29*, 314–320.

Rice, D. P., Fox, P. J., Max, W., Webber, P. A., Lindeman, D. A., Hauck, W. W., & Segura, E. (1993). The economic burden of Alzheimer's disease care. *Health Affairs, 12*(2), 164–176.

Substance Abuse and Mental Health Services Administration. (2004, July/August). Older adults: Improving mental health services. *Substance Abuse and Mental Health Services Administration News, 12*(4), 1–4.

Teo, P. (1994). The national policy on elderly people in Singapore. *Ageing and Society, 14*, 405–427.

United Nations. (n.d.). *Ageing is society-wide.* Retrieved June 30, 2004, from http://www.un.org/esa/socdev/ageing

United Nations Population Fund. (n.d.). *Population ageing and poverty.* Retrieved July 21, 2004, from http://www.unfpa.org/sustainable/ageing.htm

United Nations Population Fund. (2004). *Investing in people: National progress in implementing the ICPD programme of action 1994–2004.* Retrieved July 20, 2004, from http://www.yapi.org/girlchild/index.htm

World Health Organization. (n.d.). *Abuse of the elderly.* Retrieved July 13, 2004, from http://www.who.org

World Health Organization. (1998a). *Women, ageing and health: Achieving health across the lifespan.* Ageing and Health. Geneva: Author.

World Health Organization. (1998b). *Social determinants of health: The solid facts.* Geneva: Author.

World Health Organization. (1998c). *The world health report 1998.* Geneva: Author.

World Health Organization. (2001). *The world health report 2001.* Retrieved July 14, 2004, from http://who.int/whr2001/2001/main/en/contents.htm

World Health Organization. (2002). *Alzheimer's disease.* Retrieved July 22, 2004, from http://www.afro.who.int/mentalhealth

World Health Organization Centre for Health Development. (n.d.). Retrieved July 14, 2004, from http://www.who.or.jp/ageing/researches/index.html

Zimmerman, S., Sloane, P. D. & Eckert, J. K. (Eds.). (2001). *Assisted living: Needs, practices, and policies in residential care for the elderly.* London: The Johns Hopkins University Press.

Social Challenges and Practice Approaches from a Global Perspective

Around the world and throughout history human beings, both individually and collectively, have had their lives negatively affected by famine, poverty, disease, crime, war, and natural disasters. Although every country has to face one or more of these, each country deals with them differently. This section of the text addresses those social problems that exist in all societies, outlines differential approaches, and provides exemplars for intervening to effect change.

Wars of nations are fought to change maps. But wars on poverty are fought to map change.

Muhammad Ali

7 CHAPTER | Poverty Around the World

SCOPE OF POVERTY AROUND THE WORLD

Chronic poverty, to a large degree, is at the core of virtually all long-term human problems. As such its definition, scope, understanding, and alleviation have been fundamental concerns of the social work profession since its inception. Many refer to poverty as a relative concept. The conditions of the extremely poor on a global level are almost unimaginable to people living in industrialized societies. Yet even in these modern industrial societies many individuals suffer extreme poverty for lack of access to resources or because of catastrophic events. Fundamentally a person is considered poor if his or her resources fall below the minimum level necessary to meet basic needs. This is often referred to as a poverty line. Naturally poverty lines vary both in time and place, and different countries use different levels based on societal norms, values, and levels of development.

For the purpose of global comparison, the World Bank sets the reference lines at 1 dollar and 2 dollars per day in 1993 purchasing power parity. Based on this it was estimated in 1999 that 1.2 billion people worldwide had consumption levels below 1 dollar a day. That is equivalent to 23 percent of the population of the developing world. At the same time 2.8 billion people lived on less than 2 dollars a day. The World Bank always uses poverty lines that are based on the norms for a given society, but the unit of analysis remains one-dimensional and as a result misses much.

Recently, efforts have been made to understand non-income dimensions of poverty. The World Development Report (World Bank, 2000) assembled information on high quality social indicators for education, health, access to services, and infrastructure. It also tracks risk, vulnerability, social exclusion, access to capital, and other indices as appropriate. The new directions in the measurement of poverty include participatory approaches to identifying barriers to social participation. These methods are likely to yield more accurate and textured information and will help us understand poverty in context. Suffice it to say that a homeless individual in New York City with no visible means of support, no access to health care, and no tradable skills can be equally as miserable, despairing, and vulnerable as one in Europe, Asia, or Latin America.

Causes of Poverty

Many unfortunate and pernicious human, social, and economic problems lead to poverty or ensure that individuals and families remain in poverty. Lack of resources, unemployment, health crises, and combinations of poor endowments, unfortunate circumstances, and unwise choices all contribute to conditions of poverty, be they temporary or constant. For some time it has been recognized, however, that widespread and virtually unchangeable poverty is more often the result of events beyond individual control. These may include famine, natural disasters, economic depression, and structural inequality. While many of these causes are temporal in nature and can be overcome with residual support, the effects of structural inequality are more complex (Shah, 2002).

Shah (2002) points out that "the GDP (Gross Domestic Product) of the poorest 48 nations (i.e., a quarter of the world's countries) is less than the wealth of the world's three richest people combined." He also notes that "the combined wealth of the world's 200 richest people hit $1 trillion in 1999; the combined incomes of the 582 million people living in the 43 least developed countries is $146 billion." It is widely believed that "the impact of economic rationalist policies in Western countries is a major reason why about 100 million people exist below the official poverty line, with social safety nets becoming less and less impervious" (Cox, 1996). Many have noted that poverty in developed countries is more similar than dissimilar and that "the overall issue of poor individuals and communities can be generalized [from one country to another]. Poverty is not a result of a lack of strengths, but rather of the unavailability of structural opportunities for all" (Banerjee, 1997).

In its simplest terms, "A life free of poverty means the ability to obtain enough food, receive adequate health care, have access to clean water and sanitation, and to be a functioning member of society" (Cox, 1996) and the eradication of poverty begins with social development.

Poverty in the United States

Even though the United States is indisputably one of the wealthiest countries in the world, many of its citizens continue to live in conditions of desperate poverty. Demographically, poverty is often concentrated in rural settings or distressed inner-city neighborhoods. It affects women more than men; children more than adults; and certain racial and ethnic groups more than others.

Significant government antipoverty programs have been in place since the Great Depression: Social Security, unemployment insurance, housing, Medicaid, and food stamps, to name a few. Unfortunately many of the programs have been degraded in the past two decades, swelling the number of homeless, uninsured, and disadvantaged.

In addition, no shortage of studies and initiatives have been dedicated to identifying, understanding, and recommending policy shifts to deal with poverty in America. Some of these include the following:

- **Joint Center for Poverty Research,** a collaborative effort of Northwestern University and the University of Chicago, examines poverty in the United States from an interdisciplinary and academic research perspective. Information on grants and programs associated with poverty affecting all individuals is provided (for more information see http://www.jcpr.org).
- **The Rural Policy Research Institute** examines how policy in a number of areas (such as health care, social assistance, and community building) impacts those living in rural communities and the rural communities themselves (for more information see http://www.rupri.org).
- **The Rural Poverty Research Center** provides statistical information on and objective analyses of causes and remedies of rural poverty, a comprehensive annotated bibliography of rural poverty research, and various publications relevant to poverty in rural America (for more information see http://www.rprconline.org).

- **The Rural Assistance Center** is dedicated to health and human service information for those living in rural America. It provides information and statistics on rural living, and informational guides pertaining to services as well as methods of impacting health and human service delivery systems in rural America (for more information see http://www.raconline.org).

Social Workers and Poverty

Social workers seemingly would be at the forefront in dealing with all aspects of poverty, but the following quote suggests otherwise: "It is ironic, though, that at such a time many social workers have left the public service and community arena for private and clinical practice, serving the middle classes and the paying public" (West et al., 1998).

Campfens (1992) points out that "many of the theories that have guided us in our work have become dysfunctional in an economic, political, and social order that is constantly changing, challenging the assumptions, premises, infrastructure, and resource base upon which social work has functioned for the last few decades."

Today many social workers believe that effective poverty alleviation programs must focus on the strengths of individuals and communities as opposed to their deficits. Creative new technologies like asset mapping are helping us to identify the building blocks of community economic and social development. Kaeske (1998) asserts that "it is necessary for social workers to build coalitions that could be used to bring about a new thinking and new orientation. This should involve opening dialogue with politicians at national, regional, and global levels . . . social workers should redefine their roles in the context of structural adjustment." He also affirms that the concept of empowerment "should occupy centre stage in the intervention strategies with a view of enabling individuals, groups, and communities to gain greater control over their environment."

Poverty at the Global Level

The key issues that continue to ensure mass poverty include famine, war, natural disasters, and underdevelopment. Many agencies and programs direct their poverty alleviation efforts toward responding to these. New issues have arisen that require more complex solutions. Some of these are forced migration, trafficking, and slavery (Shah, 2002).

Clearly there is much to do in alleviating unavoidable poverty around the world. Another layer of complexity is added when the poverty is the consequence of political actions that result in forced migrations and displacement. Refugees fleeing from ethnic and political persecution, as has happened recently in the Balkans and Somalia, are often plunged into poverty without recourse to their usual social networks. Much of the knowledge and skill base of the social work profession was developed in response to the mass migration during the nineteenth century from Europe to North and South America. Settlement houses, the Salvation Army, the YMCA, and the Charity Organization Society all played major roles.

National immigration policies that allow for certain political refugees often do not recognize economic refugees. The United Nations definition of refugee is outlined in Article 1 of the Convention and Protocol Relating to the Status of Refugees. It defines a refugee as "a person who is outside his/her country of nationality or habitual residence; has a well-founded fear of persecution because of his/her race, religion, nationality, membership in a particular social group or political opinion; and is unable or unwilling to avail himself/herself of the protection of that country, or to return there, for fear of persecution" (United Nations High Commissioner for Refugees, 1951).

HUMAN TRAFFICKING

To many, slavery and human trafficking seem scourges relegated to history. Even the poorest individual still retains ownership over his or her person. In reality the nature and extent of slavery and human trafficking worldwide are cruel and enormous.

According to the United Nations Office on Drugs and Crime (1999), "Trafficking is the recruitment, transportation, transfer, harboring, or receipt of persons by improper means, such as force, abduction, fraud, or coercion, for an improper purpose, like forced or coerced labor, servitude, slavery, or sexual exploitation."

Gallagher (2001) notes that, "Despite greatly increased attention, attempts to deal with trafficking, migrant smuggling, and related exploitation at the national, regional, and global levels have been largely ineffective." She adds, "The stated purpose of the [UN] Trafficking Protocol is two-fold: first, to prevent and combat trafficking in persons, paying particular attention to the protection of women and children; and second, to promote and facilitate cooperation among states parties to this end." However, much like the illegal drug trade, human trafficking is unlikely to diminish until the demand is curbed.

Slave Labor

Anti-Slavery International (2003) describes the nature and extent of the situation:

> Millions of women, children, and men are living in slavery throughout the world. They are enslaved through bonded labor, forced labor, human trafficking, early and forced marriage, the worst forms of child labor, the commercial sexual exploitation of children, and traditional or 'chattel' slavery. Slaves are forced to work through the use or threat of violence. They are owned or controlled by an 'employer' through mental or physical threat, dehumanized, treated as a commodity or bought and sold as property. They are physically constrained or have restrictions placed on their freedom of movement.

> Women from Eastern Europe are bonded into prostitution, children are trafficked between West African countries and men are forced to work as slaves on Brazilian agricultural estates. Contemporary slavery takes various forms and affects people of all ages, sex, and race.

Box 7.1 | Exemplars from Around the World

As Midgley points out, "Social workers in industrial societies have much to learn from the Third World" (Midgley, 1990). The following are some creative initiatives that have had positive outcomes.

Philippines

The following two programs in the Philippines combine to form a multilevel strategy:

- "The [Philippine] government's National Urban Development and Housing Framework (1999–2004) emphasizes urban poverty reduction through a renewed focus on urban upgrading and slum eradication to improve urban land markets and address security of tenure for the urban poor. Poverty reduction and community participation provide a key focus to the formulation, design, and implementation of urban sector projects and programs" (Asian Development Bank, 2004).

- The multifaceted Poverty Alleviation Program in Negros Occidental province is funded by United Nations and the Philippine government, and led by a team of 16 young graduates from various disciplines. Team members link NGOs, local government offices, and local people's organizations into program developments and stimulate an expansion of each agency's work into the poverty alleviation area. They also "educate a wide range of people regarding the various areas related to poverty alleviation." Initiatives include food-for-work schemes, training opportunities, technical advice, material resource provision, and infrastructure development (Cox, 1996).

Tibet

The Tibet Poverty Alleviation Fund (TPAF) helps disadvantaged Tibetan families and communities participate actively in Tibet's rapidly expanding economy by implementing programs to help increase their incomes and living standards. It cooperates directly with local Tibetan individuals, families, and communities, implementing projects in the areas of microfinance, enterprise development, artisan development, rural employable skills, urban employable skills, maternal health, pasture preservation, and social welfare. Financing for projects comes from foundations, governments, and individual donors located in Asia, Europe, and the United States.

The TPAF selects projects in areas where needs are found to be greatest. Projects are designed to benefit rural poor and urban unemployed Tibetan populations, and to demonstrate how Tibet's public services can be strengthened to improve Tibetan livelihoods and welfare (Tibet Poverty Alleviation Fund, n.d.).

Ghana

According to Nkum (1998):

The National Programme for Poverty Reduction (NAPPR) in Ghana provides a framework for poverty alleviation with the assistance of donor agencies like the UNDP [United Nations Development Programme]. The aim is to improve the social and economic status of all individuals and to eliminate extremes of deprivation by encouraging creativity, enterprise and productivity of all citizens.

The objectives of the NAPPR are basically related to improving productivity in agriculture and small-scale enterprises, increasing access to social services, empowering women, and vulnerable groups, minimizing the effects of environmental degradation, strengthening spatial and functional linkages in human settlements, and strengthening the institutional base of communities for self reliance and participation in the development process.

Anti-Slavery International (2004) also notes:

At least ten million children around the world are working as domestic servants, many in hazardous conditions, a new ILO [International Labor Organization] report says. An estimated 90 percent are girls. Although domestic work is widely seen as a safe occupation for girls, in many cases it is extremely hazardous. Because they are hidden from view, children are vulnerable to such serious human rights abuses as being forced to work long hours, handle harmful substances, being denied their right to education, rest, play and contact with friends and family. They are also at risk of physical, mental, and sexual abuse.

| **Box 7.2** | **Research Evidence Driving the Future Agenda**
Challenges for the Future |

Global Coordination of Social Work Efforts

Because poverty and human trafficking cross all borders, it is necessary for social work efforts to do the same. However, three major obstacles impede global coordination. The first obstacle is that of co-ordination, accountability, and longevity. Without consideration of these logistical details, this truly massive endeavor would be doomed to failure. The second obstacle is that of prioritization. While almost all social workers would agree that poverty and human trafficking are major problems, it is likely that there would be a myriad of opinions regarding the prioritization of the various facets of the issues. Lastly, as a direct result of prioritization disputes, the acquisition and allocation of funds and resources would certainly become a major struggle.

Overcoming the aforementioned challenges would lead to a number of positive outcomes, including: 1) increased success at appealing to industrialized nations for support, 2) increased ability for countries to share best practices, 3) consensus regarding definitions of poverty and human trafficking, and 4) improved ability to track, apprehend, and prosecute human traffickers and slave traders/owners.

Much like trafficking, an effective response to modern slavery will require a multilateral strategy that coordinates international police and courts with properly funded NGOs.

INTERNATIONAL ORGANIZATIONS FOCUSED ON POVERTY

The World Bank Group

The World Bank Group's mission is to fight poverty and improve the living standards of people in the developing world. It is a development bank that provides loans, policy advice, technical assistance, and knowledge sharing services to low and middle income countries to reduce poverty. The WBG promotes growth to create jobs and to empower poor people to take advantage of these opportunities.

It is important to note that the World Bank Group has continually evolved throughout its history. "The Bank's mission evolved from a facilitator of post-war [World War II] reconstruction and development to its present day mandate of worldwide poverty alleviation. Whereas heavy infrastructure investment projects once dominated the Bank's portfolio, a broadened focus now includes social sector lending projects, poverty alleviation, and the Comprehensive Development Framework" (World Bank, 2004). Ruger (2005) comments on the World Bank's changing role in global health by stating, "Although it was established to finance European reconstruction after World War II, the bank today is a considerable force in the health, nutrition, and population (HNP) sector in developing countries. Indeed, it has evolved from having virtually no presence in global health to being the world's largest financial contributor to health-related projects, now committing more than $1 billion annually for new HNP projects."

In 1996, the World Bank and the International Monetary Fund (IMF) established the Heavily Indebted Poor Countries initiative, the first comprehensive approach to reduce the external debt of the world's poorest, most heavily indebted countries. This represented an important step forward in placing debt relief within an overall framework of poverty reduction.

In December 1999, the boards of the World Bank and the IMF approved a new approach to the challenge of reducing poverty in low income countries based on country-owned poverty reduction strategies. This new approach is embodied within a Poverty Reduction Strategy Paper, which is expected to serve as a framework for development assistance beyond the operations of the Fund and Bank (for more information see http://www.worldbank.org).

The International Monetary Fund (IMF)

The International Monetary Fund is a specialized agency of the United Nations system set up by treaty in 1945 to help promote the health of the world economy. Headquartered in Washington, D.C., it is governed by its almost global membership of 184 countries.

The IMF is the central institution of the international monetary system—the system of international payments and exchange rates among national currencies that enables business to take place between countries. It aims to prevent crises in the system by encouraging countries to adopt sound economic policies. It is also—as its name suggests—a fund that can be tapped by members needing temporary financing to address balance of payments problems (for more information see http://www.imf.org).

United Nations Development Programme (UNDP)

The core of UNDP's mission is eliminating poverty and meeting the Millennium Summit goal of halving extreme poverty by 2015. The UNDP assists countries in creating pro-poor policies and budgets, and improving their capacity to deliver basic services. The Sustainable Livelihoods (SL) unit of the UNDP aims to promote a holistic vision of development that includes income generation, natural resource management, and the empowered use of appropriate technology, financial services, and good governance (for more information see http://www.undp.org).

Global Partnerships

Global Partnerships helps those in poverty with the will and entrepreneurial spirit to improve their lives by supporting themselves. It creates economic opportunity for people living in poverty, helping them access the resources they need—capital, healthcare, education, and infrastructure—to generate sustainable income and positive momentum in their lives. One of Global Partnerships' programs involves the issuance of "microcredit"—small loans to people living in poverty to start or expand very small businesses (for more information see http://www.globalpartnerships.org).

Heartfelt Foundation

The Heartfelt Foundation, founded in 1979, is a volunteer-driven 501(c)(3) nonprofit organization dedicated to serving and assisting people in any form of need. The Heartfelt Foundation's work and service has extended to those in need around the world. Hospitals, orphanages, schools, families, and children have been visited, touched and assisted by Heartfelt in hundreds of global communities. Their services range from feeding those who are hungry, assisting at-risk and in-need families, supporting disadvantaged or abused children, and helping those with no homes, to providing comfort to the sick and terminal (for more information see http://www.heartfelt.org).

NetAid

NetAid is nonprofit organization that mobilizes people in developed countries to make ending extreme poverty a global priority. NetAid's programming to educate young people and inspire them to activism directly supports the global community's goal of significantly decreasing extreme poverty and related ills by 2015. NetAid was founded by Cisco Systems and the United Nations Development Programme in 1999, and continues to work in partnership with the UN and the private sector (for more information, see http://www.netaid.org).

SUMMARY

Poverty is a global issue that affects every country of the world. Various definitions of poverty exist, including specific criteria used to monetarily determine levels of individual poverty. The concept of poverty can also be considered from non-income perspectives, such as access to services, level of health, and level of education. Poverty can be caused by human, social, economic, and environmental factors. Even the most wealthy and industrialized countries in the world have major issues concerning poverty.

The social work profession plays an incredibly important role in the realm of poverty alleviation. Social workers recognize and assess current developments and trends; they raise the public, private, and governmental awareness of the issues; and they find ways to alleviate and solve major challenges being faced. It is incumbent upon social workers to unify their efforts and expand upon their traditional roles.

Despite the often grueling and discouraging nature of working to alleviate poverty, we suggest that current and future social workers have a positive attitude and perspective when dealing with the impoverished. It is imperative that social workers view themselves as change agents, charged with the task of empowering their clients to attain critical resources, increase levels of functioning, and sustain improvements.

Thinking About Practice: From Local to Global Perspectives

1. What are the challenges we face in determining a globally accepted poverty line?
2. What can social workers do to help alleviate poverty?
3. What are three non-income dimensions of poverty? Discuss why it is necessary to consider these dimensions.
4. Discuss one way in which the issue of poverty is being alleviated around the world.
5. What is the scope of human trafficking and slave labor in today's world? What action do you think needs to happen in order for these practices to be eliminated?

Social Work Practice and Social Justice Website

Please go to the Book Companion Website at http://www.thomsonedu.com/author/sowers to find a rich collection of related articles selected by the authors from Info Trac College Edition.

References

Anti-Slavery International. (2003). *Annual report 2003*. Retrieved August 4, 2004, from http://www.antislavery.org/homepage/resources/full%20annual%20report.pdf

Anti-Slavery International. (2004, June). *New report sheds light on hidden world of child domestic work*. Retrieved August 3, 2004, from http://www.antislavery.org/archive/press/press release2004childdomILO2004.htm

Asian Development Bank. (2004). *Philippines: Country strategy and program update 2004–2006*. Retrieved August 2, 2004, from http://www.adb.org/Documents/CSPs/PHI/2003/default.asp

Banerjee, M. M. (1997). Strengths in a slum: A paradox? *Journal of Applied Social Sciences, 22*(1), Fall/Winter, 45–58.

Campfens, H. (1992). The new reality of poverty and social work interventions. *International Social Work, 35*(2), 99–104.

Cox, D. (1996). Focusing on poverty: Enhancing social work's developmental relevance through poverty alleviation programs. *Journal of Applied Social Sciences, 21*(1), 27–36.

Gallagher, A. (2001). Human rights and the new UN protocols on trafficking and migrant smuggling: A preliminary analysis. *Human Rights Quarterly, 23*, 974–1004.

Kaeske, E. (1998). Structural adjustment programmes and the problem of urban poverty: An African perspective. *International Social Work, 41*(3), 311–320.

Midgley, J. (1990). International social work: Learning from the third world. *Social Work, 35*(4), 295–301.

Nkum, J. (1998). *Comparative analysis of poverty alleviation*. Retrieved August 3, 2004, from action plans in Ghana and Zimbabwe, http://www.eldis.org/static/DOC6212.htm

Ruger, J. P. (2005). Public health then and now: The changing role of the World Bank in global health. *American Journal of Public Health, 95*(1), 60–70.

Shah, A. (2002). *Causes of poverty*. Retrieved August 5, 2004, from http://www.globalissues.org/TradeRelated/Poverty.asp

Tibet Poverty Alleviation Fund. (n.d.). Retrieved August 4, 2004, from http://www.tpaf.org

West, S., Gaffney, N., Allen, T., & Barboza, D. (1998). Social work's New Deal. *Newsweek* (May), 38–40.

World Bank, The (2004). *World Bank Group historical chronology: Introduction*. Retrieved March 20, 2005, from: http://web.worldbank.org/WBSITE/EXTERNAL/EXTABOUTUS/EXTARCHIVES/0,contentMDK:20035653~menuPK:56305~pagePK:36726~piPK:36092~theSitePK:29506,00.html

World Bank, The. (2000). *World development report*. Retrieved August 3, 2004, from http://www.worldbank.org/wdr/2000/fullreport.html

United Nations High Commissioner for Refugees (1951). *Convention and protocol: Relating to the status of refugees*. Retrieved August 6, 2004, from http://www.unhcr.ch

United Nations Office on Drugs and Crime (1999). *Trafficking in human beings*. Retrieved August 5, 2004, from http://www.unodc.org/unodc /en/trafficking_human_beings.html

Civilization is a method of living, an attitude of equal respect for all men.
Jane Addams

8 CHAPTER | # Mental Health

Over the last several years, mental health has emerged as a major global issue of public health interest. Mental, physical, and social health are closely interwoven and interdependent. Recent research and better understanding of the relationships between mental, physical, and social health indicate that each is crucial to the overall well-being of individuals, societies, and countries. Unfortunately, in most parts of the world, mental health and mental disorders are not regarded with the same importance as physical health. In fact, mental health and mental disorders have been ignored or neglected in many parts of the world.

The mental health movement was first spearheaded by Dorothea Lynde Dix in 1841 in Hampden, Maine. Her reporting of the neglect, suffering, and abuse of the insane sparked the first movement to improve conditions in prisons and poorhouses. She encouraged state legislatures to support better institutions and persuaded the U.S. Congress to appropriate public land for hospitals for the deaf and the insane. Dix lobbied nationally and internationally on behalf of the mentally ill and was personally responsible for the establishment of 32 public and private institutions (Quam, 1995). The mental health movement for humane and effective treatment of the mentally ill grew out of the pioneering work of Dix.

Four hundred and fifty million people worldwide are affected by mental, neurological, or behavioral problems at any given time. Major depression ranks fourth among the ten leading causes of disease globally. Women worldwide experience higher levels of depression than men (Wetzel, 1994), and some evidence suggests that the unequal and discriminatory treatment of women is a major factor in the increased risk of women for mental illness (Wetzel, 2000). Within the next 20 years, depression is projected to become the world's second-leading cause of disease. Globally, 50 million people have epilepsy and another 24 million have schizophrenia. A million people commit suicide every year and between 10 and 20 million people attempt it. One in every four persons will be affected by a mental disorder at some time in their life. These problems are expected to increase considerably in the future (World Health Organization, 2001).

Mental problems are common to all countries. They cause immense human suffering, social exclusion, disability, and poor quality of life. They also increase mortality and cause large economic and social costs. One in every four persons going to health services has at least one mental, neurological, or behavioral disorder. Most often, these are neither diagnosed nor treated. Mental problems affect and are affected by chronic conditions such as cancer, heart disease, diabetes, and HIV/AIDS. If these problems remain untreated they can lead to poor health behavior, noncompliance with prescribed medical regimens, diminished immune function, and negative disease outcomes. Cost-effective treatments for most disorders do exist. If they are used correctly they allow affected persons to become functioning members of the community.

Yet, in most countries, major barriers exist to both the care and the reintegration of people with mental disorders. Barriers include the lack of recognition, awareness, and interventive action. Most policy makers and insurance companies, health and labor policies, and the public at large discriminate between physical and mental problems. This discrimination leads to stigma against people who need help. Most middle and low income countries devote less than 1 percent of their health expenditures to mental health, which means that mental health policies, legislation, community care facilities, and treatments for the mentally ill are inadequate to meet the need. And severely limited resources are allocated to those treatment facilities that do exist (World Health Organization, n.d.). Globally, many persons with mental health or behavioral problems are victimized for their illness and become the targets of stigma and discrimination.

Mental and behavioral disorders are estimated to account for 12 percent of the global burden of disease, yet the mental health budgets of the majority of countries constitute less than 1 percent of their total health expenditures. More than 40 percent of countries have no mental health policy that includes children and adolescents. In those countries that do have health plans, mental and behavioral disorders are often not covered at the same level as other illnesses. This creates significant economic difficulties for patients and their families (World Health Organization, 2001).

Unfortunately, even in countries with well-established mental health services, fewer than half of those individuals needing care make use of available services. This is related both to the stigma attached to individuals with mental health and behavioral disorders, and to the inadequacy of the services provided (World Health Organization, 2001). This stigma issue was highlighted in the U.S. Surgeon General's *Mental Health* report of 1999. The report noted, "Despite the efficacy of treatment options and the many possible ways of obtaining a treatment of choice, nearly half of all Americans who have a severe mental illness do not seek treatment. Most often, reluctance to seek care is an unfortunate outcome of very real barriers. Foremost among these is the stigma that many in our society attach to mental illness and to people who have a mental illness" (U.S. Department of Health and Human Services, 1999).

CONTRASTING PERCEPTIONS OF MENTAL ILLNESS

Prevailing social values related to the social perception of mental illness have had a profound impact of the care of people with mental and behavioral disorders. Throughout history, people with mental and behavioral disorders have been treated in different ways. They have been given a high status in societies that believe them to be capable of communicating and convening with gods and the dead. In medieval Europe and elsewhere they were beaten and burnt at the stake. The mentally ill have been locked up in large institutions and they have been exploited for scientific research. And, in some societies, they have been cared for and integrated into the communities to which they belong.

In the nineteenth century in Europe, mental illness was viewed in divergent ways. On the one hand, mental illness was seen as a legitimate topic for scientific inquiry. As a result of this view psychiatry grew as a medical discipline, and people with mental disorders were considered medical patients. The other view considered people with mental disorders, like those with many other diseases and undesirable social behavior, as unacceptable and untreatable. They were often isolated from society in large custodial institutions or mental hospitals, formerly known as lunatic asylums. These trends were later exported to Africa, the Americas, and Asia.

During the second half of the twentieth century, a shift in the mental health care paradigm took place, largely owing to three independent factors:

1. Psychopharmacology made significant progress, with the discovery of new classes of drugs, particularly neuroleptics and antidepressants, as well as the development of new forms of psychosocial interventions.
2. The human rights movement became a truly international phenomenon under the sponsorship of the newly created United Nations, and democracy advanced on a global basis, although at a different pace in different places (Merkl, 1993).
3. Social and mental components were firmly incorporated in the definition of health of the newly established World Health Organization in 1948. (World Health Organization, n.d.)

CORE COMPONENTS OF PRACTICE

According to the World Health Organization (n.d.), good mental health care flows from basic guiding principles. These include

- diagnosis
- early intervention
- rational use of treatment techniques
- continuity of care
- availability of a wide range of services
- consumer involvement
- partnership with families
- involvement of the local community
- integration of mental health treatment into primary health

A correct objective diagnosis is critical for the planning of individual care, since the diagnosis influences the choice of an appropriate treatment. Today, mental and behavioral disorders can be diagnosed with a high level of reliability. Because different treatments are indicated for different diseases, diagnosis is an important starting point of any intervention. A diagnosis can be made in nosological (according to a global classification and nomenclature of diseases and disorders) terms of the type and level of disability experienced by an individual. It is most preferable to provide a diagnosis in terms of both type and level Williams, 1981). Early intervention is fundamental in preventing progress towards a full-blown disease, and is critical in controlling symptoms and improving outcomes. The earlier an assessment and diagnosis is combined with a proper course of treatment, the better the potential treatment outcomes for the individual. Appropriate treatment of mental disorders should incorporate use of pharmacological, psychological, and psychosocial interventions in a clinically meaningful, balanced, and well-integrated way.

Institutionalization

Before the second half of the twentieth century people with mental disorders, like those with many other diseases and undesirable social behaviors, were isolated from society in large custodial institutions such as the so-called insane asylums. Over time, the care provided by these large institutions became repressive and regressive. The institutional use of asylums failed. This was evidenced by repeated cases of ill-treatment to patients, as well as the geographical and professional isolation of the institutions and their staffs. These institutions typically suffered from haphazard reporting and accounting procedures, bad management, poorly trained and ineffective administration, under-utilization of financial resources, lack of staff training, and inadequate inspection and quality assurance procedures. The living conditions in psychiatric hospitals throughout the world were—and in many cases still are—quite dismal. These poor conditions frequently lead to human rights violations and poor treatment outcomes. Conditions in hospitals in developed countries are sometimes better than living standards in many developing countries.

The history of harmful psychiatric institutions and adverse effects of institutionalization on patients (including the development of disabilities as a consequence of social isolation and institutional care) led to a de-institutionalization movement around the world. The de-institutionalization movement attempted to build and implement a comprehensive and cohesive network of community alternatives. According to the World Health Organization, closing mental hospitals without providing community alternatives is as dangerous as creating community alternatives without closing mental hospitals. Both have to occur at the same time, in a well-coordinated and incremental way (World Health Organization, 2001).

In most developing countries, there is no psychiatric care for the majority of the population. The scant services that are available tend to be in centralized mental hospitals, which may not be easily accessible. As a result, people often seek help there only as a last resort. The hospitals tend to be quite large and built more for ease of function for the staff than for patient treatment. In such institutions, patients are afforded very little access to society at large. For the most part, the hospitals operate under legislation that is more penal in nature than therapeutic. In addition, most developing countries do not have adequate training programs at the national level to train psychiatrists, psychiatric nurses, clinical psychologists, psychiatric social workers, and occupational therapists. Because of the lack of trained specialists, the community often turns to the available traditional healers, who do not have specialized training in dealing with mental illness (Saeed, Rehman, & Mubbashar, 2000). Human rights commissioners found deplorable conditions when they visited several psychiatric hospitals in Central America and India during the late 1990s (Levav & Gonzalez, 2000; National Human Rights Commission, 1999).

Similar conditions exist in many other psychiatric hospitals in other regions, in both industrialized and developing countries. Conditions of particular concern have included leaking roofs, overflowing toilets, eroded floors, and broken doors and windows. "Most of the patients visited were kept in pajamas or naked. Some were penned into small areas of residential wards where they were left to sit, pace, or lie on the concrete floor all day. Children were left lying on mats on the floor, some covered with urine and feces. Physical restraint was commonly misused and many patients were observed tied to beds" (World Health Organization, 2001).

Community-Based Care

The concept of community-based mental health care is a global approach rather than an organizational solution. Community-based care rejects the use of large custodial institutions and promotes a more open and flexible system of care within the community. Community-based care holds as a primary principle that the large majority of patients requiring mental health care should have the possibility of being treated at the community level. Community care focuses on the empowerment of people with mental and behavioral disorders and the involvement of affected persons and their families in the treatment process. It has as a mandate the development and provision of a wide range of services with local community settings. According to global standards of community care practice, care in the community means (World Health Organization, 2001):

- services which are close to home, including general hospital care for acute patients admissions, and long-term residential facilities in the community;
- interventions related to disabilities as well as symptoms;
- treatment and care specific to the diagnosis and needs of each individual;
- a wide range of services which address the needs of people with mental and behavioral disorders;
- services which are coordinated between mental health professionals and community agencies;
- ambulatory rather than static services, including those which can offer home treatment;
- partnership with carers and meeting their needs; and
- legislation to support the above aspects of care.

Community-based care attempts to be local and accessible and strives to address the multiple needs of individuals. It focuses on the empowerment of all persons affected by mental illness, incorporating the informal social environment as well as formal support mechanisms, and promotes the use of efficient and effective treatment techniques that enable people with mental disorders to enhance their self-help skills. Community-based care identifies available community resources and creates healthy community and service provider alliances that would otherwise remain hidden and underutilized. Use of those previously hidden resources can promote a network of social services and health care to patients and families who need support for optimal functioning.

It allows for effective management of the social and family burdens within the community context, which were traditionally alleviated by institutional care (World Health Organization, 2001). Community-based care for the mentally ill and their families is gaining recognition in the United States, Australia, Canada, China, and in some European countries. Countries in Latin America, Africa, the Mediterranean, Southeast Asia, and the Western Pacific have also introduced innovative community-based services for the mentally ill (World Health Organization, 1997).

Unfortunately, many regions and countries have not yet begun to develop community care systems. Rural areas often have inadequate mental health services. The delivery of mental health services to rural populations that are isolated, lack transportation and communication facilities, and have limited educational and economic opportunities pose unique problems and challenges. As a result, mental health services with clinical resources and specialized expertise are typically located in large metropolitan areas, leaving few alternatives for rural inhabitants in need of mental health care. A recent study of suicide in the elderly in some urban and rural areas of Hunan Province, China, showed a much higher suicide rate in rural areas (88.3 per 100,000) than in urban areas (24.4 per 100,000) (Xu et al., 2000). Rates of depression among rural women have also been reported to be more than twice those of general population estimates for women (Hauenstein & Boyd, 1994).

Community-based care still faces many operational challenges. Among the reasons for the lack of better results associated with community-based care are that some governments have not allocated the resources saved by closing hospitals to community care. Many mental health professionals have not been adequately prepared or trained to transition from practice in an institutional setting. And, because there remains a strong stigma attached to mental disorders, many communities reject the community-based model of care. In some countries, including the United States, many people with severe mental disorders are shifted to prisons or become homeless (World Health Organization, 2001). Where organized mental health services have been initiated in developing countries in recent times, such services are usually part of primary health care. Although this approach may be necessary in developing countries that lack trained professionals and the resources necessary to provide specialized services, it at least affords the ability to organize mental health services in a manner that avoids isolation, stigma, and discrimination. Even in countries, however, where pilot programs have shown the value of integrating mental health care into primary health care (for example, in Brazil, China, Colombia, India, Iran, Pakistan, Philippines, Senegal, South Africa, and Sudan), the approach has not been expanded to cover the whole country (World Health Organization, 2001).

Integrating Mental Health Service into Primary Health Care

Because mental disorders are so common, many patients are seen in primary care. However, because of the lack of specialized training in mental illness of the primary care providers, patient disorders are often not detected (Ustun et al, 1999). Mental health problems often are associated with physical disease, and emotional distress is often seen (but not always diagnosed) by primary health care professionals. With proper training, however, the integration of mental health care into basic primary health care can act as an initial screening and provide early identification and intervention. Training primary care and general health care staff in the detection and treatment of common mental and behavioral disorders is an important public health strategy. With appropriate information and training of primary health care doctors, patients discharged from psychiatric wards can be effectively followed up in a primary health care setting. Primary health care can and should play a major role in countries where community-based mental health services do not exist. In many developing countries, well-trained primary health care workers have been able to provide treatment effectively and efficiently for the mentally ill. In fact, experiences in some African, Asian, and Latin American countries show that adequate training of primary health care workers in the early recognition and management of mental disorders can reduce institutionalization and improve clients' mental health outcomes.

Suicide Prevention   Compelling evidence indicates that adequate prevention and treatment of some mental and behavioral disorders can reduce suicide rates, whether such interventions are directed towards individuals, families, schools, or other sections of the general community (McCarter, Sowers, & Dulmus, 2004). The early recognition and treatment of depression, alcohol dependence, and schizophrenia are important strategies in the primary prevention of suicide.

There are different levels of threat to consider when looking at the risk factors for suicide. James and Wherry (1991) describe these levels as a "hierarchy of behavior," a progression of suicidal thought and action that includes "suicidal threat (a statement made), suicidal gesture (attention getting action), suicidal threat (serious threat statement), suicidal attempt (dangerous attempt), and suicide (actual death)" (p. 23). On a community and society level, several risk factors may play a role in the number of suicides that are attempted or completed (McCarter, Sowers, & Dulmus, 2004). Kachur et al. (1992) and Kellermann et al. (1992) offer three indicators of higher suicide rates in a community:

1. people who live in communities with limited opportunities economically;
2. high levels of unemployment; and
3. instability in residency.

Individual and family indicators of suicide potential range from family dysfunction (DenHouter, 1981; Faber, 1978) to individual substance abuse (Evans et al., 2001; Lewinsohn, Rohde, & Seeley, 1993). One of the most discussed factors of suicide risk is depression or other types of psychopathology. Lewinsohn Rohde, and Seeley (1993), Harris and Lenings (1993), Crespi

(1990), and Wetzler et al. (1996) all consider depression a key risk factor for suicide. Other factors include previous attempts or ideation (Crespi, 1990; DenHouter, 1981) and gender (Lewinsohn, Rohde, & Seeley, 1993). Research has shown that females are more likely to attempt suicide, whereas males have higher completion rates.

Despite the seriousness of suicide, no comprehensive empirically validated treatment exists (Rathus & Miller, 2002). Prevention, however, has become a central goal (Cowen, 1985; Felner et al., 1983; Silverman & Felner, 1995) and a focus of practice in social work (Lurie & Monahan, 2001).

Educational programs to train practitioners and primary care personnel in the diagnosis and treatment of depressed patients are particularly important. In one study (Rutz, Knorring, & Walinder, 1995) on the island of Gotland, Sweden, the suicide rate, particularly of women, dropped significantly in the year after an educational program for general practitioners was introduced, but increased once the program was discontinued. In addition to implementing interventions that involve restricting access to common methods of suicide, school-based interventions involving crisis management, enhancement of self-esteem and the development of coping skills, and health decision making have been shown to lower the risk of suicide among young people (Mishara & Ystgaard, 2000). The media can also assist in prevention efforts by limiting graphic and unnecessary depictions of suicide and by deglamorizing news reports of suicides. In a number of countries, a decrease in suicide rates coincided with the media's consent to minimize the reporting of suicides.

Designing Appropriate Treatments

A correct objective diagnosis is fundamental for the planning of individual care, and for the choice of an appropriate treatment. Mental and behavioral disorders can be diagnosed with a high level of reliability (Williams, 1995). Because different treatments are indicated for different diseases, diagnosis is an important starting point of any intervention. Early intervention is fundamental in preventing progress towards a full-blown disease, controlling symptoms, and improving outcomes. Early intervention with a proper and effective course of treatment positively impacts the outcome of treatment. For example, in schizophrenia, the length of time the psychosis goes untreated, and conversely the earlier the intervention, is proving to be important. Delays in treatment are likely to result in poorer outcomes (McGorry, 2000; Thara et al., 1994).

The appropriate treatment of mental disorders often necessitates the use of pharmacological, psychological, and psychosocial interventions in a clinically meaningful, well-balanced, and integrated way. The effective management of mental and behavioral disorders requires a balanced combination of three fundamental ingredients: medication (or pharmacotherapy), psychotherapy, and psychosocial rehabilitation. These ingredients need to be skillfully assessed and utilized because the amounts needed vary as a function of the main diagnosis and any physical and mental comorbidity, the age of the patient, and the current stage of the disease. Treatment must be tailored to individual needs but these needs change as the disease evolves and as the patient's living conditions change. According to the World Health Organization (2001), a balanced combination of interventions implies adherence to the following guiding principles:

- each intervention has a specific indication according to the diagnosis, that is, should be used in specific clinical conditions;
- each intervention should be used in a given amount, that is, the level of the intervention should be proportional to the severity of the condition;
- each intervention should have a determined duration, that is, it should last for the time required by the nature and severity of the condition, and should be discontinued as soon as possible; and
- each intervention should be periodically monitored for adherence and expected results, as well as for adverse effects, and the recipient of the intervention should always be an active partner in this monitoring.

Mental disorders may at times be chronic conditions that require treatment throughout adulthood. As a result, the effective management of mental and behavioral disorders must include paying careful attention to treatment adherence, because compliance with long-term treatment is harder to achieve than compliance with short-term treatment. The fact that the existence of a mental or behavioral disorder is closely associated with poor treatment compliance on the part of the patient further complicates treatment. Considerable research has been done on factors that improve compliance with treatment. According to the World Health Organization (2001), these include:

- a trusting worker/patient relationship;
- time and energy spent on educating the patient regarding the goals of therapy and the consequences of good or poor adherence;
- a negotiated treatment plan;
- recruitment of family and friends to support the therapeutic plan and its implementation;
- simplification of the treatment regimen; and
- reduction of the adverse consequences of the treatment regimen.

Over the years, clinicians have reached consensus about the effectiveness of some interventions for the management of mental disorders. Interventions for the management of mental and behavioral disorder can be classified in three major categories: pharmacotherapy, psychotherapy, and psychosocial interventions.

Pharmacotherapy   The discovery and improvement of medicines useful for the management of mental disorders occurred in the second half of the twentieth century. These discoveries have been widely acknowledged as a revolution in the history of psychiatry and are critical to the treatment of severe mental illness (Lukens, 2003).

Four basic classes of psychotropic drugs target specific symptoms of mental disorders: antipsychotics for psychotic symptoms; antidepressants for depression; anti-epileptics for epilepsy; and anxiolytics or tranquilizers for anxiety. These drugs affect the symptoms of diseases, not the diseases themselves or their causes. The drugs are not meant to cure the diseases, but rather to reduce or control patients' symptoms or to prevent relapse. The World Health Organization's "essential drugs list" provides a listing of drugs necessary, at a minimum level, for the satisfactory management of mental and neurological disorders of public health importance (for further information see http://www.who.int/medicines). Unfortunately, persons with mental disabilities in poor or developing countries often do not have the opportunity or financial means to benefit from many of the advances in psychopharmacology.

Psychotherapy Psychotherapy refers to planned and structured interventions aimed at influencing behavior, mood, and emotional patterns of reaction to different stimuli through verbal and nonverbal psychological means. Derived from various theoretical perspectives and tested for their effectiveness, several techniques and approaches are particularly useful in the treatment of mental and behavioral disorders. Among these are behavior therapy, cognitive therapy, interpersonal therapy, relaxation techniques, and supportive therapy techniques (World Health Organization, 2001). Cognitive behavioral treatments and interpersonal therapy have been found to be effective in the treatment of phobias, drug and alcohol dependence, and psychotic symptoms such as delusions and hallucinations. They have also been shown to be effective in helping depressed patients learn how to improve coping strategies and lessen symptom distress. Encouraging evidence has recently emerged in relation to the cost-effectiveness of psychotherapeutic approaches to the management of psychosis and a range of mood- and stress-related disorders with medication (World Health Organization, 2001).

- Behavior therapy consists of the application of scientifically based psychological principles to the solution of clinical problems (Cottraux, 1993). It is based on the principles of learning theory.
- Cognitive behavioral interventions are aimed at changing thought patterns and behavior through the practice of new ways of thinking and acting, whereas interpersonal therapy stems from a different conceptual model that centers around four common problem areas: role disputes, role transitions, unresolved grief, and social deficits. Cognitive behavioral interventions are present focused and time limited and emphasize education and collaboration between the clinician and the person with an illness. They provide specific and structured approaches to identifying problem areas, identifying response patterns, and challenging and restructuring assumptions and response (Lukens, 2003).
- Relaxation aims at a reduction of the arousal state of anxiety to acceptable levels through a variety of techniques of muscular relaxation, derived from such methods as yoga, transcendental meditation, and autogenic training and biofeedback. It can be an important adjunct to other forms of treatment, is easily accepted by patients, and can be self-learned (World Health Organization, 2001).
- Supportive therapy is based on the clinician/patient relationship. Other important components of this technique include reassurance, clarification, abreaction, advice, suggestion, and teaching. Some consider this modality of treatment as the very foundation of good clinical practice and suggest its inclusion

as an intrinsic component of training programs for all those involved with clinical duties (Saleebey, 1996).

Psychosocial Interventions   Psychosocial rehabilitation provides an opportunity for individuals who are impaired, disabled, or handicapped by a mental disorder to acquire strategies and skills for independent functioning in the community. It is a comprehensive process that focuses on both improving individual competencies and introducing environmental changes (World Health Organization, 2001).

The strategies of psychosocial rehabilitation vary according to the clients' needs, the setting where the rehabilitation is provided (hospital or community), and the cultural and socioeconomic conditions of the country in which it is undertaken. Housing, vocational rehabilitation, employment, and social support networks are all aspects of psychosocial rehabilitation (Lukens, 2003). Psychosocial interventions focus on empowering the client, reducing discrimination and stigma within the community, improving individual social competence, and creating a long-term system of social support for the client. It is a major component of a comprehensive community-based mental health care plan. For example, in Shanghai, China, psychosocial rehabilitation models have been developed and effectively implemented that use primary care, family support, backup psychiatric support, community supervisors, and factory rehabilitation intervention (World Health Organization, 2001).

Psychosocial rehabilitation teaches individuals how to cope with their disabilities and promotes the acquisition of many of the practical skills needed to live and socialize in the community. By developing the social skills, interests, and leisure activities necessary to engage in normal daily living activities, individuals gain a sense of participation and personal worth. It particularly focuses on the teaching of skills for daily living including diet, personal hygiene, cooking, shopping, budgeting, housekeeping, and using various means of transport.

Aftercare   Some mental and behavioral disorders are chronic in nature although there may be some periods of remission and relapses. Because the needs of clients and their families are complex and changing, continuity of care is important. Critical measures to ensure continuity of care include:

- special clinics for groups of patients with the same diagnosis or problems;
- imparting caring skills to carers;
- the same treatment team providing care to clients and their families;
- group education of clients and their families;
- decentralization of services; and
- integration of care into primary health care (World Health Organization, 2001).

Rights of the Mentally Ill   In 1991, the United Nations General Assembly adopted principles for the protection of persons with mental illness. These principles stress the importance of improving mental health care, and

Box 8.1   Exemplars from Around the World

Geel, Belgium: The Legend of St. Dimpna as a Model of Treatment

One of the best examples of how communities can become caregivers for the mentally ill can be found in the Belgian town of Geel, the site of what is believed to be the oldest community mental health program in the western world. Since the thirteenth century, and perhaps as early as the eighth century, severely mentally ill people have been welcomed by the Church of St. Dymphna or by foster families in the town, with whom they have lived, often for several decades.

The system of care in Geel for the mentally ill and retarded is based on a religious tradition stemming from the legend of St. Dimpna. According to legend, supplemented by bits of historical fact, an Irish king made incestuous demands of Dimpna, his daughter, after the death of his wife. Dimpna escaped from her father and left the country. She was accompanied by her confessor and tutor, Gerebemus. They boarded a boat, crossed the North Sea, and landed in Belgium. The two traveled overland and hid in the region of Geel. According to legend, the king pursued and beheaded them both in approximately 600 A.D. At the moment of Dimpna's beheading it is said the king's sanity was restored. As a result, it was believed that Dimpna had miraculous powers to drive the devil or evil spirits out of persons possessed by such forces, the supposed cause of insanity at that time.

A shrine was erected in honor of Dimpna. Pilgrims, usually accompanied by relatives, traveled long distances to visit the shrine in hope of a cure. They performed rituals of penance by crawling barefoot under the tomb containing the bones of St. Dimpna. (Today, the stone floor around the tomb is worn by the feet and knees of those who wished to be cured by Dimpna of their disabilities.) The pilgrims were cared for in sickrooms adjacent to the church. When these became overcrowded, the homes of parishioners surrounding the church were used. By the middle of the fifteenth century, a sizable and steady flow of pilgrims traveled to Geel. Records of the church indicate that many of the pilgrims were cured by the "miracle of Dimpna." But many were not cured. In such cases, the natural family returned home and paid a family of Geel to house their "possessed" family member.

Initially, the motivation to house a pilgrim was primarily religious. Over time, patients were sent to Geel by welfare officials in nearby European cities as an inexpensive and convenient way to dispose of the "deviants" in their region. The expenses of wealthy patients, who came from places as distant as Russia, Brazil, and the United States, were provided by their natural families.

Currently 1,000 families within this town of 30,000 citizens care for one or a maximum of two

---

emphasize the need to develop services based on the community care model. Rights of individuals with mental disorders were particularly highlighted (United Nations, 1991). Because of the adoption of these principles, patient neglect through discrimination, carelessness, and lack of access to services, as well as through intrusive, restrictive, and regressive interventions, are recognized as a violation of human rights.

INTERNATIONAL ORGANIZATIONS ON MENTAL HEALTH

International Association for Women's Mental Health

Established in 2001 to improve the mental health of women throughout the world, the International Association for Women's Mental Health is a patients, or boarders as they are called, in their homes. Families care for a total of 1,100 individuals. The backup central hospital in Geel houses 250 in-patients. There has been no recruitment of caretakers by the government, organizations, or central administration; in fact, a waiting list has always existed. The families are not given any specific training, psychiatric history, or diagnosis before they receive an individual boarder. They are expected to rely on the intuitive understanding and skill that they have developed over years of continual exposure to other boarders within their home or neighborhood.

Hundreds of families have housed mentally disabled persons for generations. Excluding the families who "inherit" a boarder from their parents who were caretakers, other caretakers are initially motivated to take a patient for the supplemental income it offers and the work the boarder will do with the family. The policy of limiting the number of patients to two per family insures that it cannot be the sole source of income for a caretaking family. Children and boarders develop attachments, the boarders become involved in family festivities and crises, and over time, emotional bonds develop that turn the boarder into an integral part of the family group.

Most of the boarders are considered to be a chronic population in need of supportive, long-term care. The majority were referred from other traditional institutions. Many of the boarders in Geelian families are mentally ill and retarded individuals who, for the most part, are not considered to be suitable candidates for community care programs. Taking into account the type of patient Geel attracts, mainly chronic patients with no viable family or community ties, these individuals would otherwise spend their lives on the back wards of state hospitals. To the dismay of some professionals, Geelians just do not see the boarders as psychiatric patients. Boarders are included in the work and recreational activities of their families and are also free to participate on their own in the community. Boarders are quite visible in the churches, cafes, local fairs, the movie house, and at sporting events. Cafes, of which there are 143 in the town, are places of social interaction for all Geelians. Boarders socialize with others in cafes, some spend their time actively hallucinating at a corner table, and others cannot be distinguished from the "normal" customers. Although bizarrely dressed individuals may talk to themselves among a group of schoolchildren and others may endlessly pace up and down store aisles, the community does monitor certain forms of deviant behavior in public places. When a boarder begins to take off his/ her clothes or begins to direct traffic, a passerby will intervene and take the individual home. The police, too, tend to be protective of the boarders. According to the chief of police, Geel has a lower crime rate than the surrounding communities (Baxter, 1979).

not-for-profit, nongovernmental organization (for more information see http://www.womenmentalhealth.com). Its purposes include:

1. to create a network of national and international societies and sections devoted to mental health of women;
2. through international collaboration and networks, to promote research into the social, economic, ethical, legal, cultural, psychological, and biological factors which affect women's mental health; and
3. to act as international advocates for women's mental health.

International Society for Mental Health Online

ISMHO was formed in 1997 to promote the understanding, use, and development of online communication, information, and technology for the

Box 8.2	**Research Evidence Driving the Future Agenda** Challenges for the Future

Based on current research, the World Health Organization (2001) suggests the following overall recommendations to move mental health treatment forward:

- **Provide treatment in primary care.** Providing treatment in primary care enables the largest number of people to get easier and faster access to services. This gives better care and cuts waste. General health personnel should be trained in the essential skills of mental health care. Mental health should be included in training curricula.
- **Make psychotropic drugs available.** Essential psychotropic drugs should be provided and made constantly available at all levels of health care. The best drugs to treat conditions should be made available whenever possible. These drugs can ameliorate symptoms, reduce disability, shorten the course of many disorders, and prevent relapse. They often provide the first-line treatment, especially in situations where psychosocial interventions and highly skilled professionals are unavailable.
- **Give care in the community.** Community care has a better effect than institutional treatment on the outcome and quality of life of individuals with chronic mental disorders. Shifting patients from mental hospitals to care in the community

is also cost-effective and respects human rights. Mental health services should be provided in the community, with the use of all available resources. Community-based services can lead to early intervention and limit the stigma of taking treatment. This shift towards community care requires health workers and rehabilitation services to be available at the community level, along with crisis support, protected housing, and sheltered employment.
- **Educate the public.** Public education and awareness campaigns on mental health should be launched in all countries. The main goal is to reduce barriers to treatment and care by increasing awareness of the frequency of mental disorders, their treatability, the recovery process, and the human rights of people with mental disorders. The care choices available and their benefits should be widely disseminated so that responses from the general population, professionals, media, policy-makers, and politicians reflect the best available knowledge.
- **Involve communities, families, and consumers.** Communities, families, and consumers should be included in the development and decision making of policies, programs, and services. This should lead to services being better tailored to people's needs and better used. In addition,

international mental health community (for more information see http://www.ismho.org).

The International Society of Psychiatric-Mental Health Nurses

The mission of the ISPN is to unite and strengthen the presence and voice of specialty psychiatric-mental health nursing while influencing health care policy to promote equitable, evidence-based, and effective treatment and care for individuals, families, and communities (for more information see http://www.ispn-psych.org).

The Clifford Beers Foundation: The International Centre for Mental Health Promotion

Established in 1996, this foundation is dedicated to the promotion of mental health. It has developed a range of initiatives and collaborative ventures interventions should take account of age, sex, culture, and social conditions, so as to meet the needs of people with mental disorders and their families.

- **Establish national policies, programs, and legislation.** Mental health policy, programs, and legislation are necessary steps for significant and sustained action. These should be based on current knowledge and human rights considerations. Most countries need to increase their budgets for mental health programs. Mental health reforms should be part of the larger health system reforms. Health insurance schemes should not discriminate against persons with mental disorders.
- **Develop human resources.** Most developing countries need to increase and improve training of mental health professionals, who will provide specialized care as well as support the primary health care programs. Once trained, professionals should be encouraged to remain in their country in positions that make the best use of their skills. Specialist mental health care teams should include medical and non-medical professionals, such as psychiatrists, clinical psychologists, psychiatric nurses, psychiatric social workers, and occupational therapists, who can work together towards the total care and integration of patients in the community.
- **Link with other sectors.** Sectors other than health, such as education, labor, welfare, and law, and nongovernmental organizations should be involved in improving the mental health of communities. Nongovernmental organizations should be much more proactive, with better-defined roles, and should be encouraged to give greater support to local initiatives.
- **Monitor community mental health.** The mental health of communities should be monitored by including mental health indicators in health information and reporting systems. The indices should include both the numbers of individuals with mental disorders and the quality of their care, as well as some more general measures of the mental health of communities. Such monitoring helps to determine trends and to detect mental health changes resulting from external events, such as disasters.
- **Support more research.** More research into biological and psychosocial aspects of mental health is needed in order to increase the understanding of mental disorders and to develop more effective interventions. Such research should be carried out on a wide global basis to understand variations across communities and to learn more about factors that influence the cause, course, and outcome of mental disorders.

throughout the world to improve mental health of people individually and collectively (for more information see http://www.charity.demon.co.uk).

World Association for Infant Mental Health (WAIMH)

WAIMH is an interdisciplinary and international association that promotes education, research, and study of the effects of mental, emotional, and social development during infancy on later normal and psychopathological development. It advocates the development of scientifically based programs to care for, intervene, and prevent mental impairment in infancy. It also sponsors regional and biennial world congresses devoted to scientific, education, and clinical work with infants and their caregivers. It encourages the realization that infancy is a crucial period in the psychosocial development of individuals; facilitates international cooperation among individuals concerned with promoting optimal development of infants and their families; provides international networking; and sponsors the *Infant Mental Health Journal* (for more information see http://www.waimh.org).

World Federation for Mental Health

The World Federation for Mental Health was founded in 1948 to advance, among all peoples and nations, the prevention of mental and emotional disorders, the proper treatment and care of those with such disorders, and the promotion of mental health. The Federation's organizational and individual membership includes mental health workers of all disciplines, consumers/users of mental health services, family members, and concerned citizens. The specific mission of the Federation is to promote the highest possible level of mental health in its broadest biological, medical, educational, and social aspects (for more information see http://www.wfmh.org).

World Psychiatric Association (WPA)

The WPA formulates and disseminates ethical guidelines on psychiatric practice. It collaborates with the United Nations and the World Health Organization to protect the human rights of mental patients (for more information see http://www.wpanet.org).

SUMMARY

In the United States, 70 percent of the mental health service provision is provided by social workers. Throughout the world, social work is using its knowledge and expertise to promote humane and effective mental health services for vulnerable populations. Despite the progress made globally in the effective treatment of the mentally ill, mental health budgets in the majority of countries are not sufficient to meet the critical needs. Even in countries with well-established mental health services, fewer than half of those individuals needing care utilize existing services. Stigma, discrimination, and embarrassment continue to impede service provision and utilization. Recent programs designed to educate the public; involve communities, families, and consumers in the development of policies, programs, and services; and establish national policies and legislation demonstrate some initial effectiveness in improving mental health services.

Thinking About Practice: From Local to Global Perspectives

1. To what extent are communities, families, and consumers involved in the establishment of mental health policy, legislation, and programs in your community? In your nation?
2. How does the level of service provision in your community/nation compare to other countries?
3. How available are psychotropic drugs to the mentally ill population in your community? What are the obstacles to providing psychotropic drug treatment?
4. How could conditions facilitate the availability of psychotropic drugs to mentally ill persons?
5. What opportunities exist to incorporate effective programs/services offered in other countries to your community/nation?

Social Work Practice and Social Justice Website

Please go to the Book Companion Website at http://www.thomsonedu.com/author/sowers to find a rich collection of related articles selected by the authors from Info Trac College Edition.

References

Baxter, E. (1979). Geel, Belgium: A radical model for the integration of deviancy. *The Community Imperative*. Syracuse, NY: Center on Human Policy, University of Syracuse.

Cottraux, J. (1993). Behaviour therapy. In N. Sartorius, G. DeGirilamo, G. Andrews, A. German, & L. Eisenberg (Eds.), *Treatment of mental disorders: A review of effectiveness*. pp. 199–235. Geneva: World Health Organization.

Cowen, E. L. (1985). Person centered approaches to primary prevention in mental health: Situation-focused and competence-enhancement. *American Journal of Community Psychology, 13*, 31–48.

Crespi, T. (1990). Approaching adolescent suicide: Queries and signposts. *School Counselor, 37*, 256–259.

DenHouter, K. V. (1981). To silence one's self: A brief analysis of the literature on adolescent suicide. *Child Welfare, 60*(1), 2–10.

Evans, W. P., Marte, R. M., Betts, S., & Silliman, B. (2001). Adolescent suicide risk and peer-related violence behaviors and victimization. *Journal of Interpersonal Violence, 16*(12), 1330–1348.

Faber, M. (1978, February 7). *Issues in adolescent health* (Lecture). Lansing: University of Michigan.

Felner, R. D., Jason, L. A., Moritsugu, J. M., & Farber, S. S. (1983). *Preventive psychology: Theory, research, and practice*. New York: Pergamon Press.

Harris, T., & Lenings, J. (1993). Suicide and adolescence. *International Journal of Offender Therapy and Comparative Criminology, 37*(3), 263–270.

Hauenstein, E. J., & Boyd, M. R. (1994). Depressive symptoms in young women of the Piedmont: Prevalence in rural women. *Women and Health, 21*(2/3), 105–123.

James, L., & Wherry, J. N. (1991). Suicide in residential treatment: Causes, assessment, and treatment issues. *Residential Treatment for Children and Youth, 9*(2), 23–36.

Kachur, S. P., Potter, L .B., Powell, K. E., & Rosenberg, M. L. (1992). Suicide: Epidemiology, prevention, and treatment. *Adolescent Medicine, 6*, 171–182.

Kellerman, A. L., Rivera, R .P., Somes, G. L., Reary, D. T., Francisco, J., Gillentine-Banton, J., et al. (1992). Suicide in the home in relation to gun ownership. *New England Journal of Medicine, 327*, 467–472.

Levav, I., & Gonzalez, V. R. (2000). Rights of persons with mental illness in Central America. *Acta Psychiatrica Scandinavica, 101*, 83–86.

Lewinsohn, P. M., Rohde, P., & Seeley, J. R. (1993). Psychosocial characteristics of adolescents with a history of suicide attempt. *Journal of American Academy of Child Adolescent Psychiatry, 31*(1), 60–68.

Lukens, E. P. (2003). Treatments for people with severe and persistent mental illness. In R. L. English (Ed.), *Encyclopedia of social work* (19th ed.) 2003 supplement, pp. 176–186. Washington, DC: NASW Press.

Lurie, A., & Monahan, K. (2001). Prevention principles for practitioners: A solution or an illusion? *Social Work in Health Care, 33*(1), 60–68.

McCarter, A. K., Sowers, K. M., & Dulmus, C. N. (2004). Adolescent suicide prevention. In L. Rapp-Paglicci, C. Dulmus, & J. S. Wodarski (Eds.), *Preventive interventions for children and adolescents*. Hoboken, NJ: John Wiley & Sons.

McGorry, P. D. (2000). Evaluating the importance of reducing the duration of untreated psychosis. *Australian and New Zealand Journal of Psychiatry, 34*(suppl.), 145–149.

Merkl, P. E. (1993). Which are today's democracies? *International Social Science Journal, 136*, 257–270.

Mishara, B. L., & Ystgaard, M. (2000). Exploring the potential for primary prevention: Evaluation of the Befrienders International Reaching Young People Pilot Programme in Denmark. *Crisis, 21*(1), 4–7.

National Human Rights Commission. (1999). *Quality assurance in mental health*. New Delhi: National Human Rights Commission of India.

Quam, J. (1995). Dorothea Dix. In R. L. Edwards & J.G. Hopps (Eds.), *Encyclopedia of social work* (19th ed.). Washington, DC: NASW Press.

Rathus, J. H., & Miller, A. L. (2002). Dialectical behavior therapy adapted for suicidal adolescents. *Suicide and Life-Threatening Behavior, 32*(2), 146–157.

Rutz, W., Knorring, L., & Walinder, J. (1995). Long-term effects of an education program for general practitioners given by the Swedish Committee for the Prevention and Treatment of Depression. *Acta Psychiatrica Scandinavica, 85*, 83–88.

Saeed, K., Rehman, I. L., & Mubbashar, M. H. (2000). Prevalence of psychiatric morbidity among the attendees of a native faithhealer at Rawalpindi. *Journal of College of Physicians and Surgeons of Pakistan, 10*, 7–10.

Saleebey, D. (1996). The strengths perspective in social work practice: Extensions and cautions. *Social Work, 41*, 296–305.

Silverman, M. M., & Felner, R. D. (1995). Suicide prevention programs: Issues of design, implementation, feasibility, and developmental appropriateness. *Suicide and Life-Threatening Behavior, 25*(1), 92–104.

Thara, R., Henrietta, M., Joseph, A., Rajkumar, S., & Eaton, W. W. (1994). Ten-year course of schizophrenia: The Madras longitudinal study. *Acta Psychiatrica Scandinavica, 90*(5), 329–336.

United Nations. (1991). *The protection of persons with mental illness and the improvement of mental health care.* UN General Assembly resolution A/RES/46.119. Retrieved March 7, 2004 from http://www.un.org/ga/documents/gadocs.htm

U.S. Department of Health and Human Services. (1999). *Mental health: A Report of the Surgeon General.* Rockville, MD: U.S. Department of Health and Human Services, Substance Abuse and Mental Health Services Administration, Center for Mental Health Services, National Institutes of Health, National Institute of Mental Health.

Ustun, T. B., Rehm, J., Chatterji, S., Saxena, S., Trotter, R., Room, R., Bickenbach, J., & WHO/NIH Joint Project CAR Study Group. (1999). Multiple-informant ranking of the disabling effects of different health conditions in 14 countries. *Lancet, 354*(9173), 111–115.

Wetzel, J. W. (1994). Depression: Women at risk. *Social Work in Health Care, 19*(3/4), 85–108.

Wetzel, J. W. (2000). Women and mental health: A global perspective. *International Social Work, 43*(2), 205–215.

Wetzler, S., Asnis, G. M., Hyman, R. B., Virtue, C., Zimmerman, J., & Rathus, J. H. (1996). Characteristics of suicidality among adolescents. *Suicide and Life-Threatening Behavior, 26*(1), 37–45.

Williams, J. B. W. (1981). DSM-III: A comprehensive approach to diagnosis. *Social Work, 26*, 101–106.

Williams, J. B. W. (1995). Diagnostic and statistical manual of mental disorders. In R. L. Edwards & J. G. Hopps (Eds.), *Encyclopedia of social work, Vol 1* (19th ed.), pp. 729–739. Washington, DC: NASW Press.

World Health Organization. (n.d.). *Mental health.* Retrieved June 30, 2004, from http://www.who.int/mental_health/en

World Health Organization. (1997). *An overview of a strategy to improve the mental health of underserved populations: Nations for mental health.* (Report WHO/MSA/NAM/97.3). Geneva: Author.

World Health Organization. (2001). *The World Health Report 2001.* Retrieved July 7, 2004, from http://www.who.int/whr2001/2001/main

Xu, H., Xiao, S., Chen, J., & Jui, L. (2000). Epidemiological study on committed suicide among the elderly in some urban and rural areas of Hunan Province, China. *Chinese Mental Health Journal, 14*(2), 121–124.

The quality of life is determined by its activities.
Aristotle

Substance Abuse

CHAPTER 9

© The Thomson Corporation/Heinle Image Resource Bank

GLOBAL PREVALENCE AND DIFFERENTIAL SUBSTANCE USE

About 8 million people abuse opiates/heroine (United Nations International Drug Control Programme, n.d.). Heroine and opiate abuse is found throughout the world but is predominant in Southeast and Southwest Asia. Heroin abuse is far more widespread and in greater use today than it was ten years ago. Increases of opiate/heroine have been reported in Iran, Turkey, and Pakistan, and dramatic increases in the former Soviet Union countries. Heroin continues to be readily available in major urban areas in the United States.

Some 13 million people abuse cocaine worldwide, with the highest prevalence reported in the United States. Many Latin American countries also have high levels of cocaine and bazuco (coca paste) abuse. Serious cocaine usage and abuse spread to Europe between 1995 and 1997 and cocaine has become a common commodity in metropolitan areas of North America. Increases have been reported in Chile, Peru, and neighboring South American countries and along trafficking routes to America and Europe.

In the 1990s there was a sharp increase in the use of cannabis. Annually, 141 million people use cannabis. It is the most widely abused illicit drug in all parts of the world. Cannabis abuse is particularly high in western Africa, Oceania, Central America, North America, and a number of European countries.

On the basis of global 1992 data, the World Health Organization (n.d.) estimated that "over 5 million people injected drugs, that between 150,000 and 200,000 drug injectors died every year, and that at least half of those deaths were associated with HIV." It is likely that these figures underestimate the scope of the problem today (UNAIDS, n.d.).

Illicit drug use tends to fluctuate based on trafficking patterns. Supply routes, which are constantly in flux throughout the world, are influenced by the increase or decrease of law enforcement efforts, natural disasters, economics, and weather patterns. Seizures of illegal drugs have dramatically increased recently in parts of Southeast Asia and in several areas on both the east and west coasts of Africa. However, countries of Eastern Europe have now become major transit points for illegal drugs. As a result there is a sharp increase in drug injecting in these nations. Reducing the supply of illegal drugs does not necessarily help reduce drug use in areas where injecting drug use already exists. In fact, reducing the supply has been shown actually to increase risky injecting behavior. "When drugs are plentiful, many users choose to smoke rather than inject. However, injecting delivers a 'high' with a smaller drug dose than smoking, so people may switch from smoking to injecting if their usual supplies are not available. A recent study in Calcutta showed that huge seizures of heroin in the city were followed by a sharp rise in the proportion of drug users choosing to inject" (World Health Organization, n.d.).

Alcohol abusers follow a similar pattern of behavior when they are denied the ability to procure alcohol. While in prison or living on a dry reservation, for example, alcohol abusers may resort to consuming denatured alcohol.

Denatured alcohol is contained in many everyday household products such cough medicines, shaving lotion, and mouthwash. The ingestion of denatured alcohol can be extremely dangerous, often causing brain damage and death.

In almost all countries the use of heroine is illegal and carries with it strong societal taboos. In a few countries, however, users who are in treatment can get otherwise illegal drugs by prescription. Because of the illegality of drug possession and use and the strong societal taboo, most drug injectors make great efforts to hide their usage. They are extremely reluctant to come forward for help or information, even where it is available. This is particularly true for young people, who are at an extremely vulnerable stage in their lives (World Health Organization, n.d.).

The following provides an overview of drug abuse throughout the world.

Asia

Heroin is the primary drug of abuse in Asia. It is predominant particularly in the cities of Asia. There has been a steady increase in the percentage of patients who report heroin as their primary drug of abuse. The South Asian cities of Islamabad in Pakistan, Colombo in Sri Lanka, and Dhaka in Bangladesh report the highest rates of heroin use. The East Asian cities with the highest percentages of primary heroin use are Bangkok, Thailand; Kuala Lumpur, Malaysia; and Hanoi, Viet Nam. There is also a very high usage of opium as the primary drug of abuse in Hanoi. Amphetamines are the predominant drug of abuse in Manila, the Philippines, although there is also a very high rate of polydrug abuse. Also throughout Asia alcohol and cough syrup are primary substances of abuse (National Institute on Drug Abuse, n.d.).

Various means of drug administration are used throughout Asia. In Bangkok, injection is the primary method used. Smoking or "chasing the dragon" is the dominant method of drug administration in Kuala Lumpur and Islamabad. In Hanoi, inhalation is used most often.

In Viet Nam, many drug users inject drugs in "shooting galleries," slum area rooms or shacks with no basic amenities such as running water. In these dwellings dealers mix opium or heroin solution and distribute it to clients. Clients pay for a shot of the solution, which is taken from a communal pot and given to the drug user by the dealer. As many as 50 clients might share the pot of solution. Generally, they all use the same syringe and needle, which is rarely cleaned between usages. Consequently, there is a high percentage of officially diagnosed HIV infections among drug injectors in Viet Nam. A similar injecting system is common in Myanmar. "In both these countries, even shooting galleries often use home-made equipment consisting of a needle attached to an eye-dropper or polythene tube which are nearly impossible to sterilize" (United Nations Development Programme, n.d.). The National AIDS Programme (United Nations Development Programme, n.d.) estimates that over 90 percent of injecting drug users in the northern Myanmar state of Kachin are infected with HIV. The proportion is close to 80 percent in the northern Shan

State. In Myanmar, four out of five people entering drug treatment regularly share injecting equipment (National Institute on Drug Abuse, n.d.).

Australia

In Australia, cannabis is the most popular and frequently used illicit drug. There is a recent dramatic increase in the number of people seeking treatment for cannabis-related problems. A large number of those seeking treatment are experiencing psychological problems that are associated with their cannabis use. Significant symptoms from withdrawal are being reported in the areas of Brisbane and the Gold Coast. Amphetamines are the second most widely used illicit drug in Australia. Rural areas of Australia are experiencing high and increasing patterns of amphetamine use. Almost all agencies in Australia report that amphetamines are increasingly being used with other substances. For example, "marijuana and benzodiazepines are often used to medicate or soften the comedowns from amphetamine use" (National Institute on Drug Abuse, n.d.).

In addition to amphetamines, heroin is also readily available in Australia. The increased availability and use of heroin may be a result of the reduction in street prices and the increase in the purity of the heroin. There has been a sharp increase in opioid-related deaths, which now account for almost 10 percent of the deaths among Australians 24–25 years of age. Heroin is consistently the third or fourth most frequently used drug among young people, after alcohol, cannabis, and amphetamines. There is an increase in its use in Sydney and Melbourne. There has also been an increase in the use of cocaine in Sydney but its use remains very low in Melbourne, Adelaide, and Brisbane. Injection drug use is also on the rise in Australia. Basing of cocaine (crack) is most commonly found in rural areas but has also recently been reported in Brisbane and the Gold Coast. "Lysergic acid diethylamide (LSD), which has been popular in the dance party scene in Australia, is currently being marketed more broadly across the country and the increase in use is among younger age groups" (National Institute on Drug Abuse, n.d.).

Canada

Alcohol is the major substance abuse problem in Canada and cannabis is the most widely abused illicit drug. The use of substances varies greatly across Canada but is highest in British Columbia and lowest in Ontario. Cocaine/crack use is most prevalent among street youth, particularly in Vancouver and Toronto, but is low in the general population. The use of heroin is also high in the Vancouver area but is relatively low throughout the rest of Canada. LSD is the second most frequently used illicit drug in Canada, with use being primarily among youth. The highest usage of LSD occurs in British Columbia, New Brunswick, and the Nova Scotia city of Halifax, and the lowest in Toronto. The abuse of hallucinogens accounts for only a small percentage of admissions to treatment clients in Canada (National Institute on Drug Abuse, n.d.).

Recently, the British Columbia city of Vancouver opened safe-injection sites for heroin users, an action that the U.S. government strongly opposed. Local health officials hope that by opening the safe-injection sites, they will be able to reduce the spread of HIV and hepatitis C among intravenous drug users and reduce the number of heroin deaths. The first safe-injection site is located in a clinic that treats people with HIV and AIDS. According to Vancouver officials, "About 12,000 of the 1.3 million residents of the city are intravenous drug users. Nearly 40 percent of drug users have HIV or AIDS, and 90 percent have Hepatitis C. Two thousand people have died from drug overdoses on the city's streets since 1993" (Join Together, n.d.).

Europe

Prevalence levels for different drugs vary across and within European Union countries. Polydrug abuse is increasingly reported among recreational drug users and chronic drug abusers. It is estimated that there are 1.5 million chronic opiate users in the European Union, and the majority of the illicit drug abusing clients who seek treatment in the European Union are opiate abusers. There is also an increase in the use of heroin, especially by smoking. About 16 percent of the population in the European Union countries has used cannabis in their lifetime and approximately 5 percent of the population is reported currently to use cannabis. The use and availability of amphetamines continues to increase in European Union countries. Among the younger users, amphetamines are mostly taken orally, through pills or a powder that is sniffed or added to liquid. In the northern countries of the European Union, socially marginalized drug abusers continue to favor amphetamines through injection. Ecstasy appears to be the drug of choice within dance and party settings and in private social gatherings. Heavy consumers of ecstasy tend to combine it with other drugs with sedative effects, such as heroin and benzodiazepines (European Monitoring Centre for Drugs and Drug Addiction, n.d.).

In Eastern Europe evidence suggests that those who are preparing drugs engage in the particularly dangerous practice of mixing fresh blood into drug solutions. It is believed that the blood counteracts any contaminants that might exist in the home-produced drugs. This is particularly hazardous because if the blood is infected with HIV, then all the injectors drawing drug solution from that batch can become infected, even if they are using sterilized injecting equipment. "Large-scale dealers also commonly use 'slaves' to test drugs. These people draw a dose from the drug solution, inject, and report on the quality of the solution. In payment for this test, they are then allowed to draw another full dose, usually using the same unsterilized syringe. This practice can introduce the virus into drugs which are then shared by many people" (UNAIDS, n.d.).

Mexico

The most frequently abused drug in Mexico is cocaine. At least one other substance is used in combination with cocaine by many of the primary cocaine abusers. Heroin and marijuana are also frequently used by drug abusers. "Among juvenile delinquents in Mexico the most frequently abused drugs include marijuana, inhalants, cocaine, and heroin (in that order)" (National Institute on Drug Abuse, n.d.).

South Africa

Throughout South Africa alcohol is the substance most abused. In Cape Town, Port Elizabeth, and Durban, cannabis and methaqualone (Mandrax) alone or in combination are the most common illicit substances of abuse. High proportions of drug abusers in Gauteng abuse marijuana. Port Elizabeth is currently experiencing a serious problem with the abuse of over-the-counter and prescription medications. Throughout South Africa, ecstasy is used by young persons in the club scene (National Institute on Drug Abuse, n.d.).

Thailand

In Thailand, heroin is the most commonly abused drug, followed by methamphetamine and opium. An estimated 100,000 to 250,000 people in Thailand inject heroin. However, it appears that methamphetamine pills are beginning to overtake heroin as the country's drug of choice. HIV has become a prevalent and serious problem affecting approximately 40 percent of the country's heroin users. Most of the heroin abusers in Thailand inject the drug, whereas methamphetamine abusers tend to smoke the drug. Currently, it appears that the number of methamphetamine abusers is increasing and the number of heroin and marijuana abusers is decreasing (National Institute on Drug Abuse, n.d.).

Only limited treatment is available to drug users in Thailand. It is not uncommon for drug users to experience regular abuse by police, including beatings, false arrest, and forced confessions. In fact, Thailand's brutal antidrug crackdown is jeopardizing its human rights record and its success against HIV/AIDS (Human Rights Watch, n.d.). "A recent government anti-drug campaign has resulted in as many as 3,000 killings and has driven drug users underground away from lifesaving HIV prevention services. The Thai government continues to oppose needle-exchange programs, even though numerous scientific studies have proven that they reduce HIV transmission without increasing drug use" (Open Society Institute, 2004).

United States

Approximately 35.6 percent of the population of the United States (76.9 million persons) has used an illicit drug at least once during their lifetime. The most frequently used illicit drug is marijuana, followed by powder cocaine, nonprescribed analgesics, hallucinogens, inhalants, and stimulants. There has been a sharp increase in the use of illicit drugs among 12–17 year olds. Among this age group the use of marijuana has recently doubled. The use of marijuana is also substantially increasing among Black non-Hispanics. The highest overall use of illicit drugs is among young people age 18–25. Marijuana, powder cocaine, and inhalants (in that order) are the most frequently used illicit drugs. The use of marijuana among middle and high schoolers in the United States is increasing. In fact, 22 percent of eighth graders, 39.6 percent of tenth graders, and 49 percent of twelfth graders have used marijuana. There is an increasing problem of the use of crack cocaine and tranquilizers in the United States and a decrease in the use of drugs such as heroin, stimulants, and powder cocaine. Methamphetamine abuse has recently become an increasingly serious problem. Hawaii as well as the western, southern, northwestern, and midwestern states have been particularly affected (National Institute on Drug Abuse, n.d.). Methamphetamines were at one time primarily used by white males. However, there is a dramatic rise in the use of methamphetamines among Hispanics and Asian Americans, and among gay males (Hohman & Clapp, 1999) as well as females of childbearing age (Hohman, Oliver, & Wright, 2004).

CORE COMPONENTS OF PRACTICE

Prevention

A new global focus on efforts to tackle the global drug problem was introduced in 1998 by the United Nations General Assembly Special Session Devoted to Countering the World Drug Problem Together (UNGASS). Recognizing that a reduction in the demand for illicit drugs was critical to an effective international effort to fight drug abuse and trafficking, the Member States committed themselves to reducing significantly both the supply of and demand for drugs by 2008. This goal was explicitly stated and adopted by the UNGASS in their Political Declaration. "Member States also adopted the Declaration on the Guiding Principles of Drug Demand Reduction. Within the framework of this new emphasis on drug demand reduction approaches, increased attention will be given to the issue of prevention of drug abuse as a key component of demand reduction" (United Nations, 2002).

Research indicates that prevention strategies work particularly well when they are focused on the needs of young people. It is believed that because they have not yet developed strongly rooted habits, young people may be more amenable to behavior change and the adoption of safe practice. The World Health Organization (n.d.) suggests that "every opportunity must be used—beginning with primary school—to help young people learn the information and practical skills they will need to negotiate a safe path through life. Coupled with this, young people need access to prevention tools and youth-friendly services where they can get counseling."

In the past, many prevention programs have focused on efforts to deliver knowledge and effect attitude change. But current research suggests that programs based on these components alone have minimal effect on adolescent substance-using behavior, and in some cases contribute to experimentation

(Jansen, Glynn, & Howard, 1996). Single-focused prevention strategies appear ineffective in achieving long-term changes (Wallack & Corbett, 1990). Current research (National Institute on Drug Abuse, 1997, 2003) suggests that the following factors are attributable to successful prevention efforts:

- Most successful programs are comprehensive, have multiple components, and are directed at individuals, families, peers, schools, communities, the media, and the workplace.
- Prevention strategies need to use the media to educate the community, raise public awareness, develop community support, and maintain the momentum of established prevention efforts.
- Prevention strategies need to be provided in sufficient intensity and duration to achieve desired effects.
- Booster sessions are important in establishing initial progress and in maintaining effects over time.
- Prevention programming should follow a primary prevention model of targeting the large, diverse population and be adaptable to subpopulations to address differences in gender, culture or ethnicity, socioeconomic status, stage of adolescent development, and be adaptable to the type of drugs being used.
- Programs should follow a structured organizational plan that includes needs assessments, program reviews, refinement processes, and feedback to and from the community. These objectives should be time-limited and feasible according to the capabilities of each program or component.

It is critical that countries protect the rights of their young people. This should include the right to lifesaving information and services that can reduce their vulnerability to risky situations and behaviors. "Yet, in many places in the world, the necessary services are simply not available at all, or not accessible to those who need them most. In cities where injecting drug use clearly takes place and HIV prevalence is still relatively low, initiating comprehensive prevention programs now may prove critical to containing the virus with and beyond communities" (UNAIDS, n.d.).

"The prevention of alcohol dependence should be seen within the context of the broader goal of preventing and reducing alcohol-related problems at the population level (alcohol-related accidents, injuries, suicide, violence, etc.)" (UNAIDS, n.d.).

The Use of Substances and Suicide Prevention   The use of substances and suicide are inextricably linked. Compelling evidence indicates that adequate prevention and treatment of some mental and behavioral disorders can reduce suicide. Early assessment and intervention programs for alcohol dependence, schizophrenia, and depression are critical in the primary prevention of suicide. Early recognition and treatment programs can be effectively utilized when focused towards individuals, families, schools, or other sections of the general community.

The ingestion of pesticides, herbicides, medications, or other toxic substances is the preferred method for committing suicide in many places, particularly in rural areas of developing countries. For example, in 1982 the ingestion of paraquat (a herbicide) became the predominant method of suicide in Western Samoa. By reducing the availability of paraquat to the general population, Western Samoa was able to reduce the total number of suicides significantly, without a corresponding increase in suicide by other methods (Bowles, 1995). "Similar successful examples relate to the control of other toxic substances and the detoxification of domestic gas and of car exhausts. In many places, the lack of easily accessible emergency care makes the ingestion of toxic substances an unfortunately successful means of suicide" (World Health Organization, 2001).

Alcohol consumption has been increasing in recent years in the Russian Federation, and neighboring countries. The increase in the use of alcohol has been linked to an increase in rates of suicide and alcohol poisoning (Vroublevsdy & Harwin, 1998), and to a decline in male life expectancy (Leon & Shkolnikov, 1998; Notzon et al., 1998).

Harm Reduction and Control

In many cities around the world HIV disease has reached epidemic proportions. Renewed and dramatic efforts are needed to support safe behavior among the HIV infected users and among drug users in general. This is essential for drug-using and non-using communities alike (UNAIDS, n.d.). There is a high risk of HIV spreading from drug injectors to their sex partners and children. Many countries have experienced the effects of the spread of this devastating disease. Because of the critical need to support safer behavior, particularly in cities with a high prevalence of HIV, cities, governments, NGOs, and other organizations are implementing harm reduction programs.

The term "harm reduction" is used in public health settings to describe a concept aiming to prevent or reduce negative health consequences associated with certain behaviors. The American Medical Association (1997) defines harm reduction as "those practices that are employed to reduce the medical and/or public health consequences associated with use of psychoactive substances." The definition given by the International Harm Reduction Association is broader, defining harm reduction as "policies and programs which attempt primarily to reduce the adverse health, social and economic consequences of mood altering substances to individual drug users, their families, and their communities" (International Harm Reduction Association, n.d.). Harm reduction strategies have been used since the early 1980s in the form of various new policies and programs. A new global approach for harm reduction programs focuses on the use of harm reduction strategies to prevent HIV/AIDS among injecting drug users.

In contrast to a punitive approach to drug abuse, the harm reduction model views addiction as an adaptive response to a wide cross-section of individual and collective variables that may influence behavior. By retaining value-neutral views of the person and the activity, a spirit of nonjudgmentalism can pervade intervention (Rowe & Marcotte, 1998). Practitioners using the harm reduction perspective develop interventions that reduce drug-related harm without necessarily promoting abstinence as the only solution (MacMaster, 2004). Common to discussions of harm reduction (Des Jarlais, 1995; Drucker, 1995; Harm Reduction Coalition, 1996; Scavuzzo, 1996; Springer, 1991; Van Laar, de Zwart & Mensinck, 1996) are five assumptions:

1. substance use has and will be part of our world; accepting this reality leads to a focus on reducing drug-related harm rather than reducing drug use;
2. abstinence from substances is clearly effective at reducing substance-related harm, but it is only one of many possible objectives of services to substance users;
3. substance use inherently causes harm; however, many of the most harmful consequences of substance use (HIV/AIDS, hepatitis C, overdoses, automobile accidents, etc.) can be eliminated without complete abstinence;
4. services to substance users must be relevant and user friendly if they are to be effective in helping people minimize their substance-related harm; and
5. substance use must be understood from a broad perspective and not solely as an individual act; accepting this idea moves interventions from coercion and criminal justice solutions to a public health or social work perspective.

Successful harm reduction programs are based within policy, legislative, and social environment contexts that minimize the vulnerability of injecting drug users. It has been the basis of substance abuse policies and practices in several Western European countries (MacMaster, 2004). Harm reduction was originally suggested in the 1920s in the United Kingdom as part of the Rolleston Committee's recommendations regarding drug policy, and later emerged as a pragmatic response to a rise in hepatitis C rates related to injection drug use in the early 1980s (Scavuzzo, 1996). The Netherlands has used a harm reduction perspective as the underpinning of drug policy and practice for almost 30 years (Van Laar, de Zwart, & Mensinck, 1996). The Dutch have used harm reduction since the recommendations of the 1971 Hulsman Report. This report became the basis for Dutch harm reduction strategies in the Revised Opium Act of 1976 (Cohen, 1994). Switzerland and Germany have based much of their substance use policies on the concept of harm reduction (United Nations International Drug Control Programme, 1997). More recently, harm reduction strategies have been rapidly adopted by HIV/AIDS service providers in the United States because of the unquestionable link between HIV/AIDS and injection drug use (Clapp & Burke, 1999).

Harm reduction is a strategy of choice for active substance users when traditional prevention methods have been unsuccessful. Harm reduction for injecting drug users primarily aims to help them avoid the negative health consequences of drug injecting and improve their health and social status. Harm reduction approaches recognize that for many drug users total abstinence from psychoactive substances is not a feasible option in the short term. It focuses on helping drug users reduce their injection frequency and increase injection safety. It appears that in order for harm reduction strategies to be effective, however, they must be embedded into comprehensive prevention and intervention packages for injecting drug users (World Health Organization, n.d.). For instance, harm reduction techniques focusing on safer injection messages for drug injectors to reduce the spread of HIV will be most effective when the techniques are combined with messages promoting safe sex and the use of condoms. Reaching a large number of individuals who inject drugs on a regular or occasional basis is a challenge for harm reduction service providers because of the hidden—and often rapidly changing—nature of drug injecting. Consequently, harm reduction services must be informed by frequent situation assessments, which can increase understanding of local drug use patterns and contexts. Situation assessments can also provide information to communities, which in turn can act as a catalyst for learning about the necessity of evidence-based approaches to HIV prevention among injecting drug users while also reducing program controversy.

Harm reduction strategies are generally used when other prevention and treatment strategies fail. Their goals are "to reduce the direct toxicity of drugs or the indirect toxicity caused by co-ingestion, to reduce the consequences of drug use on others, and to demarginalize the user and redirect the user's life into productive pursuits" (American Medical Association, 1997). According to the World Health Organization (n.d.), harm reduction programs are important for the following reasons:

- Re-using and sharing needles, syringes, or other equipment for preparing and injecting drugs represents a highly efficient way of HIV transmission. Worldwide there may be as many as 2–3 million past and current injecting drug users living with HIV/AIDS, and more than 100 countries now report HIV epidemics that are associated with injecting drug use.
- In the absence of harm reduction activities, HIV prevalence among injecting drug users can rise to levels up to 40 percent or more within 1 or 2 years of introduction of the virus in their communities.
- HIV transmission through sharing of non-sterile injection equipment is augmented by sexual transmission both among injecting drug users and between injecting drug users and their sex partners. Hence, harm reduction carries significant HIV preventive potential for both injecting drug users and the general population.
- Interventions for injecting drug users that reduce HIV risks also have the potential to engage drug users in drug dependence treatment services that may ultimately lead to abstinence from drug use. Finally, such programs can help to avoid other harmful consequences of drug use, including hepatitis B/C infections.

Methadone maintenance programs, established in the 1960s, were the first harm reduction attempts used in the United States. Other harm reduction strategies used in the United States have focused on preventing HIV/AIDS and other diseases among injecting drug users, such as through needle/syringe exchange programs and outreach projects. "Globally, Harm Reduction has been used in providing drugs to persons who are drug dependent, substitution of drugs to the addicted persons, modification of use patterns and routes of administration, provision of safer techniques and tolls, and locations for safe drug administration" (World Health Organization, n.d.).

The following are typical components that have a significant potential to reduce individual risk behaviors associated with drug injection (World Health Organization, n.d.):

- **Needle-syringe programming (NSP)** aims to ensure that those drug users who continue injecting have access to clean injection paraphernalia, including needles and syringes, filters, cookers, drug containers, and mixing water. Specific interventions that equip drug users with sterile injection equipment usually also collect used needles and syringes, and are commonly known as 'needle exchange programs' (NEPs). Such programs can also serve as information points and may engage drug users with drug treatment services. Their ability to break the chain of transmission of HIV and other bloodborne viruses is well established. Disinfection programs have been used in settings where needle exchange is not feasible. It is hoped that drug users who disinfect their injection paraphernalia after use with chemical substances (usually household bleach) adequately decontaminate the equipment before reuse. The effectiveness of disinfection procedures depends to a large extent on the method used, is of varying efficiency, and is only seen as a second line strategy in needle-syringe programming.

- **Drug substitution treatment** involves the medically supervised treatment of individuals with opioid dependency based on the prescription of opioid agonists such as methadone. While the primary goal of drug substitution treatment is abstinence from illicit drug use, many patients are unable to achieve complete abstinence, despite improvements in their health and well being. However, there is clear evidence that methadone maintenance significantly reduces unsafe injection practices of those who are in treatment and at risk of HIV infection.

- **HIV/AIDS related treatment and care** primarily aims to help drug users living with HIV/AIDS cope with the infection. Involving HIV positive drug users in primary health care and/or anti-retroviral treatment programs provides an opportunity for them to adopt and consolidate safe behaviors and may yield significant HIV preventive effects. This applies in particular to HIV/AIDS treatment and care that is provided in the context of specific information and counseling services.

- **Information, education, and communication (IEC)** on HIV transmission through injecting drug use provides information which will assist drug users avoid or modify drug injecting behaviors. Involving injecting drug users in the development and design of information material is critical to increase its appropriateness. The content of IEC materials should cover both the risks of injection and sharing practices as well as advice on how to reduce these risks and avoid sharing of injection equipment. IEC can be delivered through a variety of channels, ranging from general awareness campaigns, the provision of targeted information through health and social services frequented by injecting drug users to delivery of information through peer and drug user networks and outreach workers. 'Risk Reduction Counseling' represents a particular method that is based on face-to-face communication and provides an opportunity for drug users to turn information into actual behavior change through a process of clarification and reinforcement. Often, risk reduction counseling is offered in the context of HIV testing and counseling.

Harm Reduction strategies have been applied for non-injecting drug users as well, such as ecstasy users. For example, "One of the main messages is to reduce the heat accompanying the intake of ecstasy by hydrating with cold water, proper air conditioning during parties, and other guidelines" (DanceSafe, n.d.). The application of harm reduction principles to other problematic substances such as tobacco and alcohol is a more recent event. Tobacco-related examples include restricting smoking to specific isolated areas, and nicotine replacement therapies. Strategies to reduce harm from alcohol have included the use of designated drivers, the "use of plastic bottles to prevent injury, vitamins added to alcoholic beverages to prevent brain damage from long term use, overnight 'bottle check' service in shelters to attract homeless people who otherwise avoid shelters in order to keep their alcohol, and 'wet hostels' where residents have access to drinks but at a strict rate of no more than one drink per hour" (Join Together, n.d.). All of these examples indicate that society is willing to tolerate the use of a certain amount of these substances. In fact, these measures have largely been accepted and supported by the public.

Comparisons between abstinence-oriented and harm reduction services often are made on a mutually exclusive basis. MacMaster (2004) asserts that this is an artificial comparison because the two perspectives can and should be incorporated to provide a more comprehensive continuum of services. However, members of the established, traditional addiction community have considered harm reduction approaches too radical and inappropriate. The result has been a fractioning of the addiction field, and the creation of divisions between segments of the addiction treatment sector, particularly in North America (Watkin, Rowe, & Csiernik, 2003).

Treatment

Alcohol Dependence   Approximately 70 million people suffer from alcohol dependence. Screening and brief interventions can be extremely effective in reducing the use of alcohol and related harms for those who are at high risk of developing alcohol-related problems (Wilk, Jensen, & Havighurst, 1997). This is particularly important because epidemiological research has shown that most alcohol-related problems arise among those who are not significantly dependent upon alcohol. This would include those individuals who drive while intoxicated and engage in other risky behaviors under the influence. It also includes those who are drinking at high risk levels but continue functioning in their daily lives by going to work, maintaining relationships, and living relatively stable lifestyles. According to the World Health Organization (2001), about 25 percent of patients attending primary health care clinics who drink at hazardous levels are dependent on alcohol.

Therapeutic treatment aims to reduce the incidence of alcohol-related morbidity and mortality. Goals of therapy also include the reduction of other social and economic problems related to chronic and excessive alcohol consumption. "Early recognition of problem drinking, early intervention for problem drinking, psychological interventions, treatment of harmful effects of alcohol (including withdrawal and other medical consequences), teaching new coping skills in situations associated with a risk of drinking and relapse, family education, and rehabilitation are the main strategies proven to be effective for the treatment of alcohol-related problems and dependence" (World Health Organization, 1996). Brief interventions by primary care professionals have been demonstrated to be effective in a number of research studies (Wilk, Jensen, & Havighurst, 1997; World Health Organization, 1996). The use of such interventions has effectively reduced alcohol consumption and heavy drinking by up to 30 percent, over periods of 6–12 months or longer. Studies have also demonstrated the cost effectiveness of these interventions (Gomel et al., 1995).

Brief interventions are primarily directed at persons who engage in risky drinking behavior but who are not alcohol dependent. The interventions may be comprised of a variety of activities that are low in intensity and of short duration. They typically consist of three to five sessions of counseling and education. Their primary goal is to prevent the onset of alcohol-related problems. Although the content of these brief interventions varies, most contain instructional and motivational components that directly address the specific behavior of drinking, combined with other components such as feedback from screening, education, skill-building, encouragement, and practical advice. They are not designed or intended to provide intensive psychological analysis or extended treatment techniques (Gomel et al., 1995).

Outpatient and inpatient treatments for patients with more severe alcohol dependence are available and have been shown to be effective. Inpatient treatment is substantially more costly than outpatient treatment (World Health Organization, 2001). Within these settings, several psychological treatments have proved to be equally effective. These include cognitive behavioral treatment, motivational interviewing, and "Twelve Steps" approaches combined with professional treatment. "Community reinforcement approaches, such as that of Alcoholics Anonymous, during and following professional treatment are consistently associated with better outcomes than treatment alone. Therapy for spouses, partners, and family members, or simply their involvement, has benefits for both initiation and maintenance of alcohol treatment" (World Health Organization, 2001).

For most addicted persons, detoxification, the treatment of alcohol withdrawal, is necessary. Detoxification is most effective when it is available within the community. The exception to this is that a community detoxification approach will be less effective for those with a history of delirium tremens, severe dependence, or an unsupportive home environment. It also appears to be less effective for those who have had several previous failed attempts at detoxification (Edwards, Marshall, & Cook, 1997).

Mandatory or coercive treatment does not appear effective for alcohol dependence. Neither civic commitment nor court-ordered treatment has been found to be beneficial (Heather, 1995). The use of medication alone has also been shown to be ineffective. However, a few drugs have been shown to be effective in the treatment for alcohol dependence when they are accompanied by a complementary psychosocial treatment for relapse prevention (National Institute on Drug Abuse, 2000).

Drug Dependence   Drug dependent persons have multiple needs. "They are at risk of HIV and other blood borne pathogens, comorbid physical and mental disorders, problems with multiple psychoactive substances, involvement in criminal activities, and problems with personal relationships, employment, and housing" (World Health Organization, 2001). As a result of these complex needs, services should be multidisciplinary in nature and utilize multiple community resources. Depending on the individual's needs, services may incorporate the use of health, social service, and criminal justice professionals and paraprofessionals as well as community volunteers.

Therapeutic goals for persons who abuse psychoactive substances include the reduction of morbidity and mortality to promote a drug-free life. "Strategies include early diagnosis, identification, and management of risk of infectious diseases as well as other medical and social problems, stabilization, and maintenance with pharmacotherapy (for opioid dependence), counseling, access to services, and opportunities to achieve social integration" (National Institute on Drug Abuse, 2000).

Methadone has long been the medication of choice for treatment of heroin addiction. However, methadone must be administered in a specialized clinic setting and has been shown to have a great potential for misuse and abuse. Buprenorphine, a new medication recently found to be effective for heroin addiction, offers great promise by helping to reduce cravings and withdrawal symptoms. Unlike methadone, it can be prescribed in a primary care setting by primary care professionals and it has low potential for misuse or abuse. The manufacturer of buprenorphine received FDA permission to market buprenorphine and buprenorphine/naloxone in October 2002 as a treatment for addictions to opiates such as heroin or prescription analgesics. However, many barriers still exist for professionals wishing to prescribe the drug. Currently, the reclassification of buprenorphine is under review and consideration by the United Nations Commission on Narcotic Drugs. "The reclassification, if approved, could limit buprenorphine availability and reduce the number of people who can be treated with the drug. Also, many insurance companies have not added buprenorphine to their formularies, and many patients lack insurance coverage. Medical detoxification is generally the first stage of treatment for dependence, however, and by itself does not change long-term drug use. Long-term care needs to be provided, and comorbid psychiatric disorders treated as well, in order to decrease rates of relapse. Most patients require a minimum of three months of treatment to obtain significant improvement" (Join Together, n.d.).

Effective treatment of dependence combines behavioral and counseling components in treatment. These treatment approaches address motivation, problem-solving abilities, coping skills, and difficulties in interpersonal relationships. Substitution pharmacotherapies are particularly useful in conjunction with behavioral and counseling approaches in the treatment of opiate addiction. The use of self-help groups as adjunctive treatments has been found to complement and extend the benefits of those treatments offered by health professionals.

The professional public health community views the injection of illicit drugs as a major public health problem. Sharing of injection equipment is associated with transmission of blood borne pathogens (especially HIV and hepatitis

B and C) and has been responsible for the spread of HIV in many countries. People who inject drugs and who do not enter treatment are up to six times more likely to become infected with HIV than those who enter and remain in treatment. "Treatment services should provide assessment for HIV/AIDS, hepatitis B and C, tuberculosis, and other infectious diseases, and whenever possible, treatment for these conditions and counseling to help patients stop unsafe injecting practices" (National Institute on Drug Abuse, 2000).

The treatment for substance dependence has made great strides. The integration of services and the collaborative nature of "shared community care" have become model best practices. Today, most general practitioners are trained in the identification and treatment of acute episodes of intoxication and withdrawal. They are able to provide brief counseling, referral as well as immunization, HIV testing, cervical screening, and family planning advice. "Drug dependence treatment is cost-effective in reducing drug use (40–60 percent), and the associated health and social consequences, such as HIV infection and criminal activity. The effectiveness of drug dependence treatment is comparable to the success rates for the treatment of other chronic diseases such as diabetes, hypertension, and asthma" (National Institute on Drug Abuse, 2000). In fact, providing treatment for substance dependence is less expensive than prior approaches such as incarceration or not treating substance dependents at all (World Health Organization, 2001).

INTERNATIONAL ORGANIZATIONS ON SUBSTANCE ABUSE

Harm Reduction Coalition (HRC)

The Harm Reduction Coalition is committed to reducing drug-related harm among individuals and communities by initiating and promoting local, regional, and national harm reduction education, interventions, and community organizing. HRC fosters alternative models to conventional health and human services and drug treatment; challenges traditional client–provider relationships; and provides resources, educational materials, and support to health professionals and drug users in their communities to address drug-related harm (for more information see http://www.harmreduction.org).

International Harm Reduction Association

The International Harm Reduction Association works with local, national, regional, and international organizations. It aims to assist individuals and communities in public health advocacy, collaboration and communication, best practices, and education, training, and research. It partners with the International Harm Reduction Development Program, the Drug Policy Alliance, the Joint United Nations Programme on HIV/AIDS, and the Australian Drug Foundation (for more information see http://www.ihra.net).

Box 9.1 | Exemplars from Around the World

Churachandpur, India

Prevention strategies are most effective if information and services are brought actively to drug users, rather than relying on users to take the initiative to seek them out. Community outreach programs greatly increase the coverage of programs designed to promote safer behavior. In the town of Churachandpur in northeast India, a program encouraging abstinence of drug use among drug users was made available through health, religious, and legal reform institutions. But the program could not reach a large enough number of the town's drug users. However, when community street outreach began with a bleach distribution program, participation in the program shot up to 80 percent in six months (UNAIDS, n.d.).

Spain

Spain implemented harm reduction programs after AIDS had become a serious epidemic among intravenous drug users in the country. The country's previous treatment programs, designed using abstinence-only objectives, had proven ineffective. As a result, a Training Program for Trainers that focused on changing the beliefs, attitudes, and behaviors of health care professionals who work with drug users was designed, implemented, and evaluated. Fifty-six public health care professionals in the country were trained. Evaluation indicated that all of the trainers received the necessary personal abilities to implement and deliver the program, and that training and abilities remained over time. The trained professionals implemented AIDS Prevention Programs with 670 intravenous drug users in their respective autonomous communities. Evaluation of these programs demonstrates an increase of safe injection practices and sexual behaviors among the intravenous drug users who participated in the programs (National Institute on Drug Abuse, n.d.).

Argentina

In Argentina, 39 percent of those diagnosed with AIDS acquired the virus through intravenous drug use. In the 1990s, some harm reduction activities oriented to drug users were implemented in the country. Using a community-based outreach approach with poor populations in Buenos Aires, officials implemented seroprevalence studies and focalized preventive campaigns oriented to drug users, their sexual partners, and children. A pilot prevention project geared toward using pharmacies to reach drug users was developed with the participation of 23 pharmacies in Buenos Aires. The focalized campaign oriented to drug users was more effective after cooperative work and agreements between 15 governmental and nongovernmental organizations in the cities of Buenos Aires and Rosario. Nine hundred intravenous drug users were reached with preventive messages in a three-month period. In each location the distribution of preventive material was in the hands of community operators (drug users and ex-drug users) and a technical advisor from each organization. Six hundred opinion surveys on the preventive materials that were distributed helped to evaluate the process. Research activities, community-based interventions, and collaborative work between different organizations made it possible to have more and better contact with the intravenous drug using population in Argentina (Rossi et al., 2001).

Join Together Online

Join Together, founded in 1991, supports community-based efforts to reduce, prevent, and treat substance. They are funded by a grant from the Robert Wood Johnson Foundation to the Boston University School of Public Health (for more information see http://www.jointogether.org).

Box 9.2	**Research Evidence Driving the Future Agenda** Challenges for the Future

- Demand and supply reduction programs have a potentially important role to play in the community response to both legal and illegal drugs provided that: "firstly, the paramount objective is always reducing harm rather than merely reducing consumption; secondly, that supply control is balanced with health and social interventions; and thirdly, that supply control is based on evidence of effectiveness and cost effectiveness. Overall, demand and supply reduction are more important for legal than illegal drugs but harm reduction is a valid response for both legal and illegal drugs" (International Harm Reduction Association, n.d.).

- A recent comparison of cities with high and low HIV prevalence in drug injectors showed that those with success in averting a drug-user epidemic had three features in common. "First, they used community outreach or peer education to reach and educate drug users, including those who would not otherwise receive HIV/AIDS information and skills or participate in treatment and prevention activities. Second, they ensured that drug users had cheap and easy access to sterile syringes through pharmacies or needle-exchange programs. And, they all started their prevention programs early on, before HIV prevalence had risen past a critical point. Mathematical modeling demonstrated that once more than 10 percent of the drug-injecting population is infected with HIV, prevalence almost invariably rises to 40 percent or 50 percent within a few years" (UNAIDS, n.d.).

- Embedding harm reduction activities into comprehensive prevention packages for injecting drug users is critical to their success. This applies in particular to combining safer injection messages with safer sex messages and condom promotion. Comprehensive HIV/AIDS programming should aim to provide opportunities for all injection drug users to access a whole range of harm reduction services. Recognizing the hidden and often rapidly changing nature of drug injecting, reaching as many individuals as possible who inject on a regular or occasional basis represents a particular challenge to harm reduction services and necessitates an in-depth understanding of local drug use patterns and contexts. For this reason, harm reduction programming should be informed by situation assessments. Situation assessments can also act as a catalyst for communities to learn about the necessity of evidence-based approaches to HIV prevention among injecting drug users and to reduce controversy about their introduction (World Health Organization, n.d.).

- Providing injecting drug users with access to information, motivational and skills training, clean injection equipment, and condoms is critical for program success. It is time intensive and requires significant human resources but has proved one of the few effective means of reducing risky behavior among injecting drug users. Health personnel can be trained at low cost to deliver harm reduction messages and skills training. Community-based HIV prevention services for injecting drug users can involve lay personnel if trained appropriately. Particularly promising are peer led approaches to outreach work that rely on the diffusion of safe injection messages into drug using networks. Intervention models designed to organize needle syringe programs through outreach networks have been shown to be particularly useful (World Health Organization, n.d.).

- Harm reduction programs aim to provide their services in close contact to injecting drug users. Often they operate out of community-based centers, and some countries have used existing infrastructure, such as health services or pharmacies. Of particular importance are approaches that reach out to where the drug users are, using vehicles and/or outreach workers. Key supplies required for the success of these programs include information material, condoms, and injection paraphernalia. Programs that reach only a minority of injecting drug users have limited effectiveness. Although they may be successful with those participants they are able to reach, this type of limited approach is not likely to impact significantly the course of the HIV epidemic at the population level. "Appropriate coverage of injecting drug users is an important target for national HIV/AIDS programming, and should include injecting drug users involved in sex work, living in prisons or forming part of ethnic minorities" (World Health Organization, n.d.).

Narconon International

Narconon International is a nonprofit public benefit organization dedicated to eliminating drug abuse and drug addiction through drug prevention, education, and rehabilitation (for more information see http://www. narconon.org).

Sober Recovery

Founded in 2000, Sober Recovery's mission is to be of service to the recovery community by providing the greatest number of resources to as many people as possible (for more information see http://www.soberrecovery.com).

United Nations International Drug Control Programme

The UNDCP is part of the United Nations Office on Drugs and Crime. It aims to limit illicit production, trafficking, and consumption of drugs worldwide. The UNDCP provides information, analysis, and expertise on the drug issue; builds local, national, and global partnerships to address drug issues; strengthens global action against drug production, trafficking, and drug-related crime; promotes efforts to reduce drug abuse, particularly among the young and vulnerable; and educates the world about the dangers of drug abuse (for more information see http://www.unodc.org).

SUMMARY

Drug and alcohol misuse and abuse are global health problems affecting all countries. Differences exist among countries with respect to laws governing drug use and the provision of services to substance abusers. Prevention initiatives directed toward young people and harm reduction strategies for substance abusers appear to be the most effective programs to date. Despite this evidence, many countries, including the United States, are reluctant to promote these services. Pilot programs across the globe point to the importance of incorporating harm reduction strategies in concert with demand and supply reduction strategies.

Thinking About Practice: From Local to Global Perspectives

1. What is the most frequently abused substance in your community/nation?
2. What policies and procedures govern substance abuse treatment in your community/nation and how do they differ from other countries?
3. How might your community/nation profit from the learning experiences of other countries in combating substance abuse?
4. What is the stigma attached to substance abuse in your community and how does it impede successful intervention programs?
5. Compare the stigma attached to substance abuse in your community to that of other countries. How are they similar or different?

Social Work Practice and Social Justice Website

Please go to the Book Companion Website at http://www.thomsonedu.com/author/sowers to find a rich collection of related articles selected by the authors from Info Trac College Edition.

References

American Medical Association. (June, 1997). *Reduction of the medical and public health consequences of drug abuse* (Report 8 of the Council on Scientific Affairs A-97). Retrieved July 14, 2004, from http://www.ama-assn.org/ama/pub/article/2036-2521.html

Bowles, J. R. (1995). Suicide in Western Samoa: An example of a suicide prevention program in a developing country. In R. F. W. Diekstra, W. Gulbinat, I. Kienhorst, & D. De Leo, *Preventive strategies on suicide* (pp. 173–206). Leiden, The Netherlands: Brill.

Clapp, J., & Burke, A. (1999). Discriminate analysis of factors differentiating among substance abuse treatment units in their provision of HIV/AIDS harm reduction services. *Social Work Research, 23*, 69–76.

Cohen, P. (1994, March 7–11). *The case of two Dutch drug policy commissions: An exercise in harm reduction 1968–1976.* Paper presented at the Fifth International Conference on the Reduction of Drug-Related Harm, Addiction Research Foundation, Toronto.

DanceSafe. (n.d.). *Promoting health and safety within the rave and nightclub community.* Retrieved July 17, 2004, from http://www.dancesafe.org

Des Jarlais, D. (1995). Harm reduction: A framework for incorporating science into drug policy. *American Journal of Public Health, 85*, 10–12.

Drucker, E. (1995). Harm reduction: A public health strategy. *Current Issues in Public Health, 1*, 64–70.

Edwards, G., Marshall, E. J., & Cook, C. C. H (Eds.). (1997). *The treatment of drinking problems: A guide to helping professions* (3rd ed). Cambridge, UK: Cambridge University Press.

European Monitoring Centre for Drugs and Drug Addiction. (n.d.). Retrieved July 17, 2004, from http://www.emcdda.eu.int

Gomel, M. K., Wutzke, S. E., Hardcastle, D. M., Lapsley, H., & Reznik, R. B. (1995). Cost-effectiveness of strategies to market and train primary healthcare physicians in brief intervention techniques for hazardous alcohol use. *Social Science and Medicine, 47*, 203–211.

Harm Reduction Coalition. (1996). *Mission and principles of harm reduction.* Oakland, CA: Author.

Heather, N. (1995). *Treatment approaches to alcohol problems: European Alcohol Action Plan.* WHO Regional Publications, European Series, No. 65. Copenhagen: World Health Organization.

Hohman, M., & Clapp, J. D. (1999). *An assessment of publicly funded alcohol and other drug treatment programs in California, 1992–1998* (Report prepared for the Senate Office of Research). Sacramento: Senate Office of Research.

Hohman, M., Oliver, R., & Wright, W. (2004). Methamphetamine abuse and manufacture: The child welfare response. *Social Work, 49*(3), 373–381.

Human Rights Watch. (n.d.). *Not enough graves: The war on drugs, HIV/AIDS, and violations of human rights in Thailand.* Retrieved July 14, 2004, from http://www.hrw.org/campaigns/aids/2004/thai.htm

International Harm Reduction Association. (n.d.). *What is harm reduction?* Retrieved July 15, 2004, from http://www.ihra.net/index.php?option=articles&Itemid=3&topid=0&Itemid=3

Jansen, M. A., Glynn, T., & Howard, J. (1996). Prevention of alcohol, tobacco, and other drug abuse. *American Behavioral Scientist, 39*, 790–807.

Join Together. (n.d.). *Harm Reduction.* Retrieved July 17, 2004, from http://www.jointogether.org/sa/issues/hot_issues/harmreduction

Leon, D. A., & Shkolnikov, V. M. (1998). Social stress and the Russian mortality crisis. *Journal of* the *American Medical Association, 279*(10), 790–791.

MacMaster, S. (2004). Harm reduction: A new perspective on substance abuse services. *Social Work, 49*(3), 356–363.

National Institute on Drug Abuse. (n.d.). *Epidemiologic trends in drug abuse.* Retrieved July 14, 2004, from http://www.drugabuse.gov/CEWG/AdvancedRep/699ADV/699adv.html

National Institute on Drug Abuse. (1997). *Preventing drug use among children and adolescents: A research-based guide* (NIH Publication No. 97-4212). Washington, DC: U.S. Government Printing Office.

National Institute on Drug Abuse. (2000). *Principles of drug addiction treatment: A research-based guide.* (NIH Publication No. 00-4180). Bethesda, MD: Author.

National Institute on Drug Abuse. (2003). *Preventing drug use among children and adolescents: A research-based guide for parents, educators, and community leaders* (2nd ed.). (NIH Publication No. 04-4212B). Washington, DC: U.S. Government Printing Office.

Notzon, F. C., Komarov, Y. M., Ermakov, S. P., Sempos, C. T., Marks, J. S., & Sempos, E. V. (1998). Causes of declining life expectancy in Russia. *Journal of the American Medical Association, 297*(10), 793–800.

Open Society Institute. (July, 2004). *Thailand: New report documents abuses in drug war.* Retrieved July 14, 2004, from http://www.soros.org/initiatives/ihrd/news/thai_20040709

Perry, C. L., & Kelder, S. H. (1992). Models of effective prevention. *Journal of Adolescent Health, 13*, 355–363.

Reback, C. J., & Grella, C. (1999). HIV risk behaviors of gay and bisexual male methamphetamine users contacted through street outreach. *Journal of Drug Issues, 29*, 155–166.

Rossi, D., Cymerman, P., Erenu, N., Faraone, S., Goltzman, P. Rojas, E., Touze, G., & Vazquez, S. (2001). Rapid assessment and response in IDUs in Buenos Aires. *2000 global research network meeting on HIV prevention in drug using populations* (pp. 42–45). Washington, DC: National Institute on Drug Abuse.

Rowe, W., & Marcotte, G. (1998). The challenge of risk reduction practices. In W. Rowe & B. Ryan (Eds.), *Social work and HIV: The Canadian experience.* Ontario: Oxford University Press.

Scavuzzo, M. (1996). *Harm reduction: A work in progress.* Minneapolis: Safe Works AIDS Project.

Springer, E. (1991). Effective AIDS prevention with active drug users: The harm reduction model. *Journal of Chemical Dependency Treatment, 4*, 141–157.

UNAIDS. (n.d.). *Report on the global HIV/AIDS epidemic June 1998: Preventing sexual transmission of HIV among young people.* Retrieved July 16, 2004, from http://www.who.int/emchiv/global_report/rep_html/report5.html

United Nations. (2002). *Lessons learned in drug abuse prevention: A global review.* New York: Author.

United Nations Development Programme. (n.d.). *The international AIDS Programme.* Retrieved July 18, 2004, from http://www.undp.org

United Nations International Drug Control Programme. (n.d.). Retrieved July 15, 2004, from http://www.unidcp.un.org

United Nations International Drug Control Programme. (1997). *World drug report.* New York: Oxford University Press.

Van Laar, M., de Zwart, W., & Mensinck, C. (1996). *Netherlands alcohol and drug report (4): Addiction care and assistance.* Utrecht, The Netherlands: Trimbos Institute.

Vroublevsky, A., & Harwin, J. (1998). Russia. In M. Grant (Ed.), *Alcohol and emerging markets: Patterns, problems and responses* (pp. 203–223). Philadelphia: Brunner Mazel.

Wallack, L., & Corbett, K. (1990). Illicit drug, tobacco, and alcohol use among youth: Trends and promising approaches in prevention. In H. Resnick, S. E. Gardner, R. P. Lorian, & C. E. Marcus (Eds.), *Youth and drugs: Society's mixed messages* (OSAP-Prevention Monograph No. 6, DHHS Publication No. 90-1689, pp. 5–29). Washington, DC: U.S. Government Printing Office.

Watkin, J., Rowe, W. S., & Csiernik, R. (2003). Prevention as controversy: Harm reduction approaches. In R. Csiernik & W. S. Rowe (Eds.), *Responding to the oppression of addiction: Canadian social work perspectives.* Toronto: Canadian Scholars Press.

Wilk, A. I., Jensen, N. M., & Havighurst, T. C. (1997). Meta-analysis of randomized control trials addressing brief interventions in heavy alcohol drinkers. *Journal of General Internal Medicine, 12,* 274–283.

World Health Organization. (n.d.) *Harm reduction approaches to injecting drug use.* Retrieved July 15, 2004, from http://who.int/hiv/topics/harm/reduction/en

World Health Organization. (1996). WHO Brief Intervention Study Group: A cross-national trial of brief interventions with heavy drinkers. *American Journal of Public Health, 86,* 948–955.

World Health Organization. (2001). *The world health report 2001—Mental health: New understandings, new hope.* Retrieved July 18, 2004, from http://www.who.int/whr2001

It was once said that the moral test of Government is how that Government treats those who are in the dawn of life, the children; those who are in the twilight of life, the elderly; and those who are in the shadows of life, the sick, the needy, and the handicapped.

Hubert H. Humphrey

Developmental/Physical Disability

CHAPTER **10**

© The Thomson Corporation/Heinle Image Resource Bank

CONTRASTING DEFINITIONS OF DISABILITY AROUND THE WORLD

People with disabilities live in every country of the world. Whether directly or indirectly, disability is something that every social worker will encounter during his or her career. Because the term "disability" is broadly defined, it is useful to explore the ways in which disability is conceptualized around the world.

As a basis, the *Declaration on the Rights of Disabled Persons* (see Appendix 1), a UN document produced by the Office of the High Commissioner for Human Rights, states: "The term 'disabled person' means any person unable to ensure by himself or herself, wholly or partly, the necessities of a normal individual and/or social life, as a result of deficiency, either congenital or not, in his or her physical or mental capabilities" (United Nations, 1975).

Each country views disability in a slightly different way. While some countries focus equally on mental and physical disabilities, other countries focus almost exclusively on the physiological functioning of an individual, with specific reference to organs, limbs, and audio-visual capabilities. Interestingly, the wording of many of the definitions may provide clues as to how people with disabilities are treated in their countries. For example, one definition states that people with disabilities are unable to do things that "normal people" can do. Another interesting point to consider is that every definition naturally focuses on the things that people with disabilities *cannot* do. While this may be the only way to define disability, it nonetheless makes it inherently difficult to employ a strengths perspective when dealing with disability.

United States

In the United States, disability is defined by the Americans with Disabilities Act (ADA) of 1990 as: 1) a physical or mental impairment that substantially limits one or more of the major life activities of the individual; 2) a record of such impairment; or 3) being regarded as having such an impairment (U.S. Department of Justice, 1990).

China

According to the *Law of the People's Republic of China on the Protection of Disabled Persons* of 1990, a disabled person is a person who suffers from abnormalities or loss of a certain organ of function, psychologically or physiologically, or in anatomical structure and has lost wholly or in part the ability to perform an activity in the way considered normal. The term "disabled persons" refers to those with visual, hearing, speech or physical disabilities, intellectual disability, mental disorder, multiple disabilities, and/or other disabilities (Law of the People's Republic of China on the Protection of Disabled Persons, 1990).

Fiji

The *Fiji National Council for Disabled Persons Act* of 1994 states that disabled persons means persons, who as a result of physical, mental, or sensory impairment are restricted or lacking in ability to perform an activity in the manner considered normal for human beings (Equal Opportunities Commission Hong Kong, 1999).

Belgium

In Belgium people with disabilities are considered those "with a significant limitation in their chances of social and vocation integration due to a deficiency or the definition of need" and conceptualized as "an alternation of mental, sensory or physical faculties which require social intervention" (Equal Opportunities Commission Hong Kong, 1999). The degree of disability, in Belgium, is usually determined on the basis of a multidisciplinary assessment.

Portugal

In Portugal, a disabled person is considered as any individual who, because of limited physical or mental capacity, encounters difficulty in obtaining or holding a job suited to his or her age, qualifications, and professional experience (Equal Opportunities Commission Hong Kong, 1999).

United Kingdom

The Disability Discrimination Act 1995 defines a disabled person as someone with a physical or mental impairment, which has a substantial and long-term adverse effect on his ability to carry out normal day-to-day activities (United Kingdom Government, 1995).

South Africa

According to the Employment Equity Act in South Africa, a disability is a long-term or recurring physical or mental impairment that substantially limits the employee's prospects of entry into, or advancement in, employment (South Africa Department of Labour, 1998).

DEMOGRAPHIC CONSIDERATIONS

Considering disability demographics is important, precisely because there are so many different definitions of disability around the world. If, for example, a country does not recognize mental disorders as disabilities, then its official total number of disabled persons may be lower than a country that does recognize mental disorders as disabilities. This possible dilemma is summarized in the following statement:

> The variety of definitions of disability used by countries for policy purposes is matched by the variety of definitions used for data gathering. If there is agreement that outcomes can be defined in the same way for persons with disabilities as for the entire population, a problem remains as to how the population with disabilities is to be defined for statistical purposes (Equal Opportunities Commission Hong Kong, 1999).

United States

The U.S. Census from 2000 counted 49.7 million people with some type of long lasting condition or disability. They represented 19.3 percent of the 257.2 million people who were aged five and older in the civilian non-institutionalized population—or nearly one person in five (U.S. Census Bureau, 2000). Consider some of the other statistics from the 2000 U.S. Census:

- 9.3 million (3.6 percent) with a sensory disability involving sight or hearing
- 21.2 million (8.2 percent) with a condition limiting basic physical activities, such as walking, climbing stairs, reaching, lifting, or carrying
- 12.4 million (4.8 percent) with a physical, mental, or emotional condition causing difficulty in learning, remembering, or concentrating
- 6.8 million (2.6 percent) with a physical, mental, or emotional condition causing difficulty in dressing, bathing, or getting around inside the home
- 18.2 million of those aged 16 and older with a condition that made it difficult to go outside the home to shop or visit a doctor (8.6 percent of the 212.0 million people this age)
- 21.3 million of those aged 16 to 64 with a condition that affected their ability to work at a job or business (11.9 percent of the 178.7 million people this age)

Canada

According to Statistics Canada 2001, one out of every eight Canadians—an estimated 3.6 million people of all ages, including children—reported some level of disability in 2001. Approximately 10 percent (2 million) of working-age adult Canadians (15 to 64) live with a disability. The three most common types of self reported disabilities were mobility, pain, and agility (Statistics Canada, 2001).

FUNCTIONAL AREAS OF PRACTICE

Work

In many countries, the rights of the disabled have become a major concern in the workplace. As mentioned earlier, viewing disability from a strengths perspective is crucial. This becomes quite evident when discussing disability in the workplace. Employers who view their disabled employees in terms of what they *cannot* do risk the possibility of marginalizing their disabled workforce. According to the South African Department of Labour, people with disabilities can demonstrate their ability and contribute equally alongside fellow workers if enterprises remove unfair discriminatory barriers to their employment and make reasonable accommodation for their needs (South African Department of Labour, 1998).

Today, government legislation and company policies often mandate fair hiring practices and reasonable accommodations for people with disabilities. In 2004, three-quarters of Scotland's businesses were facing possible fines when new disability laws, mandating workplace accessibility and employee training, were being instituted (Qureshi, 2004).

In the United States, the 1990 Americans with Disabilities Act (ADA) stipulates that employers with 15 or more employees must make reasonable accommodations for employees with disabilities (U.S. Department of Labor, 2004). Reasonable accommodations are the tools provided by employers to enable employees with disabilities to do their jobs, just as the employer provides the means for all employees to accomplish their jobs (U.S. Department of Labor, 2004).

Mobility

Many of those who do not have a disability are unaware of how difficult it might be for certain people with disabilities to negotiate the world in which we live. For example, going to the local grocery store or taking public transportation might be impossible for people with disabilities in certain localities.

Mobility was originally defined in terms of the individual's ability to move about easily and effectively in the surroundings. Certain aspects of the original scale are useful in evaluating the extent of an individual's travel. Thus, mobility can refer to the access of the individual to his or her surroundings (World Enable, 1999).

According to the Canadian Labour Congress, people with disabilities must be able to access housing, transportation, information, education and training opportunities, and support services, in order to be at work. People with disabilities are not able to participate in the workplace if they are excluded from full participation in community life (Canadian Labour Congress, 2004). This demonstrates one way in which a country can attempt to view disability from a person-in-environment perspective.

It is important to note that the ease of mobility within a country is not necessarily proportionate to its level of development or economic strength. Consider the following author's experience:

> The surprise about working in the Middle East was just how much easier it was in so many ways than living in America. In America access is always about architecture and never about human beings. Among Israelis and Palestinians, access was

rarely about anything but people. While in the U.S. a wheelchair stands out as an explicitly separate experience from the mainstream, in the Israeli and Arab worlds it is just another thing that can go wrong in a place where things go wrong all the time (Hockenberry, 1995).

Self-Care

The ability to care for oneself is often taken for granted. Many people with disabilities are unable to care for themselves and require assistance. At the same time, many people with disabilities do have the ability to take care of themselves, and others for that matter!

In 1997, the World Health Organization (WHO) defined self-care as what people do for themselves to establish and maintain health, and to prevent and deal with disease. WHO characterizes self-care broadly to encompass general and personal hygiene; lifestyle related to nutrition and physical activity; social habits and cultural beliefs; and self-medication (Shirreffs, n.d.).

An important controversy within the self-care field must be touched upon here. This controversy concerns a debate over two paradigms: the rehabilitation paradigm and the independent living paradigm. To gain an understanding of this controversy, consider the following independent living perspective:

> Since most traditional rehabilitation programs are built upon the "medical model" of service delivery, the disability rights and independent living movement promotes a completely different approach to service delivery. Independent living as a movement is quite unique compared to existing programs and facilities serving people with disabilities. Centers for independent living across the [U.S.] nation are working towards changing their communities rather than "fixing" the person with a disability (Community Resources for Independence, 2002).

This quote supports the notion that we are potentially in the early stages of a major paradigm shift, one in which we are moving from the rehabilitation model to the independent living model. While the rehabilitation paradigm focuses on the limitations and ineptness of people with disabilities, the independent living paradigm focuses on the strengths of this population. Social workers are strongly encouraged to view disability from this strengths perspective.

INTERNATIONAL ORGANIZATIONS ON DISABILITIES
World Institute on Disability

The World Institute on Disability (WID) is a nonprofit research, public policy, and advocacy center dedicated to promoting the civil rights and full societal inclusion of people with disabilities. WID's work focuses on four areas: employment and economic development; accessible health care and personal assistance services; inclusive technology design; and international disability and development.

| **Box 10.1** | **Exemplars from Around the World** |

Canada

The Canadian Labour Congress (CLC) has created a manual called *The MORE We Get Together: Disability Rights and Collective Bargaining Manual.* According to the CLC:

> The manual is a tool for union organizers and negotiators, disabled activists and their organizations, individuals with disabilities and their allies to advance issues of people with disabilities. It provides union and community activists working with people with disabilities, a comprehensive review of disability rights and collective bargaining provisions that impact on conditions of workers with disabilities (Canadian Labour Congress, 2001).

Malawi (Africa)

The disability movement in Malawi is still in its infancy because formal organizations have only recently been created. However, the movement is strong because of an umbrella organization called the Federation of Disability Organizations in Malawi (FEDOMA). Organizations within FEDOMA include one organization of the blind, one of the deaf, one of the physically disabled, and a cross-disability organization to facilitate the participation of people with disability in sport. There are also organizations of normally under-represented groups, such as people with albinism, and an organization of women with disability. The movement in Malawi is causing a paradigm shift, from perceiving disability as a charity and philanthropic issue to approaching disability from a human rights and development perspective (Danish Council of Organizations of Disabled People, n.d.).

Namibia (Africa)

In 2003, the National Federation of People with Disabilities of Namibia launched the Awareness Building Campaign. This campaign, targeting politicians, community leaders, local authorities, regional councilors, and disabled people, has focused on the rights of people with disabilities (Tjaronda, 2004).

Bangladesh

In Bangladesh an NGO called Sabalamby Unnayan Samity (Society for Self-Reliance) treats and rehabilitates disabled people. Its goal is to create confidence among the disabled, remove superstitions and wrong ideas about disability, create awareness about their rights in the society, and to make them self-reliant by providing training in different vocations and granting them loans (Alam, 2004).

India

A group called Mobility India in Bangalore holds an annual, year-long training program that offers an opportunity for trainees from many different countries to encounter up-to-date technologies for prosthetics and orthotics. The program's courses focus on primary health care, self-development and communication skills, counseling, biomechanics, documentation and organization, computer applications, human anatomy, workshop management, and materials and applied rehabilitation in prosthetics, orthotics, or community therapy. Training is completed by field placements with Mobility India's local partners in Bangalore and India abroad (Disability World, 2004).

WID serves as a center for the global exchange of information and expertise on disability and disability policy. WID's global activities include training, technical assistance, program development and evaluation, legislative and policy development, exchange programs, research, conferences, materials development and global resource, and referral. WID is committed to aiding disability organizations throughout the world to create networks, programs, and services that promote the full inclusion of disabled people in their societies (for more information see http://www.wid.org).

Box 10.2 | **Research Evidence Driving the Future Agenda**
Challenges for the Future

Defining Disability

One major challenge for the future is attaining a universally recognized definition or conceptualization of disability. A universally recognized definition would have several advantages, including the maintenance of accurate and comparable statistics from country to country, the increased ability for countries to work together to combat various disabilities, and the decreased likelihood that a person with a disability will face a stigma when traveling internationally.

It is important to note that attaining a universally recognized conceptualization of disability may be difficult due to the myriad of cultural and religious views that abound throughout the world.

Standardizing the Method for Gathering Statistics

Another challenge, one that is fundamentally attached to the notion of attaining a universal definition of disability, is the goal of implementing a standard global method for gathering statistics. By having every country gather the same statistics, it would facilitate our ability to accurately compare the level of disability from one country to the next.

Overcoming Stigmatization

Overcoming stigmatization is one of the most important challenges we have to face. Elimination of stigmas would provide people with disabilities a sense of freedom and would improve the general population's ability to see people for who they are. It is paramount that we battle ignorant and mistaken beliefs about people with disabilities.

Furthermore, overcoming stigmatization would allow governments and organizations to implement better policies and programs geared toward people with disabilities and would increase the likelihood of gathering accurate and comprehensive statistics.

Focusing on Strengths and Empowerment

A key challenge, especially for social workers, is the need to focus on the strengths of people with disabilities as opposed to focusing on the things they are unable to do. It is imperative to understand that people with disabilities do not have "problems," and that understanding is more important than charity or sympathy. Furthermore, the notion of empowerment will hopefully transfer into the governmental and organizational policies and programs.

Improving Mobility

Unfortunately, there may be a possible correlation between a country's (or company's) understanding of disability and the level of mobility afforded to its citizens (or employees) with disabilities. Mobility needs to be viewed from the perspective of an individual who is disabled and has difficulty accessing points such as doors, stairs, and workplace washrooms. For some countries, improving mobility options for the physically disabled will prove to be a major challenge. For example, they may have poor infrastructures and transportation systems that make it difficult to implement proper accommodations.

Segregated Versus Mainstreamed Programs

Another challenge, one that brings about much controversy, is the debate over segregated and mainstreamed programs. How schools should teach children with learning disabilities provides a perfect example. On the one hand, some people advocate for segregated programs that allow for learning-disabled students to receive more personalized attention, thereby increasing their likelihood of success. On the other hand, some people argue that it is necessary to include children with disabilities in the mainstream classroom, in order to reduce stigmatization and ensure continuity of learning. This particular example is appropriate because in many countries around the world children with certain disabilities do not even attend school, due to lack of accommodation and stigmatization. It is easy to see why this may be an ongoing debate.

Rehabilitation International

Rehabilitation International is a worldwide network of people with disabilities, service providers, and government agencies working together to improve the quality of life for disabled people and their families. Founded in 1922, it now has more than 200 member organizations in 90 nations.

It develops and promotes initiatives to protect the rights of people with disabilities, to improve rehabilitation and other crucial services for disabled people and their families, and to increase global collaboration towards these objectives (for more information see http://www.rehab-international.org).

Action on Disability and Development

ADD is an international development agency that supports organizations of disabled people in their campaign for the rightful inclusion of disabled adults and children in society. The agency was established in 1985 in recognition of the fact that disabled people, especially disabled women and children, are among the poorest, most disadvantaged, and socially excluded citizens (particularly in developing countries), and are often excluded from development assistance. ADD's vision is of a world where all disabled people are able to enjoy their rights, fulfill their responsibilities and obligations, and participate as fully as they choose at every level of society (for more information see http://www.add.org.uk).

TASH

TASH is an international association of people with disabilities, their family members, other advocates, and professionals fighting for a society in which inclusion of all people in all aspects of society is the norm. (The organization goes by its now well-known acronym, rather than its former name of The Association for the Severely Handicapped.) TASH is an organization of members concerned with human dignity, civil rights, education, and independence for all individuals with disabilities. It has more than 30 chapters and members hail from 34 countries and territories.

TASH believes that no one with a disability should be forced to live, work, or learn in a segregated setting, and that all individuals deserve the right to direct their own lives. TASH's mission is to eliminate physical and social obstacles that prevent equity, diversity, and quality of life. TASH's successes include legislative victories, landmark court cases, a commitment to progressive scientific inquiry, dissemination of best practice information, and the encouragement of positive portrayals in the media of people with disabilities (for more information see http://www.tash.org).

Inclusion International

Inclusion International is a global federation of family-based organizations advocating for the human rights of people with intellectual disabilities. It represents over 115 member federations in 200 countries throughout five regions—Middle East and North Africa, Europe, Africa and the Indian Ocean, the Americas, and Asia Pacific.

For more than 40 years Inclusion International has acted as a vehicle for the voices of people with disabilities and their families. The inclusion of people with disabilities into their communities, as valued neighbors and citizens, is a priority for Inclusion International and its membership. This federation is one of the largest global disability nongovernmental organizations and one of only five disability-related organizations to be officially recognized by the United Nations (for more information see http://www.inclusion-international.org).

Disability.dk

Disability.dk is a website that contains information on disability in developing countries to support NGOs, governments, and others working in the field. The site functions as a dynamic library where the newest documents and most relevant information are added. It also lists country-specific information on international organizations and donor agencies (for more information see http://www.disability.dk).

SUMMARY

Disability is a global issue that impacts every country in the world. Unfortunately, each of the world's countries seems to have its own concept of disability. While some countries focus on both physical and mental disability, other countries appear to focus entirely on physical disability. These varying conceptualizations can have a negative impact on our ability to compare the prevalence of disability from one country to another.

Disability in the workplace is an important issue for everyone. The last two decades have brought about a number of important policies and laws, in the United States and elsewhere, that protect the rights of people with disabilities. In many cases, these laws and policies have explicitly mandated that employers make reasonable accommodations when necessary. Also, it is particularly important for employers to use a strengths perspective when considering its workforce.

Other disability-related issues important for social workers are mobility and self-care, because they are closely related to the strengths perspective and to the notion of viewing clients in the context of their larger environments.

Countries around the world are enacting change in various ways. Some countries are focused on workforce issues, whereas others are focused on mobility issues. Nevertheless, some countries are in the earliest stages of organizing people and bringing attention to the need for disability rights. Other countries are advancing to the point of training people to work globally.

The future agenda is concerned with the following issues:

- defining disability on a global level;
- developing a standardized way of gathering statistics;

- overcoming the stigmatization of disability;
- focusing on a strengths perspective; and
- improving mobility.

Amongst the international organizations that focus on disability, common focal points include civil rights, education, self-sufficiency, and inclusion. These groups highlight the importance of achieving global cooperation on the disability front.

Thinking About Practice: From Local to Global Perspectives

1. How would a universal definition of disability affect the way disability statistics are gathered?
2. What is reasonable accommodation?
3. What is the United Nations' definition of disability? Do you think this definition is sufficient? Explain.
4. Discuss the difference between the "rehabilitation model" and the "independent living model." Which model do you most agree with? Explain.
5. What are the advantages and disadvantages of segregated and mainstreamed programs in the school system? Which approach do you favor and why?

Social Work Practice and Social Justice Website

Please go to the Book Companion Website at http://www.thomsonedu.com/author/sowers to find a rich collection of related articles selected by the authors from Info Trac College Edition.

References

Alam, J. (2004, April 22). *Challenging the disability: 116 cured, rehabilitated last year by a local NGO.* Retrieved April 12, 2005, from http://www. thedailystar.net/2004/04/22/d40422070375.htm

Canadian Labour Congress. (2004). *The MORE we get together.* Retrieved April 15, 2005, from http://www.clc-ctc.ca

Community Resources for Independence. (2002). *Independent living movement.* Retrieved April 14, 2005, from http://www.crinet.org/ilm.php

Danish Council of Organizations of Disabled People (n.d.). *Malawi section.* Retrieved April 10, 2005, from http://www.disability.dk

Disability World. (2004). *Prosthetics/orthotics training course to be held in India.* Retrieved April 12, 2005, from http://www.disabilityworld.org/04-05_04/news/oandpcourse.shtml

Equal Opportunities Commission Hong Kong. (1999). *Interregional seminar and symposium on international norms and standards relating to disability: Definitions of disability,* Retrieved April 10, 2005, from http://www.worldenable.net/hongkong99/hkreport9900.htm

Hockenberry, J. (1995). *Moving violations: War zones, wheelchairs, and declarations of independence.* New York: Hyperion Books.

Law of the People's Republic of China on the Protection of Disabled Persons. (1990). Retrieved April 11, 2005, from http://www.dredf.org/international/china.html

Qureshi, Y. (2004, July 25). *Firms 'oblivious' to fines risk.* Retrieved April 12, 2005, from http://scotlandonsunday.scotsman.com/politics.cfm?id=850722004

Shirreffs, M. (n.d.). *Defining self-care.* http://www.ilsina.org/index.cfm?pubentityid=147

South African Department of Labour. (1998). *Employment equity act NO. 55, of 1998: Code of good practice on key aspects of disability in the workplace.* Retrieved April 11, 2005, from http://www.labour.gov.za/docs/legislation/eea/codegoodpractise.htm

Statistics Canada. (2001). *Prevalence of disability in Canada.* Retrieved April 15, 2005, from http://www.statcan.ca

Tjaronda, W. (2004, July 23). *New campaign to raise awareness on disability.* Retrieved April 8, 2005, from http://allafrica.com/stories/200407230152.html

United Kingdom Government. (1995). *Disability Discrimination Act 1995*. Retrieved April 8, 2005, from http://www.legislation.hmso.gov.uk/acts/acts1995/1995050.htm

United Nations. (1975). *Declaration of the rights of disabled persons*. Retrieved April 7, 2005, from http://www.ohchr.org/english/law/res3447.htm

U.S. Census Bureau. (2000). *Disability status: 2000*. Retrieved April 11, 2005, from http://www.census.gov/prod/2003pubs/c2kbr-17.pdf

U.S. Department of Justice. (1990). *Americans with Disability Act*. Retrieved April 10, 2005, from http://www.usdoj.gov/crt/ada/adahom1.htm

U.S. Department of Labor. (2004). *Workplace accommodation process*. Retrieved April 8, 2005, from http://www.dol.gov/odep/pubs/ek97/process.htm

World Enable. (1999). *Interregional seminar and symposium on international norms and standards relating to disability: Definitions of disability*. Retrieved April 7, 2005, from http://www.worldenable.net/hongkong99/hkreport9907.htm

APPENDIX 1

Declaration on the Rights of Disabled Persons
Proclaimed by General Assembly Resolution 3447 (XXX)
of 9 December 1975

The General Assembly,

Mindful of the pledge made by Member States, under the Charter of the United Nations to take joint and separate action in co-operation with the Organization to promote higher standards of living, full employment and conditions of economic and social progress and development,

Reaffirming its faith in human rights and fundamental freedoms and in the principles of peace, of the dignity and worth of the human person and of social justice proclaimed in the Charter,

Recalling the principles of the Universal Declaration of Human Rights, the International Covenants on Human Rights, the Declaration of the Rights of the Child and the Declaration on the Rights of Mentally Retarded Persons, as well as the standards already set for social progress in the constitutions, conventions, recommendations and resolutions of the International Labour Organisation, the United Nations Educational, Scientific and Cultural Organization, the World Health Organization, the United Nations Children's Fund and other organizations concerned,

Recalling also Economic and Social Council resolution 1921 (LVIII) of 6 May 1975 on the prevention of disability and the rehabilitation of disabled persons,

Emphasizing that the Declaration on Social Progress and Development has proclaimed the necessity of protecting the rights and assuring the welfare and rehabilitation of the physically and mentally disadvantaged,

Bearing in mind the necessity of preventing physical and mental disabilities and of assisting disabled persons to develop their abilities in the most varied fields of activities and of promoting their integration as far as possible in normal life,

Aware that certain countries, at their present stage of development, can devote only limited efforts to this end,

Proclaims this Declaration on the Rights of Disabled Persons and calls for national and international action to ensure that it will be used as a common basis and frame of reference for the protection of these rights:

1. The term "disabled person" means any person unable to ensure by himself or herself, wholly or partly, the necessities of a normal individual and/or social life, as a result of deficiency, either congenital or not, in his or her physical or mental capabilities.

2. Disabled persons shall enjoy all the rights set forth in this Declaration. These rights shall be granted to all disabled persons without any exception

whatsoever and without distinction or discrimination on the basis of race, colour, sex, language, religion, political or other opinions, national or social origin, state of wealth, birth or any other situation applying either to the disabled person himself or herself or to his or her family.

3. Disabled persons have the inherent right to respect for their human dignity. Disabled persons, whatever the origin, nature and seriousness of their handicaps and disabilities, have the same fundamental rights as their fellow-citizens of the same age, which implies first and foremost the right to enjoy a decent life, as normal and full as possible.

4. Disabled persons have the same civil and political rights as other human beings; paragraph 7 of the Declaration on the Rights of Mentally Retarded Persons applies to any possible limitation or suppression of those rights for mentally disabled persons.

5. Disabled persons are entitled to the measures designed to enable them to become as self-reliant as possible.

6. Disabled persons have the right to medical, psychological and functional treatment, including prosthetic and orthotic appliances, to medical and social rehabilitation, education, vocational training and rehabilitation, aid, counselling, placement services and other services which will enable them to develop their capabilities and skills to the maximum and will hasten the processes of their social integration or reintegration.

7. Disabled persons have the right to economic and social security and to a decent level of living. They have the right, according to their capabilities, to secure and retain employment or to engage in a useful, productive and remunerative occupation and to join trade unions.

8. Disabled persons are entitled to have their special needs taken into consideration at all stages of economic and social planning.

9. Disabled persons have the right to live with their families or with foster parents and to participate in all social, creative or recreational activities. No disabled person shall be subjected, as far as his or her residence is concerned, to differential treatment other than that required by his or her condition or by the improvement which he or she may derive therefrom. If the stay of a disabled person in a specialized establishment is indispensable, the environment and living conditions therein shall be as close as possible to those of the normal life of a person of his or her age.

10. Disabled persons shall be protected against all exploitation, all regulations and all treatment of a discriminatory, abusive or degrading nature.

11. Disabled persons shall be able to avail themselves of qualified legal aid when such aid proves indispensable for the protection of their persons and property. If judicial proceedings are instituted against them, the legal procedure applied shall take their physical and mental condition fully into account.

12. Organizations of disabled persons may be usefully consulted in all matters regarding the rights of disabled persons.

13. Disabled persons, their families and communities shall be fully informed, by all appropriate means, of the rights contained in this Declaration.

A wise man should consider that health is the greatest of human blessings, and learn how by his own thought to derive benefit from his illnesses.

Hippocrates

Health

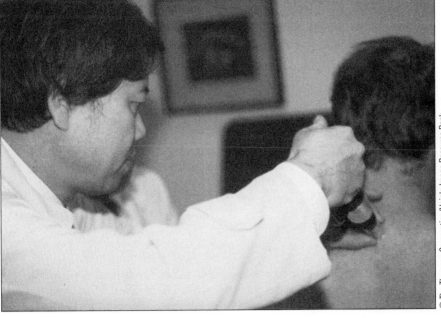

CHAPTER 11

© The Thomson Corporation/Heinle Image Resource Bank

According to the World Health Organization, health is a state of complete physical, mental, and social well-being and not merely the absence of disease or infirmity (World Health Organization, 1946). Health, of course, is an issue that concerns every person and every country of the world. Whether it's polio in Nigeria, dengue fever in China, or diphtheria in Afghanistan, health concerns will perennially plague the human experience. Consider the following statement from the World Health Organization (2003a):

> Achieving national and global health objectives requires new resources and unprecedented levels of cooperation among multilateral agencies, national authorities, communities, the private sector and other stakeholders. Such a mobilization must be based on rigorous science, but also on a clear ethical vision. . . . As globalization accelerates, the interdependence of nations is perceived clearly. Treating others justly is now both a moral imperative and an aspect of wise security policy.

MEANINGS OF HEALTH AROUND THE WORLD

United States

The United States has adopted the World Health Organization's definition of health to include one's physical, mental, and social well-being. Of these three aspects of health, social well-being presents the most difficult conceptual issues because it encompasses so many facets. Despite the fact that adequate health care is a human right established by the United Nations Universal Declaration of Human Rights, "approximately 45 million Americans, or 15.6 percent of the population, were without health insurance coverage in 2003. The number of uninsured rose 1.4 million between 2002 and 2003" (DeNavas-Walt, Proctor, & Mills, 2004).

Europe

From the European perspective, the three main determinants of health are socioeconomic status, lifestyle, and physical environment. Moreover, according to this view, lifestyle and physical environment are closely linked to socioeconomic factors. The five most important factors in a healthy lifestyle are:

1. level of nutrition;
2. physical activity;
3. tobacco use;
4. alcohol use; and
5. illegal drug use.

The eight major health factors relating to the physical environment are air quality, food safety, water, housing, work, transport, ionizing radiation, and global environmental changes (World Health Organization, 2002).

Canada

From the Canadian perspective, factors such as income, education, social support networks, the environment, and employment and working conditions determine health and well-being (Health Canada, n.d.).

HIV/AIDS

The United Nations Millennium Development Goals have set a target to halt HIV/AIDS and to reverse the spread of it by 2015 (United Nations, n.d.). HIV/AIDS is an epidemic that continues to ravage the globe. By the end of 2003, 35.7 million adults and 2.1 million children were living with HIV (UNAIDS, 2004). The disease has had a devastating effect in particular on countries in sub-Saharan Africa. This region has just over 10 percent of the world's population, but is home to more than 60 percent of all people living with HIV—some 25.4 million. In 2004, an estimated 3.1 million people in the region became newly infected, while 2.3 million died of AIDS. Among young people aged 15–24 years, an estimated 6.9 percent of women and 2.2 percent of men were living with HIV at the end of 2004 (UNAIDS, 2004). In Central Asia and Eastern Europe in 2003, there were about 1.3 million people living with HIV, a startling figure given that these two areas had only 160,000 people living with the disease in 1995 (UNAIDS, 2004). Countries such as Estonia, Latvia, Ukraine, and Russia have some of the highest infection rates in the world. In Russia alone, the rate of infection has jumped from 530,000 in 2001 to 860,000 in just two years (World Health Organization, 2004a).

Additional statistics from the UNAIDS *2004 Report on the Global AIDS Epidemic* include the following:

- More than 20 years and 20 million deaths since the first AIDS diagnosis in 1981, almost 38 million people (range 34.6–42.3 million) are living with HIV.
- Young people 15–24 year old account for nearly half of all new HIV infections worldwide.
- As of December 2003, women accounted for nearly 50 percent of all people living with HIV worldwide and for 57 percent in sub-Saharan Africa.
- Only 7 percent (400,000) of the people who need anti-retroviral treatment in developing countries have access to it at the end of 2003.
- Although global spending on AIDS has increased 15-fold, from $300 million in 1996 to just under $5 billion in 2003, it is less than half of what was needed by 2005 in developing countries.
- In 2003, almost 5 million people became newly infected with HIV, the greatest number in any one year since the beginning of the epidemic.

Prevention, Treatment, and Current Goals

The major challenges for researchers and social workers fall along two basic lines, prevention and treatment. The major hindrances to progress on both fronts continue to be lack of education and inadequate available resources.

Prevention has traditionally focused on education about safer sexual practices and the distribution of resources such as condoms and clean needles for drug users. Unfortunately, many people continue to engage in unsafe sexual behavior and risky intravenous drug use, often unaware of the various ways in which the HIV virus can be transmitted. In China, needle sharing accounted for half of the 62,000 reported HIV cases in 2002. This is a major issue for countries where the message regarding HIV has not been widely spread (Thompson, 2004).

The main type of treatment for HIV/AIDS is anti-retroviral drug treatment. The treatment consists of drugs that have to be taken for the patient's entire lifetime. Two or three drugs are usually taken at the same time because the body may become resistant to a particular drug. By taking several drugs together, it usually takes longer for an individual to become resistant (AVERT, n.d.). Unfortunately, many people around the world, especially in sub-Saharan Africa, have had little to no access to these drugs. Pharmaceutical companies have generally been unwilling to lower their costs and to provide generic brands. Global pressure and attention to this important issue, however, is slowly changing this trend.

On World AIDS Day 2003, WHO and UNAIDS released a detailed and concrete plan to reach the "3 by 5" target of providing anti-retroviral treatment to 3 million people living with AIDS in developing countries and those in transition by the end of 2005 (World Health Organization, n.d.). To reach the "3 by 5" target, WHO and UNAIDS have focused on five critical areas:

1. simplified, standardized tools to deliver anti-retroviral therapy;
2. a new service to ensure an effective, reliable supply of medicines and diagnostics;
3. rapid identification, dissemination, and application of new knowledge and successful strategies;
4. urgent, sustained support for countries; and
5. global leadership, strong partnership, and advocacy.

POLIO

Poliomyelitis (polio) is a highly infectious disease caused by a virus. It invades the nervous system and can cause total paralysis in a matter of hours. The virus enters the body through the mouth and multiplies in the intestine. Initial symptoms are fever, fatigue, headache, vomiting, stiffness in the neck, and pain in the limbs. One in 200 infections leads to irreversible paralysis (usually in the legs). Among those paralyzed, 5–10 percent die when their breathing muscles become immobilized. There is no cure for polio—it can only be prevented. Polio vaccine, given multiple times, can protect a child for life (World Health Organization, 2003b).

Although many developed countries now have minimal concerns regarding polio and polio vaccination, a handful of developing countries continue to experience substantial numbers of cases of polio infection. Fortunately, the number of children paralyzed by this devastating disease every year has fallen, from over 350,000 in 1988 to as few as 1,900 in 2003 (World Health Organization, 2003b). In addition, the number of endemic countries has fallen from 125 in 1988 to six in 2004. The six countries are Nigeria (476 cases), India (34), Pakistan (23), Niger (19), Afghanistan (3), and Egypt (1). Furthermore, cases have been reported in the following importation countries: Chad (12), Côte d'Ivoire (9), Burkina Faso (6), Benin (6), the Sudan (5), the Central African Republic (3), Mali (2), Guinea (1), Cameroon (1), and Botswana (1) (World Health Organization, 2004b).

STARVATION AND MALNUTRITION

Starvation and malnutrition are health problems that continue to plague the entire globe. Starvation is the condition in which deprivation of food has forced the body to feed on itself. Causes are famine, fasting, malnutrition, or abnormalities of the mucosal lining of the digestive system. Malnutrition is the insufficiency of one or more nutritional elements necessary for health and well-being. Primary malnutrition is caused by the lack of essential foodstuffs—usually vitamins, minerals, or proteins—in the diet (Columbia Electronic Encyclopedia, n.d.). According to the United Nations World Food Programme (2004):

- Hunger and malnutrition claim 10 million lives every year, 25,000 lives every day, and one life every five seconds.
- 842 million people—more than the populations of the United States, Canada, Europe, and Japan—in the developing world do not have enough to eat, with about one-third of these people living in sub-Saharan Africa.
- In the 1990s, global poverty dropped by 20 percent. The number of hungry people increased by 18 million.
- 315 million—more than the populations of Australia and the United States—of the world's hungry live in South Asia.
- Hunger and malnutrition are the number one risk to global health, killing more than AIDS, malaria, and tuberculosis combined.
- Poor families spend over 70 percent of their income on food. An average American family spends about 10 percent.
- One of the United Nations' eight "Millennium Goals" is halving the percentage of the world's population that is hungry.
- Micronutrient deficiencies are ranked eighth among the top ten risks to health worldwide.
- Lack of vitamin A weakens the immune system of 40 percent of children under the age of five in poor countries. A vitamin A deficiency can cause blindness and kills a million infants a year.
- Fortifying food with iron has a bigger impact on health than does immunization. Iron deficiency is the most common form of malnutrition, affecting

180 million children under four years of age and impairing the growth and mental development of 40–60 percent of children in developing countries. Over half of all pregnant women do not have sufficient iron. Every day 300 die in childbirth.

- Iodine deficiency is the main cause of brain damage in the early years of a child's life.

GLOBAL PARTNERSHIPS: A GLOBAL HEALTH EXEMPLAR

The International Federation of the Red Cross (IFRC) and the Global Network of People Living with HIV/AIDS (GNP+) is a vital global partnership that has been developed to combat health-related issues (Reinikainen, 2003). The partnership was formally launched at the UN's special general assembly on AIDS in 2001, with the support and encouragement of the United Nations Joint Programme on AIDS. It has resulted in joint missions by regional organizations of both the International Federation and GNP+ to encourage concrete cooperation, such as creating self-support groups and cooperation between national societies of both organizations. One example is the Mission to the Sudan, a new national association for Sudanese people living with HIV and AIDS, which was formed in cooperation with the Sudanese Red Crescent Society.

INTERNATIONAL HEALTH ORGANIZATIONS

World Health Organization

Since its establishment on April 7, 1948, the World Health Organization has been the United Nations' specialized agency for health. WHO's objective, as set out in its Constitution, is the attainment by all peoples of the highest possible level of health. Health is defined in WHO's Constitution as a state of complete physical, mental and social well-being and not merely the absence of disease or infirmity.

WHO is governed by representatives from 192 member states through the World Health Assembly. The main tasks of the Assembly are to approve the WHO program and budget and to decide major policy questions (for more information see http://www.who.int/en).

United Nations World Food Programme

In late 1961, the Food and Agriculture Organization, a large autonomous agency within the UN, and the UN General Assembly adopted parallel resolutions establishing the World Food Programme (WFP). The three-year experimental program was not due to enter into operation until January 1963. It turned out that it was up and running several months early, after an earthquake hit Iran, a hurricane swept through Thailand, and newly independent Algeria

Box 11.1	**Research Evidence Driving the Future Agenda** Challenges for the Future

Achieving a world in which all people are healthy is a daunting task. However, there is a definite agenda that researchers and social workers can follow in order to move closer to attaining such a lofty goal.

Definition of Health

An important yet often overlooked aspect of health is the question of how it is defined and conceptualized around the world. Do countries have vastly different notions of what it means to be healthy? Does a country's view of what it means to be healthy have a direct effect on the way it approaches the health of its citizens? Furthermore, is it necessary or even possible for all countries to operate under the same working definition of health? Answers to these questions may help us determine the course of future global cooperation.

Increased Global Cooperation

Cooperation, knowledge sharing, and resource distribution are all key factors in the treatment, prevention, and eradication of disease. With regard to securing the health of the world's citizens, certainly a considerable gap is forming between developed and undeveloped countries. Some world health officials believe that many developed countries wait until diseases reach epidemic proportions before they are willing to become involved. All countries must realize that disease is a universal problem that fails to recognize borders and jurisdictions. Hence, the main challenge for social workers becomes one of policy change.

Another issue stemming from global cooperation is the visibility of current initiatives. Aside from the initiatives being spearheaded by the World Health Organization, it is difficult to find instances of people, organizations, and countries cooperating on a global level. Increasing visibility will certainly create necessary synergies.

Government Accountability

Government accountability must be another item on the future agenda. Without accountability many of the world's poorest citizens will likely continue to fall short of health-related goals. It is important to ensure that governments that seek assistance from other countries or organizations are actually paying their fair share of costs. It is also necessary to ensure that the funds being funneled into various countries are actually being properly allocated to the appropriate agencies and initiatives. As the journal *New Scientist* (2004) has noted:

> Money to tackle this and other crises is in short supply. After opening the conference, the UN secretary-general Kofi Annan criticized governments in the U.S. and Europe for not supporting the Global Fund to Fight AIDS, Tuberculosis, and Malaria, which was set up to mount aggressive campaigns against all three diseases. The fund needs $3.5 billion to support its programme in 2005, but it looks as if Europe is dragging its heels over its expected $1 billion contribution, and the U.S. intends to halve the $1.2 billion it was expected to chip in. Instead, the U.S. government is directing money to poor countries though its own channels.

Striking a Balance

While the severity and prevalence of diseases such as HIV/AIDS, tuberculosis, and polio dominate research, treatment, and education, it is necessary to strike a balance between focusing on these diseases and those of equal potential urgency. Diseases such as cholera, malaria, and yellow fever, for example, continue to be dangerous and debilitating diseases in many parts of the world. By not paying attention to these types of diseases, a great disservice is being paid to millions of people. It's worth mentioning as well that if these so-called "lesser diseases" are not treated, people face a higher risk of contracting more severe diseases.

Attaining Goals

The attainment of specific goals is another agenda item for future research. Both the United Nations and the World Health Organization have outlined specific health-related goals that social workers and researchers around the world can strive toward.

was overwhelmed by 5 million returning refugees. Food aid was urgently needed and WFP was tasked to supply it.

WFP is now the United Nations' frontline agency mandated to combat global hunger, which afflicts one out of every seven people on earth. In emergencies, WFP delivers food aid to save the lives of victims of war, civil conflict, and natural disasters. After the critical stage of an emergency has passed, WFP uses food aid to help communities rebuild their shattered lives (for more information see http://www.wfp.org).

Project HOPE (Health Opportunities for People Everywhere)

It is Project HOPE's mission to achieve sustainable advances in health care around the world by implementing health education programs, conducting health policy research, and providing humanitarian assistance in areas of need. The organization thereby contributes to human dignity, promotes global understanding, and enhances social and economic development. The essence of Project HOPE is teaching; the basis is partnership (for more information see http://www.projhope.org).

International Federation of Red Cross and Red Crescent Societies

The International Federation of Red Cross and Red Crescent Societies is the world's largest humanitarian organization, providing assistance without discrimination as to nationality, race, religious beliefs, class, or political opinions. Founded in 1919, the International Federation comprises 181 member Red Cross and Red Crescent Societies (with more in formation), a Secretariat in Geneva, and more than 60 delegations strategically located to support activities around the world. The Red Crescent is used in place of the Red Cross in many Islamic countries.

The Federation's mission is to improve the lives of vulnerable people by mobilizing the power of humanity. Vulnerable people are those who are at greatest risk from situations that threaten their survival, or their capacity to live with an acceptable level of social and economic security and human dignity (for more information see http://www.ifrc.org).

Post-Polio Health International

Post-Polio Health International's mission is to enhance the lives and independence of polio survivors and home ventilator users through education, advocacy, research, and networking (for more information see http://www.post-polio.org).

HealthNet International

Netherlands-based HealthNet International was established in 1992 to bridge the gap between humanitarian relief and structural support for health sector recovery in the aftermath of crises. The organization works with the local population in war-affected countries on structural development of health care. HealthNet International specializes in health systems development, health financing, community-based mental health, and disease control (for more information see http://www.healthnetinternational.org).

International Society of Travel Medicine

ISTM is committed to the promotion of healthy and safe travel. In cooperation with national and international health care providers, academic centers, the travel industry, and the media, ISTM advocates and facilitates education, service, and research activities in the field of travel medicine. This includes preventive and curative medicine within many specialties, such as tropical medicine, infectious diseases, high-altitude physiology, travel-related obstetrics, psychiatry, occupational health, military and migration medicine, and environmental health (for more information see http://www.istm.org).

UNAIDS

UNAIDS, the Joint United Nations Programme on HIV/AIDS, is the main advocate for global action on the epidemic. It leads, strengthens, and supports an expanded response aimed at preventing transmission of HIV, providing care and support, reducing the vulnerability of individuals and communities to HIV/AIDS, and alleviating the impact of the epidemic (for more information see http://www.unaids.org).

International Council of AIDS Service Organizations

ICASO is a global network of nongovernmental and community-based organizations. It was formed in 1991 with secretariats in five geographic regions, and a central secretariat based in Canada. In 1995 ICASO was incorporated under Canadian law, and it's accredited to the United Nations Economic and Social Council. ICASO's mission is to:

- mobilize communities and their organizations to participate in the response to HIV/AIDS;
- articulate and advocate the needs and concerns of communities and their organizations;
- ensure that community-based organizations, particularly those with fewer resources and within affected communities, are strengthened in their work to prevent HIV infection, and provide treatment, care, and support for people living with and affected by HIV/AIDS;
- promote the greater involvement of people living with and affected by HIV/AIDS in all aspects of prevention, treatment, care and support, and research; and

- promote human rights in the development and implementation of policies and programs responding to all aspects of HIV/AIDS (for more information see http://www.icaso.org).

SUMMARY

Two important goals are to devise a universally recognized definition of health and to achieve global health through global cooperation. Specific micro and macro level changes can be made in order to help alleviate issues pertaining to health on a global level. Various countries around the world conceptualize health in different ways, ranging from mental and physical fitness to lifestyle and socioeconomic status.

HIV/AIDS is a deadly disease that continues to be a pervasive problem throughout the world, especially in sub-Saharan Africa. It has quickly spread to millions of people over a short period of time. New forms of treatment continue to be employed throughout the world. HIV/AIDS prevention continues to be primarily focused on education about safe sexual practices. Polio has been widely controlled throughout the world, but continues to have devastating effects in a handful of developing countries.

Starvation and malnutrition also remain widespread throughout the world, as is demonstrated by numerous alarming statistics on the pervasiveness of the problems. The link between hunger and disease should not be overlooked. Key challenges and topics for the future global health agenda include the definition of health, the need for global cooperation, and government accountability. An examination of various international organizations focused on health demonstrates that the issue is being approached from different perspectives, including that of poverty alleviation, education, sustainable growth, and the prevention and treatment of diseases.

Thinking About Practice: From Local to Global Perspectives

1. How does the World Health Organization define health? Do you feel this is a sufficient definition of health? Why?
2. What are some of the issues that prevent the achievement of global health?
3. What are some of the ways in which various countries conceptualize health?
4. What is the scope of HIV/AIDS today? How is it being treated and prevented?
5. Discuss two of the challenges that must be considered for the future agenda. Can you think of and discuss a challenge that was not considered?

Social Work Practice and Social Justice Website

Please go to the Book Companion Website at http://www.thomsonedu.com/author/sowers to find a rich collection of related articles selected by the authors from Info Trac College Edition.

References

AVERT. (n.d.). *AIDS & HIV antiretroviral drug treatment in resource poor communities.* Retrieved March 21, 2005, from http://www.avert.org

Columbia Electronic Encyclopedia. (n.d.). Retrieved March 23, 2005, from http://education.yahoo.com/reference/encyclopedia

DeNavas-Walt, C., Proctor, B., & Mills, R. J. (2004). Income, poverty, and health insurance coverage in the United States: 2003. *U.S. Census Bureau Report, August 2004.* Retrieved March 21, 2005, from http://www.census.gov/prod/2004pubs /p60-226.pdf

Health Canada. (n.d.). *Healthy living.* Retrieved March 20, 2005, from http://www.hc-sc.gc.ca

New Scientist. (2004). Broken promises: What hope is there of stopping AIDS if rich nations won't pay up. *Reed Business Information US.* Retrieved March 26, 2005, from http://www.lexis-nexis.com

Reinikainen, P. (2003). *Partnerships key to defeating HIV/AIDS.* Retrieved March 21, 2005, from http://www.ifrc.org

Thompson, D. (2004). Injecting drug use fueling spread of HIV in China. *The Population Reference Bureau.* Retrieved March 20, 2005, from http://www.prb.org

UNAIDS. (2004). *2004 report on the global AIDS epidemic.* Retrieved March 22, 2005, from http://www.unaids.org/bangkok2004/report.html

United Nations. (n.d.). *UN Millennium Development Goals.* Retrieved March 25, 2005, from http:// www.un.org/millenniumgoals

United Nations World Food Programme. (2004). *Hunger facts.* Retrieved March 26, 2005, from http://www.wfp.org

World Health Organization. (n.d.). *The 3 by 5 initiative.* Retrieved March 20, 2005, from http://www.who.int/3by5/en

World Health Organization. (1946). *Preamble to the constitution of the World Health Organization.* Retrieved March 21, 2005, from http://www3. who.int/whosis/faqs/faqs.cfm#top

World Health Organization. (2002). *The European health report 2002.* Retrieved March 20, 2005, from http://www.euro.who.int/ europeanhealth report

World Health Organization. (2003a). *The world health report 2003: Shaping the future.* Retrieved March 21, 2005, from http://www.who.int/ whr/2003/en

World Health Organization. (2003b). *Poliomyelitis.* Retrieved March 21, 2005, from http://www. who.int/mediacentre/factsheets/fs114/en/

World Health Organization. (2004a). *AIDS epidemic poses serious threat to Europe.* Retrieved March 18, 2005, from http://www.who.int/3by5/ mediacentre/news24/en

World Health Organization. (2004b). *New polio cases confirmed in Guinea, Mali and the Sudan.* Retrieved March 16, 2005, from http://www.who.int/mediacentre/news/releases/ 2004/pr57/en

I have always found that mercy bears richer fruits than strict justice.
Abraham Lincoln

12 CHAPTER | Crime and Justice

RESTORATIVE JUSTICE

For social workers, the topic of crime and justice must begin with the concept of restorative justice. This is because the principles and methods of restorative justice are in direct accordance with social work's core values and beliefs, and because social work has a natural inclination towards a bio-psychosocial approach. According to Van Wormer (2002), "Restorative justice is the growing movement that aims to change the direction of criminal law by focusing it on the needs of victims and on repairing communities. Unlike retributive justice, which focuses on punishment of the guilty offender, restorative justice takes a more caring approach. Proponents of this nonadversarial model adopt a different lens for viewing crime and rectifying the harm done by the crime."

Restorative Justice Online (2003) provides a useful introduction to the concept of restorative justice:

> Restorative justice is a systematic response to wrongdoing that emphasizes healing the wounds of victims, offenders and communities caused or revealed by criminal behavior. Practices and programs reflecting restorative purposes will respond to crime by identifying and taking steps to repair harm, involving all stakeholders, and transforming the traditional relationship between communities and their governments in responding to crime. Three principles form the foundation for restorative justice: 1) Justice requires that we work to restore those who have been injured, 2) Those most directly involved and affected by crime should have the opportunity to participate fully in the response if they wish, and 3) Government's role is to preserve a just public order, and the community's is to build and maintain a just peace.

The motivation for restorative justice is the deep concern for the broader quality of social life. It places an emphasis on the coming together of the parties associated in the specific offense to resolve collectively how to deal with the repercussions of the offense and its implications for the future (Marshall, 1996). Restorative justice is usually the first option in dealing with crimes; however, it does not necessarily mean that every crime must be dealt with restoratively. There have been cases in which other intervention models have better suited the circumstances.

When considering juvenile justice, it is difficult to determine where the line should be drawn between the two vastly different models of restorative justice and retributive justice. The difficulty lies in the gray area of "responding to youths who have offended in terms of their social or psychological needs, and punishing them for what they have done" (Doob & Tonry, 2004). Many youth justice systems struggle with this issue. It has been difficult for policy makers to form clear lines between utilization of each model.

MINIMUM AND MAXIMUM AGES OF YOUTH COURT JURISDICTION BY COUNTRY

Doob and Tonry (2004) state, "While it has been difficult for many countries to define a clear and concrete definition of youth justice systems, countries have

Table 12.1
Minimum and
Maximum Ages
of Youth Court
Jurisdiction by
Country

Jurisdiction	Minimum Age	Maximum Age
Canada	12	17
Netherlands	12	17
Germany	14	17
England	10	17
Scotland	8	15
United States (average; varies by state)	10	17
Sweden	15	Not applicable
Denmark	15	Not applicable
New Zealand	14	16

Source: Doob & Tonry, 2004

been able to identify specific ages in the minimum and maximum ages of youth court jurisdiction." The following table shows the maximum and minimum ages of youth court jurisdiction for various countries. The "Maximum Age" column indicates that a person is considered a youth until he or she has reached the next birthday (i.e., a person in Canada is considered a youth until his or her eighteenth birthday). Minimum ages vary widely, from 8 to 15. In most countries adult court jurisdiction begins at age 18. Denmark and Sweden have no specialized youth court, so "adult" jurisdiction begins at age 15 (Doob & Tonry, 2004).

JUVENILE JUSTICE AROUND THE WORLD

Youth justice systems differ all over the world. One attribute they all have in common, however, is an ongoing tension between treatment and punishment in the response to youth crime (Walgrave, 2004). Similarly, every country has different laws and policies for youth and adult offenders in the restorative justice system. It is difficult to generalize about the global youth justice system because of these vast differences among countries.

The United States and England focus on punishment as the principal aim in youth justice, and their youth justice systems bear a resemblance to their adult courts. In the United States, until recently this included the possibility that people convicted of capital crimes committed as minors could be executed. As one of the only countries in the world to conduct such executions, the United States faced a tremendous amount of condemnation and pressure from the global community. In 2004, however, the U.S. Supreme Court ruled that people who commit murder while under the age of 18 could no longer be executed for their crimes.

In the legal systems of Scandinavian countries, youths cannot even commit a crime until they are 15 years of age. Misconduct by youths who are younger than 15 is dealt with by social welfare agencies. After this age they are deemed an adult and their offenses are processed in the court system. Similarly, consequences to crimes committed by youth in New Zealand are almost never handled in court. In the New Zealand restorative justice system, youth cases are dealt with in conferences (Doob & Tonry, 2004).

The Scottish youth justice system focuses on preventive goals as opposed to retributive goals. "In Scotland, a unified welfare-based system, committed to the prevention of harm to children, encompasses children who offend and children in social jeopardy. It uniquely and radically separates functions between the courts as factual and legal arbiters and children's hearings as treatment tribunals" (Bottoms & Dignan, 2004).

In Hong Kong, a highly urbanized "special administrative region" of China, juvenile delinquency is not as serious a problem as it is in similar populations among developed countries. Social work and criminal justice professionals play an important role through welfare and statutory criminal justice strategies. Probation and community service offer the only community-based sentencing options for juvenile offenders (Wong, 2000). According to Wong, juveniles in Hong Kong who have gone through mandatory detention appear to have attained more deviant values and behavior than they had before they were arrested.

In the Netherlands, an emphasis is placed on the young offenders and not on the use of repressive measures. The social work practice in the Netherlands places a commitment on welfare values and having welfare institutions respond actively to youth offenders. According to Hunger-Tas (2004), "Changed criteria make waiver of young offenders to adult courts easier, but the numbers waived have fallen, and most who are waived receive community penalties. Statutes have authorized longer confinement terms for young offenders, but the use of long sentences has declined. There has been a substantial increase in the use of community penalties, including community service and victim compensation, and new programs have given the police greater powers to take action against alleged offenders."

Germany has the lowest youth incarceration rate in all of Europe, due to the facts that offenders are dealt with specifically by judges and the system uses special sanctions for youth. Changes in incarceration rates for youth in Germany began in the early 1920s when German Youth Court was established. It is emphasized that juveniles should be treated differently from adults. Also, educating youth is a valuable piece in Germany's juvenile justice system (Albrecht, 2004).

ADULT CRIMINAL JUSTICE IN THE UNITED STATES

The United States is second to Russia in having the highest rates of imprisonment in all industrialized nations. Imprisonment rates in the United States are six to ten times higher than the imprisonment rates of most industrialized nations (Mauer, 2003).

The United States has extremely high rates of imprisonment, with 702 inmates per 100,000 population. The homicide rate in the United States is about four times that of most Western European countries. Sentencing practices in the United States are harsher than those in other nations. Current policies affect African-American males in the United States more than any other group of people. Nearly a quarter of all inmates in U.S. prisons have been incarcerated for drug charges (Mauer, 2003). The United States imprisons more people for longer amounts of time than similar nations (Lynch, 1995). Political policy makes a difference in the number of adults imprisoned in the United States—in recent decades the criminal justice system has increasingly been used as a weapon in the "war on drugs." Mauer (2003) states:

> Within the U.S., policy changes adopted under the rubric of the "get tough" movement and the "war on drugs" have contributed substantially to the rising prison population. In the 1990s, these trends have been exacerbated by such policies as the "three strikes" laws adopted by half the states and "truth in sentencing" policies in some 30 states.

The high rates of incarceration in the United States impact many different areas of the country. In some states, individuals who have been convicted of a drug felony may be barred from receiving welfare benefits, they may not be permitted to live in public housing, they may lose their right to vote, and they may not be able to gain financial aid for higher education. Families and communities also feel the effects of the high rate of incarceration in the United States.

Nationally, some 1.5 million children have a parent who has been incarcerated. These children must live with the stigmas and stereotypes that shadow having an incarcerated parent. Economically, at a state level, money spent on corrections systems competes directly with vital services such as support for higher education. Communities are affected when resources are diverted to the prison system rather than affordable housing and crime prevention programs (Mauer, 2003). The United States also utilizes stricter sentencing policies then many other nations. When criminologist James Lunch compared sentencing practices in the United States to other nations, such as Canada and England, he found that the United States incarcerates more people and for longer periods of time (Mauer, 2003).

The United States utilizes prisoner reentry programs that emphasize the transition from prison to community. For example, before living completely independently, a person being released from prison may have an allotted amount of time in which he or she can live in a halfway house. Such programs initiate treatment within the criminal justice system and allow for a community program to provide continuity of care. Studies show that, compared to conventional parolees, graduates of these programs are less likely to be arrested again, to commit a new drug-related offense, or to violate their parole (Seiter & Kadela, 2003).

CRIMINAL JUSTICE FROM THE SOCIAL WORK PERSPECTIVE

There has been a conflict between the key characteristics of social work practice and the values of the criminal justice system. Social work practice emphasizes the dignity and self-determination of each individual client. The criminal justice system places an emphasis on order, control, and punishment. After the 1980s, this conflict caused a weakening in the active role that social workers played in the criminal justice system. The United States has utilized social workers in preparing presentence investigations. The social worker's role in such investigations is to assess the client's strengths and weaknesses and to prepare recommendations for a judge to formulate into a program of treatment (Gumz, 2004). Gumz states:

> It is essential for social workers to continue to pursue their commitment to social justice. Social work can invigorate its presence in corrections by affirming its traditional commitment to social justice—one of the primary tenets of the profession. The concept of social justice in social work has usually stressed distributive justice, calling for a more equitable distribution of goods and services in society. In addition, social work as a profession needs to affirm the concept of restorative justice, which offers a holistic approach toward work in corrections in which justice for the victim, offender, and the community are all relevant.

INTERNATIONAL ORGANIZATIONS ON CRIME AND JUSTICE

United Nations Office on Drugs and Crime

UNODC is a global leader in the fight against illicit drugs and international crime. Established in 1997, UNODC has approximately 500 staff members worldwide. It relies on voluntary contributions, mainly from governments, for 90 percent of its budget. The three pillars of the UNODC work program are:

- Research and analytical work to increase knowledge and understanding of drugs and crime issues and expand the evidence-base for policy and operational decisions;
- Normative work to assist countries in the ratification and implementation of international treaties, the development of domestic legislation on drugs, crime and terrorism, and the provision of secretariat and substantive services to the treaty-based and governing bodies; and
- Field-based technical cooperation projects to enhance the capacity of member states to counteract illicit drugs, crime, and terrorism (for more information see http://www.unodc.org/unodc/index.html).

Box 12.1 | Exemplars from Around the World

New Zealand

The "Children, Young Persons, and Their Families Act" of 1989 incorporated family group conferences into New Zealand's youth justice system. In this system, the only time an offender under the age of 14 is prosecuted is when he or she has committed the crime of murder or manslaughter. Offenders who are 14 to 17 years old are referred to a group conference before formal sentencing (Morris, 2004). The conference is lead by a youth justice coordinator who is usually a social worker. Other attendees are the subject's family members, the victim, and the victim's supporters. The conference is not over until each person in the conference agrees upon the outcome. Morris (2004) states:

> The family group conference operates at two distinct and key points: as an alternative to courts (for young people who have not been arrested), and as a mechanism for making recommendations to judges before sentencing (for young people who have been arrested). This means that the police cannot refer young offenders who have not been arrested to the youth court without first having a family group conference; most of these conferences end in an agreement that does not involve a court appearance. It also means that judges cannot sentence young offenders who have been arrested without first referring them to a family group conference and taking into account its recommendations. This key positioning of family group conferences is consistent with the restorative justice value of empowering young people, families, and victims by giving them a role in the decisions about how best to respond to offending and thereby reducing the powers of professionals who must take these parties' views into account.

New Zealand's family group conference system has been successful, as is evidenced by satisfaction levels reported by offenders, families, and victims. Usually, each party is more satisfied with the conference than with the process of the justice system (Morris, 2004). Success is also evidenced by the fact that the group conference system has kept youths out of courts and criminal custody. Finally, it enables the offenders, victims, and respective families to help in the decision process. Ultimately, this system has held young offenders accountable for their actions and has empowered the victims to experience closure to the crimes committed against them (Morris, 2004).

China

The Chinese system for dealing with criminal offenders is different from most other countries. China reforms inmates through labor and education. They have an optimistic view that this process makes the perpetrator become a wholly new person. According to Chen (2004), "Dramatized throughout the Chinese correctional program is the paternalistic dictum that the individual can and should be reasoned with and guided toward positive ends and, therefore, that correctional officials must be to inmates as parents are to their children, as doctors are to patients, and as teachers are to students." In Chinese society, the offender is looked upon as the victim of negative influences in the environment; he or she is not seen as a deficient person (Chen, 2004).

According to Wong (2000), "Rehabilitation and correctional services, statutory measures such as detention centers, training centers, reformatory schools, and probation homes have been established to deal with young convicted offenders. Those who are found guilty of less serious offences but who are not suitable for a custodial sentence are put under community supervision by a probation order or community service order." China's system relies on an optimistic view of human nature. China's system is also unique in that it believes that correctional officials should take a basically paternalistic attitude toward inmates. This provides the perpetrator with support from the system.

Box 12.2	**Research Evidence Driving the Future Agenda** Challenges for the Future

Increasing Best-Practice Sharing

One of the most important challenges for social workers dealing with crime and justice is increasing best-practice sharing on a global level. As we have seen from exemplars like New Zealand and China, there are certainly effective methodologies and philosophies that can be leveraged by other countries. Despite the fact that countries approach crime and justice in vastly different ways, there is much to be learned through dialogue and research. It is imperative that social workers be included in these dialogues, to ensure that the most highly regarded and sought after practices are in accordance with social work's core values and beliefs.

Applying an Interdisciplinary Approach

For restorative justice to be successful, an interdisciplinary approach must be undertaken. It is imperative that social workers, law enforcement agencies, relevant community groups, and criminal justice factions work together to help victims and offenders come to an appropriate and curative resolution to the relevant damage that has been done. The challenge for the future is achieving interdisciplinary approaches on national and global levels. While this may be a daunting task, social workers—because of the profession's tradition of treating victims, offenders, and fellow contemporaries alike with dignity and respect—are in a unique position to add stability and balance to interdisciplinary teams.

Effect of Public Opinion on Criminal Justice Policies

Public opinion is a major factor when it comes to dealing with violations of the law. As we have mentioned, public opinion has been gradually leaning toward favoring retributive justice in many countries. Therefore, social workers face the challenge of changing the public perception of crime and justice.

Empirical Evidence for Restorative Justice

In this age of empirically based practice, it is necessary for social workers to meet the challenge of conducting and reporting research that supports the use of restorative justice. Furthermore, it is important for social workers to disseminate their findings to their interdisciplinary counterparts, as well as to the general public. Strong research evidence is the best way for social workers to influence public opinion, change policies and procedures, and maintain credibility.

The Role of Social Workers in Criminal Justice

Social workers must also face the challenge of securing their role in the criminal justice field. As we have seen, the role of social workers has been diminishing for a variety of reasons. By swaying public opinion, lobbying for policy changes, conducting research, and employing techniques based on empirical findings, social workers can help to safeguard their place in the criminal justice arena.

Centre for International Crime Prevention

CICP is the United Nations office responsible for crime prevention, criminal justice, and criminal law reform. The Centre is part of the United Nations Office for Drug Control and Crime Prevention. It pays special attention to combating transnational organized crime, corruption, and illicit trafficking in human beings (for more information see http://www.uncjin.org/CICP/ cicp.html).

International Centre for the Prevention of Crime

ICPC is a network of organizations and people who value human security as a common good. It bridges the gap between policy makers, practitioners, and researchers. The Centre serves as a global forum to monitor developments, exchange knowledge and experience, and debate ideas about effective and sustainable ways to prevent crime and build safer communities (for more information see http://www.crime-prevention-intl.org).

International Centre for Criminal Law Reform and Criminal Justice Policy

The International Centre's mission is to improve the quality of justice through reform of criminal law, policy, and practice. The Centre promotes democratic principles, the rule of law and respect for human rights in criminal law, and the administration of criminal justice domestically, regionally, and globally. The primary role of the Centre is to provide advice, information, research and proposals for policy development, and legislation (for more information see http://www.icclr.law.ubc.ca).

Office of International Criminal Justice

The OICJ is a nonprofit educational organization with offices in Illinois, Indiana, and Texas. OICJ offers a global perspective on contemporary and historical criminal justice news and trends. Their publications, conferences, and travel programs bring together academics, criminal justice practitioners, journalists, and the public (for more information see http://www.oicj.org).

International Association of Chiefs of Police

Founded in 1893, the IACP's goals are to advance the science and art of police services; to develop and disseminate improved administrative, technical, and operational practices, and promote their use in police work; to foster police cooperation and the exchange of information and experience among police administrators throughout the world; to bring about the recruitment and training of qualified persons in the police profession; and to encourage adherence of all police officers to high professional standards of performance and conduct (for more information see http://www.theiacp.org).

International Association of Prosecutors

A nongovernmental and nonpolitical organization, the IAP is the first and only world organization of prosecutors. Membership of the IAP is open to lawyers who are, or have been, prosecutors, who join as individual members; and to prosecution services, associations of prosecutors, and crime prevention agencies, which join as organizational members (for more information see http://www.iap.nl.com).

Terrorism Research Center

The TRC is an independent institute dedicated to the research of terrorism, information warfare and security, critical infrastructure protection, and other issues of low-intensity political violence and "gray-area phenomena." The TRC seeks to represent a new generation of terrorism and security analysis, combining expertise with technology to maximize the scope, depth, and impact of its research for practical implementation. The TRC provides core expertise in terrorism, counter terrorism, critical infrastructure protection, information warfare and security (including design review, technical assessments, policy development and review, and training), vulnerability and threat assessment, systems engineering, encryption, intelligence analysis, and national security and defense policy (for more information see http://www. terrorism.com).

SUMMARY

A fundamental aspect of restorative justice is repairing the harm that has occurred as a consequence of a person's crime. Restorative justice provides all parties involved in the crime, and affected by the crime, the opportunity to achieve a satisfactory outcome in the situation. Restorative justice contrasts with the many theories of retributive justice, which utilize only discipline as a form of punishment and restoration for a crime. Restorative justice is a way in which the consequences of a person's actions can be formulated through the community as a whole.

Key characteristics of social work practice clash with certain values of the criminal justice system. The clash can be seen when looking at the order, control, and punishment of the retributive criminal justice system and comparing it to the values placed on dignity and self-determination by the social work profession. It is important for the clinician to find a balance between characteristics like these that are on extreme opposite sides of the spectrum. A clinician must also remember the importance that education plays in fighting crime and in preventing future crime. Exemplars from around the world show criminal justice systems have made changes that can reduce the number of incarcerated people. It is important to evaluate and critically think about the changes these countries have made when trying to determine what changes would best benefit other nations facing similar challenges.

Thinking About Practice: From Local to Global Perspectives

1. What is the difference between restorative justice and retributive justice?
2. Is restorative justice useful in all circumstances? Explain.
3. What are the similarities and differences between juvenile justice systems around the world?
4. What are the distinguishing features of China's and New Zealand's approaches to crime and justice?
5. How does the concept of restorative justice reflect the values and beliefs of the social work profession?

Social Work Practice and Social Justice Website

Please go to the Book Companion Website at http://www.thomsonedu.com/author/sowers to find a rich collection of related articles selected by the authors from Info Trac College Edition.

References

Albrecht, H. (2004). Youth justice in Germany. *Crime and Justice, 31,* 443.

Bottoms, A., & Dignan, J. (2004). Youth justice in Great Britain. *Crime and Justice, 31,* 21.

Chen, X. (2004). Social and legal control in China: A comparative perspective. *International Journal of Offender Therapy and Comparative Criminology, 48*(5), 523–536.

Doob, A. N., & Tonry, M. (2004). Varieties of youth justice. *Crime and Justice, 31.*

Gumz, E. J. (2004). American social work, corrections and restorative justice: An appraisal. *International Journal of Offender Therapy and Comparative Criminology, 48*(4).

Hunger-Tas, J. (2004). Youth justice in the Netherlands. *Crime and Justice, 31,* 293.

Lynch, J. (1995). Crime in international perspective, in J. Wilson and J. Petersilia (Eds.). *Crime.* San Francisco: Institute for Contemporary Studies (22–23).

Marshall, T. (1996). The evolution of restorative justice in Britain. *European Journal of Criminal Policy and Research, 4,* 21–23.

Mauer, M. (2003). Comparative international rates of incarceration: An examination of causes and trends. *Presented to the U.S. Commission on Civil Rights,* 1–16.

Morris, A. (2004). Youth justice in New Zealand. *Crime and Justice, 31,* 243.

Restorative Justice Online (2003). Introduction: What is restorative justice? Retrieved March 15, 2005, from: http://www.restorativejustice.org/rj3/intro_default.htm

Seiter, R. P., & Kadela, K. R. (2003). Prisoner reentry: What works, what does not, and what is promising. *Crime and Delinquency, 49*(3), 360.

Van Wormer, K. (2002). Restorative justice and social work. *Social Work Today, 2*(1).

Walgrave, L. (2004). Restoration in youth justice. *Crime and Justice, 31,* 543.

Wong, D. (2000). Juvenile crime and responses to delinquency in Hong Kong. *International Journal of Offender Therapy and Comparative Criminology, 44*(3), 279–292.

The more we study the social problems of our time, the more we realize that the mechanistic world view and the value system associated with it have generated technologies, institutions, and life styles that are profoundly unhealthy.

Noel de Nevers (1972)

Stress, Trauma, and Crisis Intervention

CHAPTER **13**

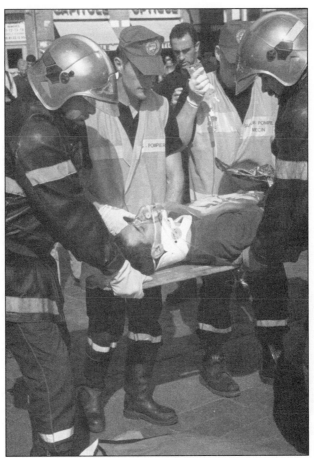

197

Natural and human-made disasters often strike communities with little or no warning. Changing climate patterns from long-term atmospheric cycles and global warming are expected to increase. Recent events around the globe underscore our lack of preparedness and ability to respond to the aftermath of disasters. Our ability to transmit images quickly across the world brings home how families, communities, and individuals suffer when disasters strike. Technological disasters, terrorism, and war also place added stressors on people and infrastructures, both environmental and human-made. When disasters strike, whether natural or human-made, individuals, families, and communities suffer trauma and stress in multiple dimensions of their daily lives, including their health, community infrastructure, property, jobs, personal belongings, and social ties (Dukfa, 1988; Zakour, 1996). Often the most serious and long lasting harm from disasters occurs to people who are poor or otherwise vulnerable (Rogge, 2003). Social workers need to be trained to respond to these growing threats.

NATURAL DISASTERS

Natural disasters have killed around 128,000 people and affected another 136 million every year over the last ten years (Heiberg, 1999). Both the severity and frequency of natural disasters has increased (United Nations, 1996). It is believed that the changing climate is responsible for the unusual combinations of hurricane, flood, and drought patterns. According to the International Federation of Red Cross and Red Crescent Societies (1999), the world can expect to see even more extreme weather patterns that will cause many more disasters. Although the number of people who died from natural disasters decreased from the 1970s to the 1990s (from 2 million during the decade of the 1970s to under 800,000 during the 1990s), the number of people adversely affected from these disasters tripled and the economic losses were five times greater—approximately $629 billion (International Federation of Red Cross and Red Crescent Societies, 2002). Consider, for example, recent examples of natural disasters around the world:

- On December 26, 2004, a massive undersea earthquake measuring 9.0 on the Richter scale struck off the coast of northern Sumatra. The quake triggered a powerful tsunami that swept the coasts of neighboring countries and caused serious damage and loss of life. At least five million people were affected in Indonesia, Sri Lanka, Maldives, India, Thailand, Seychelles, and Myanmar. The death toll exceeded 280,000 people and more than 1 million persons were displaced as a result of the destruction (World Health Organization, n.d.).
- The recent deaths of more than 13,000 French elderly in the European heat wave during the summer of 2003 revealed serious weaknesses in the social foundation of urban communities. The breakdown occurred in community services, neighborhood networks, and governmental agencies that were responsible for warning of impending dangers to at-risk elderly (Langer, 2004).

- It is estimated that more than two million people died in the famine that plagued North Korea in 1997 and 1998 (McGregor, 1998).
- In 1997, the United Nations estimated that 4.7 million North Koreans were in danger of starvation (Washington Post, 1997).
- The 1998 earthquake in Afghanistan claimed 4,500 lives (United Nations Office for the Coordination of Humanitarian Affairs, 1998).
- The earthquake that shook Bhuj in the Indian state of Gujarat on January 26, 2001, was the most deadly earthquake to strike India in its recorded history. One month after the earthquake, figures from the Indian government placed the death toll at 19,727 and the number of injured at 166,000. Indications are that 600,000 people were left homeless, with 348,000 houses destroyed and an additional 844,000 damaged. The Indian State Department estimated that the earthquake affected, directly or indirectly, 15.9 million people out of a total population of 37.8 million. More than 20,000 cattle were reported killed. The government estimated that the direct economic losses were $1.3 billion (Cooperative Institute for Research in Environmental Sciences, 2001).
- On September 21, 1989, a Class IV hurricane, Hugo, struck the South Carolina coast of the United States, carrying 175 mile-per-hour winds and a tidal surge between 12 and 23 feet. The eye of the hurricane entered the mainland north of Charleston. In a nearby national forest, from 70 to 80 percent of all trees were destroyed. In Charleston County, 80 percent of all structures endured roof damage, 6,000 homes were destroyed, over 12,000 homes were rendered uninhabitable, and 65,000 people required temporary shelter (Mullins & Burbage, 1989).

The most vulnerable tend to be hit hardest when natural disasters strike. Over 90 percent of all deaths caused by disaster occur in developing countries. The economic losses to developing countries are generally about twenty times greater than in industrial countries. These statistics are particularly alarming given that almost a billion people currently reside in unplanned urban shanty-towns. Global warming is affecting patterns of wind, rain, and sun and making it more difficult to predict the scope and ferocity of natural disasters. With global deforestation and damage to our natural ecological defenses, the poor people of the world are at greater risk than ever before (Heiberg, 1999). "Flawed development (e.g., rapid unplanned urbanization, deforestation) is exposing more people to disasters. Risk-blind development is one factor in increasing vulnerability. Another is the absence of effective disaster preparedness and mitigation measures (e.g., flood-proof dykes, early warning systems, evacuation routes, shelters, relief stockpiles, disaster response teams, public awareness)" (International Federation of Red Cross and Red Crescent Societies, 2002).

Children are especially vulnerable to negative short-term effects associated with trauma related to natural disasters. Previous research specific to natural disasters and school-age children reveals short-term effects that include apathy and aggression (Bloom, 1986; Galante & Foa, 1986), sleep disturbances, decrease in appetite, increase in somatic complaints (Dollinger, 1985;

Dollinger, O'Donnell, & Staley, 1984), and separation anxiety (Dollinger, 1985; Sugar, 1988). Children have also been shown to demonstrate an increase in fears (Bloom, 1986; Dollinger, 1985; Dollinger, O'Donnell, & Staley, 1984). Although some children have long-term emotional difficulties, some have exhibited play involving the traumatic event (Galante & Foa, 1986; Saylor, Swenson, & Powell, 1992; Sugar, 1988) and few children exhibit psychiatric disorders as a result of disaster (Earls et al., 1988). Recent research suggests that help from mental health professionals for families with children may be most effective if it can be given fairly intensively during the six months immediately following a natural disaster (Swenson et al., 1996).

Planning and preparedness are critical elements in mitigating the damage from natural disasters and managing the aftereffects. For maximum benefit, preparedness plans need to be widely disseminated, carefully implemented, and specifically followed (United Nations Environment Programme, 2001). No multilateral treaty currently exists outlining the rights of victims of natural disasters to receive humanitarian aid. The lack of such a treaty and the uncertainty among states and nations about delivering humanitarian aid have created barriers to delivering aid in a cooperative and timely fashion. This is particularly alarming given the increasing frequency of natural disasters. However, the International Committee of the Red Cross is working to promote the status of humanitarian assistance in times of natural disaster as a human right and is recommending the adoption of a global agreement on the issue (Hardcastle & Chua, 1998).

ENVIRONMENTAL DEGRADATION

Some disasters are triggered by environmental degradation. Some disasters are made worse by environmental degradation. Either way, in countries that are affected by overcultivation, erosion, severe deforestation, and overgrazing of marginal lands, the effects of natural or human-made disasters are more devastating. We know that the frequency and magnitude of natural disasters are increasing and it appears that some are increasing because of environmental degradation—the disturbance of formerly stable ecosystems (United Nations Environment Programme, 2001). Recent research findings indicate that "countries which suffer most from natural disasters are those in which environmental degradation is more severe, i.e., those with severe deforestation, soil-erosion, over-cultivation, and over-grazing" (United Nations Environment Programme, 2001). Because environmental degradation can transcend national boundaries, and because it can negatively impact large numbers of people's lives, every nation and state must become part of the solution to combat destruction of critical environments. For example, recently South Asia has been hit hard by many preventable natural disasters caused by the loss of forests and other natural vegetation around the world (United Nations Environment Programme, 2001).

Toxic chemical contamination can also negatively affect the environment. Over recent years the earth has become increasingly contaminated with toxic chemicals, resulting in increased frequency and quantity of exposure. Hundreds of new chemicals are developed every year and released into the environment, in addition to the thousands already being released. Exposure to chemicals does not always result in toxic effects. The dose-response relationship is different for every chemical and for every individual. This variation is due to the structure of the chemical, how it is metabolized, the rate it is absorbed into the body, and the amount that is excreted. An individual's susceptibility to chemical exposure depends largely on age. The most vulnerable populations to chemical exposure are the very young and the very old (Darby et al., 2004).

Convincing evidence is accumulating that children's chronic exposure to the 80,000-some chemicals in the air, water, and on land is harming their physical, mental, and emotional well-being (Rogge, 2003). Childhood cancer, asthma and other respiratory problems, developmental disabilities including attention hyperactivity deficit disorder and aggression, endocrine and immune system damage, and loss of IQ are among the documented and suspected consequences of chemical exposure (Rogge, 2003). Children at greatest risk are those who live in poverty.

Research has identified a strong correlation among race, ethnicity, and geographical locations of toxic waste sites. Some experts have referred to this phenomenon as environmental racism, referring to the intentional placement of hazardous waste sites, landfills, incinerators, and polluting industries in communities inhabited predominantly by minority groups and the working poor.

TECHNOLOGICAL DISASTERS

The second half of the twentieth century was a period of rapid technological and social change. Springing from the earlier industrial revolution, our present and recent past is distinguished by continual technological development. Transformation of industry and application of modern technologies now touch the lives of humanity around the globe to an extent and at a pace unparalleled in any earlier periods of change. Over the last fifty years the very industrial processes that have brought convenience and material well-being to large segments of the human race have also caused an increasing frequency of disastrous accidents around the world (Granot, 1998). The risks associated with high-tech systems are apparent in the disastrous events of our recent past. The disasters at Chernobyl and Bhopal have served to focus the attention of the public, the media, and government officials on the potentially disastrous effects of technology (Pidgeon et al., 1992). In the past, up until the end of the 1970s, human-made accidents were often considered unfortunate sudden failures, without specific responsibility, instead of the outcomes of earlier processes that resulted in disaster. But some improvement in the prevention and mitigation of major industrial disasters has been made. There has been growing concern after the effects of recent industrial accidents have been realized. This has brought to the forefront the need to develop strategies and systems to develop public policies and attempts to control the risks of industrial and technological processes. As a result, there is a current emphasis on the responsibilities of management in preventing and reducing the risks of technological disasters. The critical role that emergency services play after a disaster has occurred is now quite clear.

Many industrial and technological organizations must frequently deal with hazardous material in quantities that exceed the threshold for adverse health effects. The most fundamental factor that determines the scale of the hazard is the inventory of the hazardous material. The larger the inventory of hazardous material, the greater the potential loss should an accident occur. Failure of an organization's ability to control the hazardous material can result in a human-made disaster, no matter how secure the surrounding area may be (Shaluf et al., 2002). A human-made disaster may be defined as "the event that causes extensive damage and social disruption, involves multiple stakeholders and unfolds through complex technological, organizational, and social processes" (Shrivastava et al., 1988). A few examples of devastating human-made technological disasters include:

- Malaysia has experienced repeated disasters that can be tied to the fast pace of industrial development. The disasters have occurred in various economic sectors, including the fireworks industry and the chemical industry. For example, in a 1991 fireworks tragedy 23 persons died and 103 persons sustained injuries of varying degrees of seriousness.
- On April 26, 1986, the world's worst nuclear power accident occurred at Chernobyl in the former U.S.S.R. (now Ukraine). The Chernobyl nuclear power plant located 80 miles north of Kiev had four reactors. While testing one of the reactors, numerous safety procedures were disregarded. At 1:23 A.M. the chain reaction in the reactor spun out of control and exploded in a fireball that blew off the reactor's heavy steel and concrete lid. The accident killed more than 30 people immediately, and as a result of the high radiation levels in the surrounding 20-mile radius, 135,000 people had to be evacuated. About 760 children in the contaminated "safety zone" have been reported to have thyroid cancer. Birth defects have more than doubled and there have also been isolated cases of liver and rectal cancer, which is uncommon in young children.
- In Baia Mare, Romania, on January 31, 2000, a tailings dam at a Romanian gold mine ruptured. Over the course of four days the spill released water contaminated with cyanide, a leeching agent used to extract gold, into the Somes River, a tributary of the Szamos, Tisza, and Danube rivers. The cyanide reached levels of over 700 times normal concentrations, and killed all living species in its path. The poisoned water flowed into Hungary and Yugoslavia on the Szamos and Tisza rivers and back into Romania on the Danube. This international incident, with potential long-term effects for the people and environment of Eastern Europe, highlights the risk inherent in mining activity and the need for effective emergency planning (United Nations Environment Programme, 2001).

General agreement exists as to the criteria used to define a human-made disaster in terms of consequences (Center for Research on the Epidemiology of Disasters, 2002; Keller & Al-madhari, 1996; Keller et al., 1997; De Sousa, 2000; United Nations Environmental Programme, 2002). The criteria requires that for an accident to be considered as a human-made disaster, at least one of the following criteria be fulfilled (United Nations Environment Programme, 2001):

- three or more fatalities;
- ten or more injuries;
- 50 or more people evacuated; and
- damage costs exceeding $1 million.

Technological disasters can have devastating effects. They have the potential to kill large numbers of people and the consequences can leave organizations depleted and unable to recover. In recent decades, much has been learned about the causes and prevention of technological disasters. Particular progress has been made in the areas of assessment of industrial design; legislation regarding design, operations and inspection; and mitigation. However, many organizations have not learned the lessons or implemented appropriate preventive strategies. No matter how much attention is devoted to the planning, operations, and inspection of industrial areas, accidents will occur on occasion and need to be contained with minimum consequences to the plant, the public, and society generally. The lack of preventive strategies on the part of some organizations underscores the importance of citizens playing a far more active part in decisions about technology.

TERRORISM, ARMED CONFLICTS, AND WAR

Contemporary armed conflicts are increasing and becoming ever more complex. They form part of the increasingly visible globalization that affects economies and communication. Armed conflict displaces civilians, exposes them to ill treatment, and separates them from their families. Military and militia campaigns can displace vast populations in a few hours or days. Armed conflicts are no longer international in the traditional sense, but are rooted in complex national or regional realities, with history, culture, and ethnic origins playing an important role (Heiberg, 1999). Recent examples abound:

- In September 2004, gunmen, some wearing bomb belts, seized a school in southern Russia on the first day of classes. The terrorists demanded an end to the war in Chechnya. On the third day of the hostage taking, an emergency services van pulled up to the school building to collect 20 bodies of persons killed by the hostage-takers. As the workers began to enter the building, an explosion sounded and some of the more than 1,000 hostages—including children—tried to flee. The terrorists began gunning them down and the military returned fire. Russian and foreign news agencies reported that more than 200 hostages, many of them children, were killed, and at least 650 were hospitalized with injuries.

- In what is considered the largest ongoing humanitarian emergency in the world, in 2004 over 1 million people were displaced by violence in Sudan. Between 100,000 and 140,000 Sudanese refugees have crossed the border into Chad. Inside Sudan, large numbers of persons are seeking safe refuge from the violence (Medecins Sans Frontieres, 2004).
- On September 11, 2001, a hijacked airline en route from Boston to Los Angeles with 92 people aboard crashed into the north tower of the World Trade Center in New York City. A second hijacked airline with 65 persons aboard crashed into the south tower of the World Trade Center 18 minutes later. A third hijacked plane, with 45 people aboard, crashed in southwestern Pennsylvania. A fourth hijacked plane with 64 persons aboard crashed into the Pentagon in Washington, D.C. The day's death toll reached almost 3,000, including more than 400 firefighters, policemen, and emergency personnel who were among the first to respond at the World Trade Center. Most of the approximately 50,000 people employed at the World Trade Center were employees of 430 businesses from 26 countries.

The health and well-being of large numbers of children around the world are threatened every day by war and organized violence. When children and their families are forced to find refuge in another country, substantial psychosocial problems are likely to develop. Problems may be associated with the trauma of the preflight experiences and the difficulties of resettlement (Angel, Hjern, & Ingleby, 2001). In fact, research indicates that organized violence in the home country is an important risk factor for mental health problems among refugees in exile. About 35–50 percent of children of resettled refugee families suffer from poor mental health (Almqvist & Brandell-Forsberg, 1995; Hjern, Angel, & Jeppsson, 1998; Ljungberg-Miklos, 1989; Montgomery, 1998).

How traumatic experiences are realized and internalized, however, and the extent of mental health trauma, may differ significantly among populations (Krupinski & Burrows, 1986) and within populations (Angel, Hjern, & Ingleby, 2001). In fact, it appears that the relationship between war stressors and the development of mental health symptoms is unpredictable. Children and adults alike may experience very differing effects from the exact same traumatic event. Many factors need to be considered, at the individual, family, and wider community levels (Angel et al., 2001), when assessing children and adults who have undergone stressful events. For instance, not all cultures share the traditional value attached in Western cultures to sharing distress, such as through verbal psychotherapy (Summerfield, 1999; Wellenkamp, 1997). In fact, disclosure appears to produce very different consequences in different cultural settings. In cultures where disclosure is discouraged, the use of disclosure as a therapeutic tool (such as talking about the war and war memories) is likely to be associated with short-term negative mental health outcomes for the trauma survivor. But in cultures where disclosure is encouraged, this therapeutic tool is likely to increase support and emotional involvement for the victim, resulting in more positive mental health outcomes (Angel, Hjern, & Ingleby, 2001).

It is important that mental health interventions using a verbal therapeutic approach be adapted to the context in which they are to be implemented.

DISASTER MANAGEMENT, PLANNING, AND CRISIS INTERVENTION

Social workers have a long history of responding to disaster trauma. As disasters have magnified in frequency and intensity, however, so has the complexity of disaster response, relief, and recovery efforts. Moreover, pre-disaster management, including assessment, mitigation, and preparedness, and post-disaster relief are relatively new arenas for social workers and other professionals. Many groups and organizations, which operate under various auspices, assumptions, and values, are now involved in the delivery of an array of post-disaster services (Soliman & Rogge, 2002). Despite the best of intentions, organizational variations in modes of communication, application requirements, scheduling, and eligibility standards increase the likelihood of inconsistency, conflict, and poor coordination in post-disaster service delivery (Gillespie et al., 1993; Seaman, 1999).

All forms of catastrophe, including terrorist attacks and armed conflicts, strain people's abilities to understand, cope, and respond. They also have a major impact on health and psychosocial functioning. Whether directly exposed to the event, or as a remote observer, most people are affected by such tragedies (Department of Mental Health and Substance Dependence, 2001). For social workers to respond in a timely and appropriate manner to the likely psychological distress experienced by trauma survivors, it is critical that social workers understand the nature of the problems survivors may experience, the types of help they may need, and the level of preparedness of the health and human service delivery systems in place to respond to those needs. Collecting information in the days and weeks following a disaster presents special challenges for social workers; foremost among them is the need for investigators to attach the highest priority to standards of privacy, dignity, and courtesy in the interactions with participants who were affected in any way by the event. Any information gathering activities, according to the National Institute of Mental Health (2001), "must acknowledge and adhere to the imperatives of doing no harm, placing the care and safety of victims and survivors above all else, and coordinating with local assistance efforts."

Research gathered by the WHO's Department of Mental Health and Substance Dependence (2001) offers important lessons learned about responses to catastrophes:

- Intense emotional reactions in the face of these events are expected and normal.
- There is a trajectory of responses over time, most often starting early and subsiding within weeks and months. But for some people, the onset of responses may be delayed. In others, the reactions may become long-term, leading to considerable disability.

- Responses will be highly individual in nature, often quite intense, and some-times conflictual. The vast majority of reactions are in the normal range and the intensity will diminish for most people over time without the need for professional help. Support from family and friends is critical. For some, how-ever, the degree of exposure may lead to more serious and prolonged reac-tions.
- The range of feelings experienced may be quite broad. People may describe intense feelings of sadness followed by anger. Others may experience fearful-ness and hypervigilance to the environment, among numerous other reac-tions.
- There may be temporary disruptions in normal coping mechanisms for many people, and some may go on to develop problems with sleep, nightmares, concentration, intrusive thoughts, and a preoccupation with reliving the events. These reactions are generally short lived but if they persist, profes-sional consultation should be sought.

The Department of Mental Health and Substance Dependence (2001) provides the following guidelines for providing help in the aftermath of a catastrophe:

- Create opportunities for people to talk and share experiences in supportive groups. This is often done best in familiar surroundings such as religious places, schools, or community centers.
- Provide accurate and practical information, especially concerning the larger recovery efforts. Special attention to the needs of relief applicants is necessary as relating to the rules and regulations of the relief organizations during the crisis.
- Give particular consideration to the needs of special groups such as children, those who have been most intensely exposed or had a history of previous events (exposure to trauma), rescue workers, and people with pre-existing mental health conditions.
- Children and adolescents will need the support of their caregivers. This support should reflect accurate concerns, and diminish any words or actions that would increase the child or adolescent's anxiety. Caregivers should offer reassurance as to their presence and availability during this time. Exposure to television, movies, or print matter that offers too graphic depictions of the destruction or victims should be limited.
- As many as 30 percent of people who experience the most direct exposure to the events may go on to develop more serious mental health concerns and should be referred for services if they develop persistent issues.

Social and community-based organizations must build the capacity neces-sary to partner with governmental and disaster relief organizations if mitigation attempts and post-disaster relief efforts are to be successful. Building capacity should focus on pre-disaster planning and action, including interdisciplinary community assessments of disaster potential, mitigation strategies and policy development, network building and resource mobilization, and education

| Box 13.1 | **Exemplars from Around the World** |

India

One of the most important and cost-effective measures for disaster-prone areas is flood forecasting and early warning systems. In India a cabinet-level committee on natural calamities was established that developed and implemented a five-year plan to extend and improve forecasting networks. As part of this plan, ten high-power cyclone detection radars were installed along the east and west coasts of the country. The plan also calls for the extension of the cyclone warning systems to all vulnerable areas. To identify potentially vulnerable areas, contour mapping of coastal areas is being conducted. Governmental officials are using contingency planning as a means to minimize flood-related crop losses. In addition, India is now employing the use of a new drought forecasting technique, utilizing regional and global parameters physically related to the southwest monsoon. "This, together with grain provision, access to health facilities and protection of cattle, has enabled the country to significantly improve its drought management systems" (United Nations Environment Programme, 2001).

Bangladesh

Bangladesh has set up a Natural Disaster Prevention Council. The council has taken over the coordinating functions of the government in the fields of natural disaster forecasting, management and post-disaster relief, and rehabilitation work (United Nations Environment Programme, 2001).

United States

In the United States, Columbia University is undertaking a comprehensive community-based assessment of environmental risks to African-American and Latino infants and children. Researchers in the center are studying the health consequences of residential sources of pollution and the relationship of the effects of inadequate nutritional status to increased negative impacts of environmental toxicants. Research scientists work closely with members of the local community to advance society's understanding of how environmental agents affect children's health. New and improved policies and practices will be informed by these research findings.

(Rogge, 2003). According to Rogge (2003, pp. 5–6), social work has an opportunity to build professional capacity to:

- define disasters and traumatic events and understand their nature;
- account for the needs of culturally diverse people and of vulnerable populations before, during, and after disasters and traumatic events happen;
- help communities assess, plan, and act to reduce damage and loss from such phenomena;
- increase community effectiveness in responding to disaster, through coordinated planning, training, and other action before the fact;
- respond to disaster and traumatic events with a knowledge and skill set that minimizes the hardships that citizens experience alone;
- engage in agency, service delivery system, and community-wide action to improve the quality of life as communities strive to recover from disaster;
- apply disaster and traumatic event-related knowledge and skills to improve policy and practice; and
- create disaster management strategies at individual, local, organizational, regional, national, and global levels.

| Box 13.2 | **Research Evidence Driving the Future Agenda**
Challenges for the Future |

- Community-based approaches to disaster mitigation lead to more accurate definition of problems and solutions, because they draw on local expertise in living with disasters. They can deploy low-cost, appropriate technologies effectively. They are more likely to be sustainable because they are "owned" by the community and build up local capacity. However, community-based approaches need to partner with government to increase outreach and have greater impact (International Federation of Red Cross and Red Crescent Societies, 2002).

- Innovative approaches to risk reduction from natural disasters appear promising. One of the most exciting is the "sustainable livelihoods" perspective, which analyzes the range of vulnerabilities poor communities face and the assets to which they have access. Vulnerability and Capacity Analysis (VCA) is a valuable new field tool being used to assess communities' disaster resilience and mobilize risk reduction (International Federation of Red Cross and Red Crescent Societies, 2002).

- Disclosure or verbal psychotherapy has differing effects depending on the individual and culture. In cultures where disclosure is discouraged, talking about the traumatic event may cause short-term negative mental health outcomes. Mental health interventions using a verbal therapeutic approach should be adapted to the cultural context in which it is implemented.

- Help from mental health professionals for children and families experiencing trauma from natural disaster experiences is most effective if given fairly intensively during the six months immediately following a natural disaster. In cultures where disclosure is acceptable, helping the parents to cope adaptively with the immediate aftermath of the disaster, to recognize their children's needs, and to discuss the event openly are important elements to effective helping.

- Implementation of comprehensive land use plans have been instrumental in incorporating hazard mitigation and preparedness provisions into the development process. For instance, provision of green belts on river banks reduces flood damage; parks and open spaces in a city can provide temporary shelters during earthquakes. Similarly, slum and squatter settlement improvement schemes that are being undertaken in many areas have also helped reduce the risk of disasters (United Nations Environment Programme, 2001).

INTERNATIONAL ORGANIZATIONS

Centre for Research on the Epidemiology of Disasters

CRED was established in 1973 as a nonprofit institution with international status under Belgian law. It is located within the School of Public Health of the Universite Catholique de Louvain in Brussels. With a special focus on public health, epidemiology, and structural and socioeconomic aspects, CRED promotes research, training, and information dissemination on disasters. It aims to enhance the effectiveness of developing countries' disaster management capabilities as well as foster policy-oriented research (for more information see http://www.cred.be/cred1/who.htm).

International Committee of the Red Cross

The ICRC was established in 1863. As an impartial, neutral and independent organization, it serves as the guardian of international humanitarian law. Its exclusively humanitarian mission is to protect the lives and dignity of victims of war and internal violence and to provide them with assistance. It directs and co-ordinates international relief activities in situations of conflict. It also works to prevent suffering through the promotion and strengthening of humanitarian law and universal humanitarian principles. The ICRC is the founding body of the International Red Cross and Red Crescent Movement (for more information see http://www.icrc.org).

Medecins Sans Frontieres (Doctors Without Borders)

Medecins Sans Frontieres is the world's largest medical assistance organization. It is an independent humanitarian medical aid agency committed to providing medical aid wherever needed, regardless of race, religion, politics, or sex. It works to raise awareness of the suffering of people around the world. Following natural disasters, MSF sends in medical teams, equipment, and supplies (for more information see http://www.msf.org).

United Nations Environment Programme

The UNEP provides leadership and encourages partnerships in caring for the environment by "inspiring, informing, and enabling nations and peoples to improve their quality of life without compromising that of future generations" (for more information see http://www.unep.org).

SUMMARY

Natural and human-made disasters are occurring at a greater frequency than ever before. Social workers can and should play a vital role in preventing and responding to natural and human-made disasters. Although social workers have a long history of responding to disaster trauma, pre-disaster management is a new arena for social workers and other professionals. All social workers need to be trained in risk and crisis management. Given the increased frequency of catastrophes, the social work profession must increase its efforts in research, planning, and social policy to better prepare all social workers in this arena.

Thinking About Practice: From Local to Global Perspectives

1. How well is your community/state/nation prepared to respond to a natural disaster? Assess the local, state, and national preparedness plans from early warning to post-disaster relief. Are there other strategies that could be put in place?
2. To what extent are social workers in your community prepared to respond in case of a natural or human-made catastrophe? Interview social workers in your community. Is additional training needed?
3. Locate and review the disaster response plan for your community in the event of terrorism or armed conflict. Does your community have one? If not, why? If so, is the plan comprehensive in scope? What is the social work role in the plan? Do you

think there are other strategies that need to be put in place?

4. When was the last natural or human-made disaster in your community, or close to your community?

What devastation occurred? How could the response have been improved?

Social Work Practice and Social Justice Website

Please go to the Book Companion Website at http://www.thomsonedu.com/author/sowers to find a rich collection of related articles selected by the authors from Info Trac College Edition.

References

Almqvist, K., & Brandell-Forsberg, M. (1995). Iranian refugee children in Sweden: Effects of organized violence and forced migration on preschool children. *American Journal of Orthopsychiatry, 65*, 225–237.

Angel, B., Hjern, A., & Ingleby, D. (2001). Effects of war and organized violence on children: A study of Bosnian refugees in Sweden. *American Journal of Orthopsychiatry, 71*(1), 4–15.

Bloom, G. E. (1986). A school disaster: Intervention and research aspects. *Journal of the American Academy of Child Psychiatry, 25*, 336–345.

Center for Research on the Epidemiology of Disasters. (2002). *The OFDA/CRED international disasters database.* Retrieved August 2, 2004, from http://www.cred.be/emdat/disda2.htm

Cooperative Institute for Research in Environmental Sciences. (2001). *The Gujarat earthquake.* Retrieved August 18, 2004, from http://cires.colorado.edu/~bilbaum/gujarat2001.html

Darby, K. H., Ellis, R. A., Sowers, K. M., & McCarter, A. K. (2004). Chemical exposure. In L. Rapp-Paglicci, C. N. Dulmus, & J. S. Wodarski (Eds.), *Handbook of preventive interventions for children and adolescents* (pp. 174–197). Hoboken, NJ: John Wiley & Sons.

Department of Mental Health and Substance Dependence. (2001). *How to address psychosocial reactions to catastrophe.* Geneva: World Health Organization.

De Sousa, A. B., Jr. (2000). Emergency planning for hazardous industrial areas: A Brazilian case study. *Risk Analysis, 20*(4), 483–493.

De Nevers, N. (Ed.). (1972). *Technology and society.* Reading, MA: Addison-Wesley.

Dollinger, S. J. (1985). Lightning-strike disaster among children. *British Journal of Medical Psychology, 58*, 375–383.

Dollinger, S. J., O'Donnell, J. P., & Staley, A. A. (1984). Lightning-strike disaster: Effects on children's fears and worries. *Journal of Consulting and Clinical Psychology, 52*, 1028–1038.

Dufka, C. L. (1988). The Mexico City earthquake disaster. *Social Casework, 69*(3), 162–170.

Earls, F., Smith, E., Reich, W., & Jung, K. G. (1988). Investigating psychopathological consequences of a disaster in children: A pilot study incorporating a structured diagnostic interview. *Journal of the American Academy of Child and Adolescent Psychiatry, 27*, 90–95.

Galante, R., & Foa, A. (1986). An epidemiological study of psychic trauma and treatment effectiveness in children after a natural disaster. *Journal of the American Academy of Child Psychiatry, 25*, 357–363.

Gillespie, D. F., Colignon, R. A., Banerjee, M. M., Murty, S. A., & Rogge, M. E. (1993). *Partnerships for community preparedness.* Boulder, CO: Institute of Behavioral Science, University of Colorado Press.

Granot, H. (1998). The dark side of growth and industrial disasters since the Second World War. *Disaster Prevention and Management, 7*(3), 195–204.

Hardcastle, R. J., & Chua, A. T. L. (1998). *Humanitarian assistance: Towards a right of access to victims of natural disasters.* Retrieved August 14, 2004, from http://www.icrc.org

Heiberg, A. N. (1999). Keynote address by Dr. Astrid N. Heiberg, President of the International

Federation of Red Cross and Red Crescent Societies. *International Review of the Red Cross, 836*, 837–841.

Hjern, A., Angel, B., & Jeppsson, O. (1998). Political violence, family stress and mental health of refugee children in exile. *Scandinavian Journal of Social Medicine, 26*, 18–25.

International Federation of Red Cross and Red Crescent Societies. (1999). *World disasters report 1999*. Geneva: Author.

International Federation of Red Cross and Red Crescent Societies. (2002). *World disasters report 2002*. Geneva: Author.

Keller, A. Z., & Al-madhari, A. F. (1996). Risk management and disasters. *Disaster Prevention and Management, 5*(5), 19–22.

Keller, A. Z., Manikin, M., Al-shammari, I., & Cassidy, K. (1997). Analysis of fatality, injury, evacuation and cost data using the Bradford Disaster Scale. *Disaster Prevention and Management, 6*(1), 11–21.

Krupinski, J., & Burrows, G. (1986). Psychiatric disorders in adolescents and young adults. In J. Krupinski (Ed.), *The price of freedom* (pp. 123–135). New York: Pergamon Press.

Langer, N. (2004). Natural disasters that reveal cracks in our social foundation. *Educational Gerontology, 30*(4), 275–286.

Ljungberg-Miklos, J. (1989). The mental health of refugee children. *Socialmedicinsk Tidskrift, 66*, 18–24.

McGregor, R. (21 February 1998). Hidden holocaust. *The Australian*.

Medicins Sans Frontieres. (2004). *Sudan crisis: Fleeing the hidden war*. Retrieved August 14, 2004, from http://www.msf.org/countries

Montgomery, E. (1998). Refugee children from the Middle East. *Scandinavian Journal of Social Medicine, 54*, 1–152.

Mullins, S., & Burbage, J. (1989). *And Hugo was his name: Hurricane Hugo, a diary of destruction, September 21, 1989*. Sun City West, AZ: C. F. Boone Publishing.

National Institute of Mental Health. (2001). *Research in response to terrorist acts against America: Addendum to: Rapid assessment post-impact of disaster research grant program*. Retrieved August 20, 2004, from http://grants.nih.gov

Pidgeon, N., Turner, B., Toft, B., & Blockley, D. (1992). Hazard management and safety culture.

In D. Parker & J. Handmer (Eds), *Hazard management and emergency planning: Perspectives on Britain*. London: James & James.

Rogge, M. (2003). The future is now: Social work, disaster management, and traumatic stress in the 21st century. *Journal of Social Service Research, 30*(2), 1–6.

Saylor, C.F., Swenson, C. C., & Powell, M. P. (1992). Hurricane Hugo blows down the broccoli: Preschoolers' postdisaster play and adjustment. *Child Psychiatry and Human Development, 22*(3), 139–149.

Seaman, J. (1999). Malnutrition in emergencies: How can we do better and where do the responsibilities lie? *Disasters, 23*(4), 306–315.

Shaluf, I. M., Ahmadun, F., Said, A. M., Sharif, R., & Mustapha, S. (2002). Technological man-made disaster precondition phase model for major accidents. *Disaster Prevention and Management, 11*(5), 380–388.

Shrivastava, P., Mitroff, I., Miller, D., & Migliani, A. (1988, July). Understanding industrial crisis. *Journal of Management Studies, 25*(4).

Soliman, H. H., & Rogge, M. E. (2002). Ethical considerations in disaster services: A social work perspective. *Electronic Journal of Social Work, 1*(1), 1–23.

Sugar, M. (1988). Children in a disaster: An overview. *Child Psychiatry & Human Development, 19*, 163–179.

Summerfield, D. (1999). A critique of seven assumptions behind psychological trauma programmes in war affected areas. *Social Science and Medicine, 48*, 1449–1462.

Svedin, C. G., Back, K., & Wadsby, M. (1994). Mental health among immigrant and refugee children of divorced parents. *Scandinavian Journal of Social Medicine, 22*, 178–186.

Swenson, C. C., Saylor, C. F., Powell, M. P., Stokes, S. J., Foster, K. Y., & Belter, R. W. (1996). Impact of a natural disaster on preschool children: Adjustment 14 months after a hurricane. *American Journal of Orthopsychiatry, 66*(1), 122–130.

United Nations. (1996). *Agenda for development*. UN doc. A/AC.250. Retrieved August 13, 2004, from http://www.un.org

United Nations Environment Programme. (2001). *State of the environment, South Asia 2001*. Retrieved August 19, 2004, from http://www. unep.org

United Nations Environment Programme. (2002). *UNEP-APELL* Disasters Database. Retrieved August 10, 2004, from http://www.unepie.org/pc/apell/disasters/lists/ disasterdate.html

United Nations Office for the Coordination of Humanitarian Affairs. (12 February 1998). UN, IRC seek $2.5 million for Afghan air drop. *Reuters.*

Washington Post. (27 May 1997). Koreans agree on food aid to the North. Washington, DC: Author.

Wellenkamp, J. (1997). Cultural similarities and differences regarding emotional disclosure: Some examples from Indonesia and the Pacific. In J. Pennebaker (Ed.), *Opening up: The healing power of expressing emotions* (pp. 293–311). New York: Guilford Press.

World Health Organization. (n.d.). *Three months after the Indian Ocean earthquake-tsunami.* Retrieved May 13, 2005, from http://www.who.int/crises/international/asia_tsunami/3months/en/index.html

Zakour, M. J. (1996). Disaster research in social work. In C. L. Streeter & S. A. Murty (Eds.), *Research on social work and disasters,* (pp. 7–26). New York: Haworth.

Macro Perspectives

Social work practice occurs at the intersection between the individual and environment. The vision of social work has been to help societies realize their greatest potential for all of their citizens. The most recent focus has been on strengthening communities rather than on change directed toward one person or one family at a time. Community empowerment has shown to have great promise by helping communities take charge of their own destiny. This section highlights promising community development models designed to empower and strengthen communities.

The universal brotherhood of man is our most precious possession.
Mark Twain

14 CHAPTER | Community Development

COMMUNITY ORGANIZATION/COMMUNITY DEVELOPMENT

Community organization has long been considered one of the social work profession's major methodologies for improving the well-being of neighborhoods and communities. Community organizers have in the past worked for governments, municipalities, and large institutions engaged in social planning. Others employing a community development approach have worked in nongovernmental organizations or for interested groups focused on a particular goal, such as the development of services, neighborhood improvement, and various goals and priorities as determined by the community. Historically the focus in the United States was often on poverty alleviation at the community level using existing social and economic structures.

Gilchrest (2003) noted that, "Traditionally, community development has tended to prioritize or focus on areas experiencing multiple disadvantage or where there is a perceived need for local infrastructure and capabilities to be improved." This being the case, social workers around the world are forced to decide how the term "disadvantaged" is defined. Similar to the issue of poverty, there is no standard and globally recognized definition of this term. Conceptualizing this term is important for social workers, especially for those who are working globally.

O'Neil and O'Neil (2003) make a similar point, "Community development, a term used to depict professional activities to improve the well-being of community residents, has a history that cuts across various disciplines. Generally, it involves a range of practices dedicated to improving the strength and effectiveness of community life."

Increasingly community empowerment became the preferred strategy, "The definitions of empowerment include concepts of giving power, authorizing, or enabling relationships within the following domains: personal/individual and family, social-cultural, political, social and economic" (O'Neil & O'Neil, 2003).

Edwards (n.d.) noted, "Against the background of economic globalization and financial meltdown, social inequality and exclusion are increasing both within and between countries, threatening livelihoods, peace and stability the world over."

Brocklesby and Fisher (2003) concluded that "by the late 1990s, the idea of sustainable livelihoods had consolidated into an approach, or a number of very similar approaches, developed and/or implemented by intergovernmental organizations, bilateral donors, non-governmental organizations and research institutes."

Some countries have found it difficult to work with NGOs and include citizens from disadvantaged neighborhoods in the planning and decision-making process.

United Kingdom

The UK government has focused attention on Britain's most disadvantaged communities and, through its neighborhood renewal strategy, is targeting resources on areas experiencing particularly high levels of unemployment, poor health, low educational achievement and rising crime. Different interpretations abound of what this means in practice, but nevertheless there is a broad agreement that communities should be included in decision-making about things that affect them (Gilchrist, 2003).

Gilchrist's point is important because it establishes unemployment, poor health, low educational achievement, and rising crime as specific criteria that can be used to determine whether a community is in need of development. In other words, these criteria are all universally recognized indicators that can potentially be used in a standardized way of viewing community development needs. Gilchrist (2003) goes on to say:

> Many government agencies and civil servants find managing their relationships with community and voluntary organizations difficult and frustrating, and are only beginning to appreciate the vital complexity and dynamism of the sector, let alone the myriad of identity- and interest-based communities within British society.

Here Gilchrist highlights the importance of collaboration between governments and NGOs. This is significant because governments play a key role in community development by providing economic and legal support.

Czech Republic

"There is limited transparency and openness of planning and decision-making processes in the Czech Republic," note Jindrova, Djorgov, and Nizu (2003). "This again relates to that long period in our [Czech citizens'] recent history when we had centralized decision-making in government and no one at the local level was invited to think about or participate in any planning or decision-making."

The preceding quote speaks to the fact that people must be included in the processes that are affecting their lives. Successful community development is based on the premise that the people see themselves as active participants.

In the Czech Republic, the public and also nongovernmental, nonprofit sectors are not seen as important partners in community development. There is quite a strong historical resistance towards cooperation and exchange of information among nonprofit organizations. In the Czech Republic, extremely limited funding is available for all types of activities, so there is very strong competition between organizations and this creates a difficult situation for cooperation (Jindrova, Djorgov, & Nizu, 2003). These authors point out a potentially overlooked aspect of community development, that of competition amongst NGOs for funding. This is an important consideration, especially given the aforementioned need for governmental involvement.

Ireland

Community development has moved from the margins to become a central aspect of Ireland's antipoverty and social inclusion action. There is a commitment to move to more open and accountable government, evidenced by developments such as the requirement that government departments prepare a "strategy statement" providing a link between government policy and its implementation, and the passage in 1998 of freedom of information legislation (Lee, 2003).

NONGOVERNMENTAL ORGANIZATIONS

Nongovernmental organizations are perhaps the most substantial change agents in the realm of community development. NGOs have a tremendous amount of power because they often act as intermediaries between governments and citizens. The following can serve as a working definition for nongovernmental organizations.

The World Bank defines NGOs as private organizations that pursue activities to relieve suffering, promote the interests of the poor, protect the environment, provide basic social services, or undertake community development. In wider usage, the term NGO can be applied to any nonprofit organization that is independent from government. NGOs are typically value-based organizations, which depend, in whole or in part, on charitable donations and voluntary service. Although the NGO sector has become increasingly professionalized over the last two decades, principles of altruism and voluntarism remain key defining characteristics (Shreve, 2004).

SAMPLE OF NATIONAL AND INTERNATIONAL NONGOVERNMENTAL ORGANIZATIONS

Iran

Centre for Sustainable Development and Environment: Its projects include Water for Peace and Prosperity, sustainable pastoral development, anti-desertification, and food sovereignty (for more information see http://www.cenesta.org).

Africa

New Partnership for Africa's Development: Its projects include economic development, job creation, conflict resolution, and support to grass-root organizations (for more information see http://www.nepad.org).

USA

National Coalition for the Homeless: The coalition's work focuses on housing, economic justice, health care justice, and voting rights. Methods include grass-root organizing, public education, policy advocacy, and technical assistance (for more information see http://www.nationalhomeless.org).

Center for Community Change: Its work focuses on helping low income people, building effective organizations in order to improve their communities, and promoting public policies. The group also advocates comprehensive immigration reform (for more information see http://www.communitychange.org).

Brazil (Land Redistribution)

Movimento dos Trabalhadores Rurais Sem Terra (Brazil's Landless Workers Movement): The main focus is land reform, given that 60 percent of Brazil's farmland is unused, while 25 million peasants subsist with temporary agricultural jobs (for more information see http://www.mstbrazil.org).

United Kingdom

British Overseas NGOs for Development (BOND): This is a network of more than 280 voluntary organizations working on global development and education. It focuses on enhancing civil society to combat poverty and to demand accountability and action from governments (for more information see http://www.bond.org.uk).

India

Association for Stimulating Know How (ASK): ASK helps build the capacities of community-based organizations (CBOs) and NGOs for self-development, provides women with options and choices for social and economic empowerment, promotes socially responsible business practices, brings positive and strategic change in the life of children in difficult circumstances, and mainstreams social development principles in infrastructure development projects (for more information see http://www.askindia.org).

Nepal

MS Nepal: This group focuses on creating better conditions for the poor and marginalized and promoting global justice (for more information see http://www.msnepal.org).

HOUSING

Many view affordable housing as a basic focus of community development. A person's shelter provides not only protection from the elements, but also establishes the basis for social inclusion and community involvement. According to Article 25(1) of the United Nations Universal Declaration of Human Rights, "everyone has the right to a standard of living adequate for the health and well-being of himself and of his family, including food, clothing, and housing" (United Nations, 1998).

Housing itself is an important productive asset that can cushion the effects of economic reform, so the shape of housing policy and the form of land market regulation can create or deny poor people the opportunities they need to use these assets to advance or protect their interests (Edwards, n.d.).

Despite the economic strength of the United States, homelessness and inadequate housing continue to be major problems. Extraordinary numbers of rural citizens continue to live in dwellings with minimal amenities and unsafe conditions. Some of the country's most distressed communities are located in inner-city slums that continue to deteriorate in spite of various programs and promises.

In the United States a lack of affordable housing and the limited scope of housing assistance programs are the primary causes of homelessness. The growing gap between the number of affordable housing units and the number of people needing them has created a housing crisis for poor people. Consider the following statistics:

- Overall, 14.4 million families have critical housing needs.
- Between 1973 and 1993, 2.2 million low-rent units disappeared from the market. These units were either abandoned, demolished, converted into condominiums or expensive apartments, or became unaffordable because of cost increases (Daskal, 1998).
- At the same time, the number of low income renters increased, due to factors such as eroding employment opportunities and the declining value and availability of public assistance.
- In 1999, there were only 4.9 million rental units affordable and available to 7.7 million extremely low income renter households; this represented a shortage of 2.8 million units (U.S. Census Bureau, 1999).
- It would take annual production of more than 250,000 units for more than 20 years to close the housing affordability gap.
- In 1997, 3 million low to moderate income working families spent more than one-half of their income on housing. By 2001 this number had jumped to 4.8 million—a 67 percent increase (National Coalition for the Homeless, 2002).

According to the National Coalition for the Homeless (2002):

Homelessness and poverty are inextricably linked. Poor people are frequently unable to pay for housing, food, childcare, health care, and education. Difficult choices must be made when limited resources cover only some of these necessities. Often it is housing, which absorbs a high proportion of income that must be dropped. Being poor means being an illness, an accident, or a paycheck away from living on the streets.

INTERNATIONAL ORGANIZATIONS ON COMMUNITY DEVELOPMENT

United Nations Human Settlements Programme (UN-HABITAT)

UN-HABITAT is mandated by the UN General Assembly to promote socially and environmentally sustainable towns and cities with the goal of providing adequate shelter for all. UN-HABITAT runs two major worldwide campaigns—the

Box 14.1   Exemplars from Around the World

Carmelita, Guatemala

In Carmelita, the Guatemalan government has established 13 locally managed forest concessions in the jungle village. The cooperative that works the 130,000-acre concession in the rain forest consists of 56 impoverished families from the jungle village. The concessions are logged in accordance with rules laid down by the Forest Stewardship Council, a nonprofit organization based in Bonn, Germany. Environmental organizations credit the approach with reducing deforestation and protecting watersheds and wetland areas while providing a steady income for local residents (Replogle, n.d.).

Ghana

The Ghana Community School Alliances Project, a community-mobilization initiative funded by USAID, fosters community participation in more than 300 primary schools throughout Ghana to build an environment of mutual respect, responsibility, and action among community members, schools, and education administrators as they work to meet the learning needs of Ghanaian children. In addition, the project trains district-level education mangers to use data for decision making at the local level (Education Development Center, n.d.).

Indonesia

In the aftermath of the December 2004 Indian Ocean tsunami, Mercy Corps field managers quickly mobilized local workers to rebuild schools, clean up water systems, and repair commercial fishing boats. Through innovative cash-for-work programs, tsunami survivors earned income to support their families and reclaim their lives (Mercy Corps, n.d.).

Global Campaign on Urban Governance and the Global Campaign for Secure Tenure. Through these campaigns and by other means, the agency focuses on a range of issues and special projects that it helps implement. These include supporting a joint UN-HABITAT/World Bank slum-upgrading initiative called the Cities Alliance; promoting effective housing development and housing rights policies and strategies; helping to develop sustainable cities and urban environmental planning and management; and advocating for post-conflict land management and reconstruction in countries devastated by war or natural disasters (for more information see http://www. unchs.org).

CARE International

CARE works with poor communities in more than 70 countries around the world to find lasting solutions to poverty. It looks at the big picture of poverty and goes beyond the symptoms to confront underlying causes. It has a broad range of programs based on empowerment, equity, and sustainability. CARE seeks to tap human potential and leverage the power of individuals and communities to unleash a vast force for progress.

CARE's mission is to serve individuals and families in the poorest communities in the world. Drawing strength from its global diversity, resources, and experience. CARE promotes innovative solutions and advocates for global responsibility. It facilitates lasting change by:

- strengthening capacity for self-help;
- providing economic opportunity;

Box 14.2 | Research Evidence Driving the Future Agenda
Challenges for the Future

International Definition of Community Development

As we have seen with other issues, establishing a global definition of community development is important. This is especially the case if increased global cooperation is expected. More so than defining the concept, it would be ideal for all government officials and individual citizens to view community development as a critical issue for all people. Viewing community development in this light would allow for the global sharing of best practices.

Ending Relocation of Poor for Profit-Driven Motives

As land and resources continue to become scarcer, the practice of relocating the poor and disadvantaged for profit-driven real estate development is likely to increase. Because social workers have the special responsibility of advocating on behalf of the poor and vulnerable, this is an area where they can make a substantial difference.

Increased Attention on Factors That May Lead to Homelessness

People become homeless for a variety of reasons. Causes of homelessness typically include unemployment, mental disorder, drug addiction, and domestic violence. Although it is important to solve the issue of homelessness, it is more important to tend to the reasons why people become homeless in the first place. Social workers can make a significant difference by helping people and communities to develop in such a way as to prevent homelessness from occurring.

Increasing Governmental Ownership of Homelessness

Social workers and other individuals can do only so much when it comes to community development. Real change can be enacted only when governments take responsibility for their homeless populations. The homeless population is often forgotten because it lacks the power and voice necessary to move the government to action. Furthermore, in this climate of devolution it is becoming increasingly more difficult to determine if the ultimate responsibility for homelessness should rest with the local, the state, or the federal government.

Improving Collaboration among NGOs

Improving collaboration among nongovernmental organizations is another area in which social workers can make a substantial difference. NGOs play an important role in providing disadvantaged people with the resources and power they need in order to develop their communities. In addition to working with each other, NGOs also have the responsibility of advocating on behalf of the poor and vulnerable by convincing governments to pay attention to this population.

Cultural Training for Social Workers

Social workers who wish to work globally face the monumental task of entering another culture that must be understood and respected in order for change to occur. Therefore, social workers must receive cultural training that will allow them to move successfully from one country to the next.

Educating the Public

It is necessary to educate the general public regarding community development. This would allow people to better understand their environment and would enable them to become active participants in the changes that are being made around them.

- delivering relief in emergencies;
- influencing policy decisions at all levels; and
- addressing discrimination in all its forms (for more information see http://www.careinternational.org).

World Neighbors

World Neighbors is a grass-root development organization working in partnership with the rural poor in hundreds of villages throughout Asia, Africa, and Latin America. World Neighbors brings people together to solve their problems and meet their basic needs. By supporting community self-reliance, leadership, and organization, World Neighbors helps people address the root causes of hunger, poverty, and disease.

World Neighbors helps people develop and sustain their own programs. Most programs begin using locally available resources and simple, low-cost technologies. As people gain the skills and confidence they need to solve problems, local leaders and organizations emerge to carry on the work and multiply results. World Neighbors' role is to strengthen these basic human resources for long-term development (for more information see http://www.wn.org).

Habitat for Humanity International

Habitat for Humanity International is a nonprofit, ecumenical Christian housing ministry. HFHI seeks to eliminate poverty housing and homelessness from the world, and to make decent shelter a matter of conscience and action. Habitat invites people of all backgrounds, races, and religions to build houses together in partnership with families in need. Habitat has built more than 175,000 houses around the world, providing safe, decent, affordable shelter for more than 900,000 people.

Through volunteer labor and donations of money and materials, Habitat builds and rehabilitates simple, decent houses with the help of the homeowner (partner) families. Habitat houses are sold to partner families at no profit, and financed with affordable, no-interest loans. The homeowners' monthly mortgage payments are used to build still more Habitat houses (for more information see http://www.habitat.org).

International Relief and Development

IRD is a private voluntary organization (PVO) dedicated to improving the quality of life of people in the most economically deprived parts of the world by facilitating and supporting assistance tailored specifically to their needs. IRD works with a wide range of organizations (domestic and foreign government agencies, international organizations, international and local PVOs, and U.S. corporations) to implement targeted, cost-effective relief and development programs. Through these programs IRD helps communities to develop, rehabilitate, and maintain their infrastructure—roads, primary health clinics, school buildings, water sanitation, small dams, and street lights—in order to improve citizens' quality of life (for more information see http://www.ird-dc.org).

Homeless International

Homeless International is a British-based charity that supports community-led housing and infrastructure-related development in partnership with local organizations in Asia, Africa, and Latin America. It was established in 1989 following the 1987 United Nations International Year of Shelter for the Homeless. The initiatives are all led, developed, and managed by the local community groups themselves.

Homeless International: 1) supports partners through long-term development initiatives, 2) advocates through sharing information and influencing policy, 3) provides financial services by scaling up access to credit for the poor through loans and guarantees, 4) organizes technical assistance by providing practical forms of specialist help, and 5) carries out research by aiming to explore long-term solutions to poverty (for more information see http://www.homeless-international.org).

International Association for Community Development

The IACD is a not-for-profit, nongovernmental organization belonging to its members. Its mission is to act as the recognized international forum for the promotion of: 1) community development practice, research, and policy analysis, 2) advocacy for community development values and approaches in international forums, 3) links amongst community development practitioners, associations, educators, and policy makers, and 4) community empowerment and the creation of an effective voice at local, regional, and global levels for community development and communities (for more information see http://www.iacdglobal.org).

EnterpriseWorks/Volunteers in Technical Assistance

EnterpriseWorks has recently merged with Volunteers in Technical Assistance, which has a 45 year history of empowering the poor in developing countries. The merged agency continues to be a private, nonprofit, international development organization, registered as a private voluntary organization with USAID. The organization offers services in a variety of areas including information dissemination, the design and installation of specialized communications systems, preparation and publication of technical materials, disaster information coordination, and management of long-term development programs.

VITA was founded on the premise that information is an essential part of improving the quality of life in developing countries. In 2004, VITA's original service, the Technical Inquiry Service, observed its 45th year of operation. During this time it has provided information to almost 300,000 individuals and groups, responding to their expressed needs. Importantly, those that have used and benefited from VITA's services represent the very groups that most development agencies have targeted as priorities—the poor and disadvantaged (for more information see http://enterpriseworks.org/vita.asp).

SUMMARY

As Mark Twain noted, the "universal brotherhood of man" is indeed our most precious possession. This concept of the universal fellowship of humanity is especially important when we consider community development, an area of paramount significance for social work because it touches upon the fundamental belief that social workers must view the entire system of an individual or family in order to be effective. This includes issues relating to community development, housing, and homelessness, and how government agencies, nongovernmental organizations, and nonprofits can address these concerns.

An important issue when considering global social work is the determination of what is meant by community development around the world. Furthermore, how do countries view community development, what level of importance do they place on it, and how do they determine which communities need to be developed? It is necessary to consider the fact that not every country has the same concept of what it means to be disadvantaged or poor, thus leading to different attitudes and policies regarding community development.

Governments have the major responsibility of recognizing adequate housing as a fundamental human right. For the betterment of all societies, governments must view community development, housing, and homelessness as critical issues. Community development is doomed to failure without governmental support, effective policies, and economic funding. Additionally, governments must assume responsibility for protecting citizens who are in jeopardy of losing their homes due to profit-driven real estate development.

Empowerment is essential to the discussion of community development because the ultimate goal of development should always be creation of sustainable livelihoods. Although it is important to build an infrastructure and provide financial support, it is even more important to ensure that the people of a given community can sustain themselves when support is reduced or ceases altogether. Also, making people aware of the planning and decision-making processes that affect their lives will allow them to become active participants in the construction of their own realities.

Thinking About Practice: From Local to Global Perspectives

1. What are some of the ways in which a community can become developed?
2. Why is it important to understand how different countries conceptualize community development?
3. Why do social workers need to be culturally competent when attempting to develop communities locally or globally?
4. What is empowerment? Why is it important?
5. What roles do nongovernmental organizations play in community development?
6. How does the World Bank define nongovernmental organizations (NGOs)?

Social Work Practice and Social Justice

Please go to the Book Companion Website at http://www.thomsonedu.com/author/sowers to find a rich collection of related articles selected by the authors from Info Trac College Edition.

References

Brocklesby, M. A., & Fisher, E. (2003). Community development in sustainable livelihoods approaches: An introduction. *Community Development Journal, 38*(3), 185.

Daskal, J. (1998). *In search of shelter: The growing shortage of affordable rental housing.* Washington, DC: Center on Budget and Policy Priorities.

Education Development Center. (n.d.). *Ghana community school alliances (CSA) project.* Retrieved August 27, 2005, from http://main. edc.org/search/projectView.asp

Edwards, M. (n.d.). *Civil society's role in promoting inclusiveness.* Retrieved August 27, 2005, from http://www.unchs.org/mdg/documents/global/ Vol4_No4 _civil_societys_role_in_promoting_inclusiveness.doc

Gilchrist, A. (2003). Community development in the UK: Possibilities and paradoxes. *Community Development Journal, 38*(1), 16–25.

Jindrova, P., Djorgov, V., & Nizu, F. (2003). Community development in East and Central Europe: Three cameos. *Community Development Journal, 38*(1), 59–68.

Lee, A. (2003). Community development in Ireland. *Community Development Journal, 38*(1), 48–58.

Mercy Corps. (n.d.). *Restoring lives in Indonesia.* Retrieved August 27, 2005, from http://www. mercycorps.org

National Coalition for the Homeless. (2002). *Why are people homeless?* Retrieved August 26, 2005, from http://www.nationalhomeless.org/causes. html

National Coalition for the Homeless (n.d.). *People need affordable housing.* Retrieved August 27, 2005, from http://www.nationalhomeless.org/ facts/ housing.html

O'Neil, G. S., & O'Neil, R. (2003). Community development in the USA: An empowerment zone example. *Community Development Journal, 38*(2), 120.

Replogle, J. (n.d.). *Village in Guatemalan rain forest thrives with ecological logging: Lumber sold in U.S. through program that certifies wood.* Retrieved August 27, 2005, from http:// www. sfgate.com/egi-bin/article.cgi? file=c/a/2005

Shreve, C. (2004). *Non-governmental organizations research guide.* Retrieved August 27, 2005 from http://docs.lib.duke.edu/igo/guides/ngo

United Nations (1998). *Universal declaration of human rights.* Retrieved March 21, 2005, from: http://www.un.org/Overview/rights.html

U.S. Census Bureau (1999). American housing survey. Retrieved August 27, 2005 from http://www. huduser.org/datasets/ahs/ahsdata99.html

The Future of Global Social Work Practice

Internationalization and globalization are already becoming realities. Our world has become easier to navigate but at times no easier to understand. War, poverty, disease, and population displacement affect all parts of the world. We cannot escape the impact of tragedies taking place in other parts of the world. Our hope for a peaceful, thriving, and sustainable environment for future generations depends on finding solutions to the world's problems today. Social workers can make a positive difference on the global stage. This section of the text outlines steps being taken to internationalize and globalize the profession of social work and provides a roadmap for the future.

Does not the perspective of a better future depend on something like an international community of the shaken which, ignoring state boundaries, political systems and power blocs, starting outside the high game of traditional politics, aspiring to no title and appointments, will seek to make a real political force out of a phenomenon so ridiculed by the technicians of power—the phenomenon of human conscience?

Vaclav Havel

15 CHAPTER | Future Trends in Global Social Work Practice

Great challenges lie ahead as social work continues to move toward becoming a globalized profession. One of these challenges will be for the profession to evolve a concept of social work that can bridge the differing philosophies of society's role in meeting human needs. At the same time, social work needs to maintain its unique function as the profession that addresses both individual and family needs, and simultaneously remains concerned with changing society to reduce or eliminate factors that contribute to people's problems in social functioning (Morales & Sheafor, 2001). Prevalent social work practice models may no longer be appropriate as social problems become more interconnected and nations increasingly interdependent. Development of a practice framework is needed that can articulate the connection between poverty, environmental resource depletion, social injustice, global militarism, and worldwide consumption patterns. This will require a shift in thinking regarding problem identification and our professional social work practice response (Mary & Morris, 1994).

Another major challenge for global social work is the tendency in social work to dichotomize between global and domestic social work issues. In general, U.S. social work, the dominant profession in domestic social work, has remained uninvolved in global social development agencies and disinterested in the development education movement or in social work policies that have global implications (Healy, 1995).

Since the nineteenth century, social work has attained a significant degree of professionalization. This professionalization has been reflected in the existence of international associations that have sought to promote social work's interests and to enhance its professional development worldwide. Despite the growth of social work as a global profession, most social workers are poorly informed about the activities of their colleagues in other countries. As the global social work profession evolves, a growing emphasis must be placed on knowledge dissemination and the cross-national application of social science knowledge. Knowledge can and should be increased by investigating social phenomena in multiple countries and societies (Midgley, 1995). And, with the increasing sensitivity that social workers have recently gained to cultural differences in this increasingly multicultural world, there is a corresponding increase in the need to generate theories and practice methods that are appropriate to specific social and cultural situations (Midgley, 1989).

Unfortunately, despite the potential benefits of learning from the Third World, social workers remain largely ignorant of the experiences of their colleagues in developing nations. Midgley (1990) challenges the one-way international flow of ideas and practices and calls upon social workers from the West to become open to learning from the Third World. Third World social workers lack easy access to publication sources that can disseminate their ideas, and because of financial constraints, they cannot readily attend international meetings and conferences. Although many Western social workers travel to developing countries, they seldom study local approaches with a view to learn from them or test them in their own countries. The global social work community needs to foster mutual exchanges of experiences and information between social workers in different societies. More opportunities for the representation of Third World social workers at international gatherings are needed, and publication sources should provide a forum for disseminating Third World experiences. Third World social workers also should be used as consultants to programs in industrial countries, where their knowledge can be applied (Midgley, 1990).

Governments of developing countries often employ helping professionals, such as social workers, who are involved in various community development, social planning, and social action models of community organization (Kawewe & Dibie, 1999; Midgley, 1995). The training of these workers, however, generally emphasizes Western social work conceptual frameworks and intervention skills, which they struggle to apply to the indigenous context of developing countries (Abrahams et al., 1994; Guzzetta 1996). Additionally, the worldwide adoption of U.S. textbooks and concepts embeds the prevailing Western cultural imperialism of social work education, with its emphasis on individual treatment models (Kawewe & Dibie, 1999). These models render social workers ineffective in societies where the community, rather than the individual, is the appropriate level of attention (Abrahams et al, 1994; Guzzetta, 1996). Many developing world social workers have successfully determined that imported Western individualistic paradigms of social work and education are irrelevant to their cultural premises of collective coexistence (Kawewe & Dibie, 1999). Social work that favors the traditional Western aftereffect/treatment modality over an equally important prevention/reform strategy is a major limitation in a developing world setting (Kawewe & Dibie, 1999). Some Western social workers argue that the West would equally benefit from the prevention/reform strategy successfully used in developing countries. As Kawewe and Dibie (1999, p. 9) point out, effective and enduring grass-root efforts in developing countries have shown to be useful in "helping people build up skills to solve problems now and in the future." Broad participation by progressive social workers in international professional organizations could help to make the world a better place for humankind through cross-pollination of ideas, while honoring the history and culture of nation-states.

National Association of Social Workers Initiatives

The National Association of Social Workers (NASW) is currently pursuing and promoting global relations. Guided by its International Activities Committee, formed in 1986, it seeks to adopt a variety of mechanisms to increase the globalization of the association. As part of its global outreach activities, NASW has sponsored international meetings and travel opportunities. During the 1980s and 1990s many state NASW chapters forged partnerships with social workers and associations in other countries. The NASW and a number of state chapters have sponsored study tours in various countries around the world.

Council on Social Work Education Initiatives

The Council on Social Work Education has a long history of commitment to international education. It established an International Commission in 1978 to enhance global opportunities in the social work curriculum. More recently it established the Katherine A. Kendall Institute for International Social Work Education. Its mission is to foster the mainstream development of international content in social work education and to increase the cross-organizational collaboration in project development as well as research and data collection and dissemination. It also promotes the implementation of programs and initiatives within the global social work education community. Even more recently the council established the Commission on Global Education, which interfaces with other international organizations such as the International Association of Schools of Social Work (IASSW). In addition to promoting international programs and projects, the commission also provides guidance for the development of international content in the social work curricula. The council strongly advocates that schools internationalize curricula and provide students with worldwide opportunities.

INTERNATIONAL HUMAN SERVICE ORGANIZATIONS

Amnesty International

Amnesty International was founded in 1961. It is a Nobel Prize–winning grass-root activist organization with over 1.8 million members worldwide. Amnesty International conducts research and action focused on preventing and ending abuses of the rights to physical and mental integrity, freedom of conscience and expression, and freedom from discrimination, within the context of its work to promote all human rights (for more information see http://www.amnesty.org).

Human Rights Watch

HRW is an independent, nongovernmental organization supported by contributions from private individuals and foundations worldwide. Its goals are to prevent discrimination, to uphold political freedom, to protect people from inhumane conduct in wartime, and to bring offenders to justice (for more information see http://www.hrw.org).

International Council for Caring Communities

ICCC is a not-for-profit organization that has Special Consultative Status with the Economic and Social Council of the United Nations. It acts as a bridge linking government, civil society organizations, the private sector, universities, and the UN in their efforts to promote innovative perspectives on a multigenerational society. Since its inception, ICCC has been committed to the principle that private enterprises and individuals can help society improve communities and social public activities. It attempts to stimulate and highlight innovative concepts that deal creatively with the challenges of global longevity. Through educational programs, conferences, technical support, and international student architectural competitions, ICCC promotes a global dialogue on the impact of ageing (for more information see http://www.international-iccc.org).

International Federation of Red Cross and Red Crescent Societies

A global humanitarian organization, the International Federation was founded in Paris in May 1919 after World War I to assist with cooperation between the different national humanitarian organizations. It is the world's largest humanitarian organization and currently has 173 chapters worldwide. They are active in disaster relief, blood collection, refugee locating, and civilian medical training (for more information see http://www.ifrc.org).

Organisation for Economic Co-operation and Development

The OECD is an intergovernmental organization that consists of 30 member countries sharing a commitment to democratic government and the market economy. Its work covers economic and social issues, from macroeconomics to trade, education, development, and science and innovation. It plays a major role in fostering good governance in the public service sector and in corporate activity. It assists governments to ensure the responsiveness of key economic areas. It helps policy-makers adopt strategic orientations by identifying emerging issues. By identifying policies that work, it helps policy-makers adopt strategic orientations for policy development (for more information see http://www.oecd.org).

Peace Corp

First organized in 1961, the Peace Corps sends American volunteers to different nations to assist in a variety of social, economic, and agricultural projects (for more information see http://www.peacecorps.gov).

Open Society Institute

OSI is a private operating and grant-making foundation founded by philanthropist George Soros and based in New York City. It partners with the Soros foundations network, a group of autonomous foundations and organizations in more than 50 countries. OSI and the Soros foundations network implement a range of initiatives that aim to promote open societies by informing government policy and supporting education, media, public health, and human and women's rights, as well as social, legal, and economic reform (for more information see http://www.soros.org).

United Nations

The UN serves as the primary agency to coordinate the efforts of countries to overcome oppression, facilitate the delivery of health and welfare services that cross international boundaries, and promote social justice. The International Association of Schools of Social Work (IASSW) represents social work educators at the United Nations. Here, it holds special consultative status and has been active in shaping policies focusing on children, women, older people, and migrants in a range of areas, including social development, poverty, mental health, human insecurity, and antiracism (for more information see http://www.un.org).

United Nations Educational, Scientific and Cultural Organization

Founded in 1945, UNESCO functions as a laboratory of ideas and standard-setting to forge universal agreements on emerging ethical issues. The organization also serves as a clearinghouse for the dissemination and sharing of information and knowledge while helping member states to build their human and institutional capacities in diverse fields. It promotes international cooperation in the fields of education, science, culture, and communication (for more information see http://www.unesco.org).

United Nations Population Fund

UNFPA (the acronym harks back to the agency's original name, the United Nations Fund for Population Activities) is the world's largest international source of funding for population and reproductive health programs. UNFPA works with governments and nongovernmental organizations in more than 140 countries, at their request, and with the support of the global community. It supports programs that help women, men, and young people plan their families and avoid unwanted pregnancies; undergo pregnancy and childbirth safely; avoid sexually transmitted infections; and combat violence against women (for more information see http://www.unfpa.org).

United States Agency for International Development

USAID has two responsibilities: international private investment and operating the Agency for International Development (AID). AID provides funding for international projects and is very concerned about HIV/AIDS, child welfare, population growth, and basic education. USAID is an independent federal government agency that extends assistance to countries recovering from disaster, trying to escape poverty, and engaging in democratic reforms (for more information see http://www.usaid.gov).

World Bank Group

The World Bank Group's mission is to fight poverty and improve the living standards of people in the developing world. It is a development bank that provides loans, policy advice, technical assistance, and knowledge sharing services to low and middle income countries to reduce poverty. The Bank promotes growth to create jobs and to empower poor people to take advantage of these opportunities (for more information see http://www.worldbank.org).

GLOBAL SOCIAL WORK EDUCATION

The active social work global presence is more often found at the university level than at the practice level. This has important implications relating to the need to go beyond the classroom and into the practice arena. Social work education needs to become much more proactive in developing a practice-relevant international curriculum that provides students with international practice as well as content. In adapting to more current global concerns, there is a need to develop a curriculum that reflects the universal nature of social work (Caragata & Sanchez, 2002).

Examples of active global cooperation and collaboration in social work and human relations include the two international organizations that provide the basic leadership for the globalization of social work—the International Federation of Social Workers (IFSW) and the IASSW—and the Alliance of Universities for Democracy.

The IFSW was formed in 1928 following the International Conference on Social Work held in Paris. Today organizational members of IFSW are from approximately 70 countries, representing 500,000 social workers. The activities of IFSW include publication of a newsletter, operation of a commission that advocates for the protection of human rights throughout the world, the development of a statement of ethical guidelines for social workers, and maintenance of updated policy positions on global social welfare issues.

The IASSW was formed in 1948 and now includes more than 400 member social work educational associations. Its primary concerns are incorporating global content into social work education programs, providing consultation to the United Nations and the United Nations Children's Fund, and facilitating the transfer of academic credit among schools from different countries. The International Exchanges and Research Task Force of the IASSW aims to bring schools of social work together so that they can undertake joint projects and exchange curriculum materials. The IASSW also funds small projects that enable social work educators to promote the ideas and practices of global social work.

The Alliance of Universities for Democracy is a consortium of 94 universities in Europe and the United States. It was established in 1990 to enhance the role of universities in promoting democratic institutions, economic development, education, philanthropy, and human rights in the newly established democracies of Central and Eastern Europe. The alliance promotes collaborative work among universities, drawing on social workers for expert participation (Boyle, 2003).

SUMMARY

Governments, nongovernment organizations, and organizations across the globe employ helping professionals such as social workers who are involved in various community development, social planning, and social action models of community organization. Social workers working with individuals, families, groups, communities, and organizations are needed to work with all populations and across a multitude of problems. Social workers must be better prepared, however, to work across cultures and with indigenous groups.

Thinking About Practice: From Local to Global Perspectives

1. Go to the Council on Social Work Education website (http://www.cswe.org) and review their site on international/global activities. What is the emphasis on cross-pollination of ideas between different cultures and nation-states? How could the initiatives be improved?

2. Evaluate your own readiness to work with different cultures and with different nation-states. How might you increase your skills and knowledge to be better prepared?

Social Work Practice and Social Justice Website

Please go to the Book Companion Website at http://www.thomsonedu.com/author/sowers to find a rich collection of related articles selected by the authors from Info Trac College Edition.

References

Abrahams, C. K., Ariyasena, S., Chandrasekere, S., Kotelawala, P., Kurundukumbura, B., & Mayakaduwa, A. (1994). *A manual for social development practice* (2nd ed.). Toronto: Canadian Scholars/Colombo.

Boyle, S. W. (2003). *Introduction to social work* (9th ed.) Boston: Allyn & Bacon.

Caragata, L,. & Sanchez, M. (2002). Globalization and global need: New imperatives for expanding international social work education in North America. *International Social Work, 45*(2), 217–238.

Guzzetta, C., (1996). The decline of the North American model of social work. *International social work, 39* (3), 301–315.

Healy, L. (1995). International social welfare: Organizations and Activities. In R. Edwards & J. G. Hopps (Eds.), *Encyclopedia of social work* (19th ed.). Washington, DC: NASW Press.

Kawewe, S., & Dibie, R. (1999). United Nations and the problem of women and children abuse in Third World nations. *Social Justice, 26*(1), 78–98.

Mary, N. L., & Morris, T. (1994). The future and social work: A global perspective. *Journal of Multicultural Social Work, 3*(4), 89–101.

Midgley, J. (1989). Social work in the Third World: Crisis and response. In P. Carter, T. Jeffs, & M. Smith (Eds.), *Social work and social welfare yearbook* (pp. 33–45). Milton Keynes, England: Open University Press.

Midgley, J. (1990). International social work: Learning from the Third World. *Social Work, 35*(4), 295–300.

Midgley, J. (1995). International and comparative social welfare. In R. Edwards & J. G. Hopps (Eds.) *Encyclopedia of social work* (19th ed.) Washington, DC: NASW Press.

Morales, A. T., & Sheafor, B. W. (2001). *Social work: A profession of many faces* (9th ed). Boston: Allyn & Bacon.

The true civilization is where every man gives to every other every right that he claims for himself.

Robert Ingersoll

Conclusion

A challenge for the next generation of social workers will be to evolve a concept of social work that will bridge the differing philosophies of society's role in meeting human needs, as well as to maintain social work's unique function as the profession that addresses both individual and daily needs, and simultaneously is concerned with changing society to reduce or eliminate factors that contribute to people's problems in social functioning (Morales & Sheafor, 2001). Toward that end, the social work profession must more fully embrace principles of social and political justice (Siepel, 2003), and schools of social work must become more active agents of social change. Schools of social work should train students to become working partners with professions and community agencies to participate in efforts towards social change (Cloward, 1998). Because social problems are complex and embedded in international structures, social workers must increase their efforts to interact with international bodies (Cox, 1990).

Recognition of the importance of international social issues has increased. There is a growing realization that no nation can solve its social problems alone. "Experience with the spread of AIDS, drug trafficking, and addiction; the disaster at the Chernobyl nuclear power plant; and migration underscores the reality of global interdependence [MM1]" (Healy, 1995, p. 1509). As stated in the 1995 annual report of the United Nations, "Never before have so many courageous and committed people been involved in world betterment. Never before have nations recognized so clearly that their fate is bound up with each other" (Boutros-Ghali, 1995, p. 362). This growing awareness increases the demand for social workers who have social development skills and who are prepared to respond effectively respond to these global challenges (Johannesen, 1997).

Welfare, economic, and foreign policies are increasingly becoming globally interdependent (Drover, 2000). Drover (2000) proposes a useful concept for citizenship that transcends borders. He suggests that three essential components of social citizenship in a global era, which transcend traditional social rights and provide a practical map for action, are: 1) active citizenship; 2) extra-statism; and 3) diversity. Active citizenship implies reciprocity based on mutual recognition of a person's equal worth. It is action and services based on caring rather than dependency. Extra-statism assumes that rights are grounded in personhood rather than a specific location. Examples include the right to clean air and unpolluted water, and entitlement to social services. Diversity assumes an inclusive model of citizenship that includes cultural diversity and gender as essential parts of global social citizenship. This would negate homogeneity of treatment or general understanding that excludes different groups of people.

The key to understanding the role of social workers in a globalized world lies in the promotion of ideas of global citizenship, expressed through an articulation of human rights and the intentional inclusion of marginalized groups. This approach reaches across the entire range of social work practice in any context. And because human rights are universal, it firmly locates social work as global practice, requiring us to link the personal to the political in the very broadest sense. The value base of social work requires that our internationalist human rights practice be inclusive, and that we work in solidarity with the marginalized in order to achieve the ideal of globalization (Ife, 2000).

References

Boutros-Ghali, B. (1995). *Confronting new challenges: Annual report on the work of the organization.* New York: United Nations.

Cloward, R. A. (1998). The decline of education for professional social work. *Social Work, 43*(6), 584–586.

Cox, D. (1990). An international overview. In H. Campfens (Ed.), *New reality of poverty and struggle for social transformation* (pp. 53–55). Vienna: International Association of Schools of Social Work.

Drover, G. (2000). Redefining social citizenship in a global era. In B. Rowe (Ed.), *Social work and globalization* (pp. 29–49). Ottawa, Ontario: Canadian Association of Social Workers.

Healy, L. (1995). International social welfare: Organizations and Activities. In R. Edwards & J. G. Hopps (Eds.), *Encyclopedia of social work* (19th ed.). Washington, DC: NASW Press.

Ife, J. (2000, July 30–August 2). *Local and global practice: Relocating social work as a human rights profession in the new global order.* Paper presented at the Conference of the International Association of Schools of Social Work, Montreal, Canada.

Johannesen, T. (1997). Social work as an international profession. In M. C. Hokenstad & J. Midgley (Eds.), *Issues in international social work.* Washington, DC: NASW Press.

Morales, A. T., & Sheafor, B. W. (2001). *Social work: A profession of many faces* (9th ed). Boston: Allyn & Bacon.

Siepel, M. (2003). Global poverty: No longer an untouchable problem. *International Social Work, 46*(2), 191–207.

Credits

Chapter 3

page 31-32: Excerpt from United Nations Population Fund. (n.d.). Culture matters: Working with communities and faith-based organizations: Case studies from country programmes. Retrieved July 10, 2004, from http:// www.unfpa.org.

page 32: Excerpt from United Nations Population Fund. (n.d.). Culture matters: Working with communities and faith-based organizations: Case studies from country programmes. Retrieved July 10, 2004, from http://www.unfpa.org.

page 34-35: Excerpt from International Federation of Social Workers. (1996). International policy on human rights. Hong Kong.

page 35: Excerpt from International Federation of Social Workers. (n.d.). The ethics of social work principles and standards. Retrieved March 10, 2003, from http://www.ifsw.org/Publications/4.4.pub.html.

page 35-36: Excerpt from International Federation of Social Workers.

(n.d.). The ethics of social work principles and standards. Retrieved March 10, 2003, from http://www.ifsw.org/Publications/4.4.pub.html.

page 36-38: Excerpt from International Federation of Social Workers. (n.d.). The ethics of social work principles and standards. Retrieved March 10, 2003, from http://www.ifsw.org/Publications/4.4.pub.html.

page 40-42: Excerpt from International Federation of Social Workers. (n.d.). The ethics of social work principles and standards. Retrieved March 10, 2003, from http://www.ifsw.org/Publications/4.4.pub.html.

Chapter 4

page 58-59: Excerpt from United Nations Children's Fund. (n.d.). Convention on the Rights of the Child. Retrieved July 7, 2004, from http://www.unicef.org/crc.

page 64-65: Excerpt from International Federation of Social Workers. (2000). International statement on

youth. pp. 2-5. Retrieved July 20, 2004, from http://www.ifsw.org.

Chapter 5

page 82-83: Excerpt from International Federation of Social Workers. (1999). International policy on women. Helsinki: Finland.

page 99-100: Excerpt from International Federation of Social Workers. (1999). International policy on older persons. New York.

Chapter 6

page 103-104: Excerpt from United Nations Population Fund. (n.d.). Population ageing and poverty. Retrieved July 21, 2004, from http://www.unfpa.org/sustainable/ageing.htm.

Chapter 8

page 134-135: Excerpt from World Health Organization. (2001). The World Health Report 2001. Retrieved July 7, 2004, from http://www.who.int/whr2001/2001/main.

Index